HORSES
Through Time

HORSES
Through Time

Edited by Sandra L. Olsen

ROBERTS RINEHART PUBLISHERS
FOR
CARNEGIE MUSEUM OF NATURAL HISTORY

To Mary Littauer
and the memory of
Sandor Bökönyi,
whose quests for knowledge
about horses
reach deep into prehistory

International Standard Book Number 1-57098-060-8
Library of Congress Catalog Card Number 96-068566

Published by Roberts Rinehart Publishers
5455 Spine Road
Boulder, Colorado 80301

Published in the UK and Ireland by
Roberts Rinehart Publishers
Trinity House, Charleston Road
Dublin 6, Ireland

Distributed in the U.S. and Canada by Publishers Group West

Cover and book design by Paulette Livers Lambert

Manufactured in Hong Kong

Crowell Hadden, Jr.

Front jacket photograph: Thunder Gulch, the 1995 Kentucky Derby winner, just
before crossing the finish line at Churchill Downs. (© Churchill Downs, Inc. and
Kinetic Corporation)

Back jacket photograph: Reconstructed Hyracotherium
(Photo by Melinda McNaugher)

Frontispiece: A Kazak man with his horse in northwest China.
(Photo by Sandra Olsen)

CONTENTS

PREFACE *vii*

ABOUT THE AUTHORS *ix*

One **INTRODUCTION** *1*
Sandra L. Olsen

Two **THE ANCESTRY OF THE HORSE** *11*
Richard C. Hulbert, Jr.

Three **HORSE HUNTERS OF THE ICE AGE** *35*
Sandra L. Olsen

Four **BRIDLING HORSE POWER**
THE DOMESTICATION OF THE HORSE *57*
David W. Anthony

Five **HORSES IN HISTORY** *83*
Juliet Clutton-Brock

Six **IN THE WINNER'S CIRCLE**
THE HISTORY OF EQUESTRIAN SPORTS *103*
Sandra L. Olsen

Seven **HOOVES ACROSS THE STEPPES**
THE KAZAK LIFE-STYLE *129*
Victor Shnirelman, Sandra L. Olsen, and Patricia Rice

Eight **THE PROLIFERATION OF HORSE BREEDS** *153*
D. Phillip Sponenberg

Nine **THE ADVANCEMENT OF EQUINE MEDICINE** *175*
Corinne Raphel Sweeney

Ten **THE LIVING RELATIVES OF THE HORSE** *191*
Susan L. Woodward

APPENDIX General Information on the Horse *209*

INDEX *215*

Preface

The authors in this volume were chosen for their expertise in their respective disciplines, and we are, indeed, fortunate to have brought together some of the very best scholars in the world for this task. While there have been many books published on horses in recent years, most are generalized popular volumes by single authors. Although these are fine publications, this book is unique in that each chapter is written by an expert on its subject. It is important to recognize that these contributors not only possess a thorough knowledge of the work of others in their field, but are themselves pushing forward with research that is revolutionizing equine-related science. Whereas all the contributors are accomplished writers in the scientific journals of their own disciplines, this is the first compilation of their works to present their research and recent discoveries in a format suitable for a general audience. For myself as editor, preparation of this volume has been a most edifying and enlightening undertaking. I believe that all readers—both laypeople and scholars—will find *Horses Through Time* entertaining and educational and that it will fuel an already widespread interest in the role of horses in our society, both past and future.

This volume would be nothing more than a dream in a curator's mind without the contributions of many people and institutions. First, I would like to pay tribute to the Carnegie Museum of Natural History, which, in addition to providing considerable financial assistance, has generously allowed members of our Division of Education and myself virtually unlimited time to work on the production of this book. Without the unwavering support of James E. King, Director of Carnegie Museum of Natural History, this volume would not have been possible. Louise Craft, Managing Editor in the Division of Education, and her assistant, Elizabeth Mertz, have suffered all the trials and tribulations associated with the gestation and delivery of this publication and have shown remarkable dedication and perseverance.

One person deserves a very special thanks for her contribution to this book. Mary Littauer reviewed the entire manuscript in detail, adding immeasurably to its accuracy through her vast knowledge of virtually everything related to the horse. We were, indeed, very fortunate to have benefited from her critical eye. All those who have met Mary, and there are certainly many, agree that she is unsurpassed in her wisdom regarding horses. Although she could have easily written a comprehensive volume on the subject based on her own scientific research and experience, she instead kindly agreed to devote an enormous amount of her time to improve this book. Any errors that may occur in this volume regarding equestrian history most probably arose after Mary carefully combed through it.

Facing page, glazed earthenware horse from the Tang Dynasty. (See page 95.) (Courtesy of Carnegie Museum of Art; photography / Peter Harholdt)

PREFACE

To the authors I would like to offer my gratitude for their fine contributions and their patience for the duration of the production period. We, the authors and the editors, also owe much to the reviewers, artists, photographers, and museums who have added immeasurably to the style, accuracy, and presentation of *Horses Through Time*. Institutions that have made special contributions include the British Museum, Buffalo Bill Historical Center, Carnegie Museum of Art, Carnegie Museum of Natural History, Harness Racing Museum and Hall of Fame, International Museum of the Horse, Kentucky Derby Museum, Kinetic Corporation, Natural History Museum of Basel (Switzerland), Robert Harding Picture Library, Royal Armouries of HM Tower of London, Senckenberg Natural History Museum (Germany), and the Spanish Riding School.

Special persons who shared their knowledge and helped with various aspects of the book include Gail Brownrigg, Mary Dawson, Dennis Foster, Deborah Harding, Richard Harington, Janet Hitchen, Melinda McNaugher, Daniel Opplinger, Nancy Perkins, Barbara Pitman, Jenifer Raisor, Christine Randall, Patricia Rice, G. Richter, and Randall White. It is impossible to thank all of the generous people who took time from their busy schedules to assist, inform, facilitate, and contribute to the production of this book. There were so many with whom I spoke on the telephone who offered their help, despite never having met me or heard of me until they answered the phone. I do not know whether horse enthusiasts are "a breed apart," but it seems to me that they have an infinite capacity for kindness and amazing energy when it comes to spreading the word about horses. I hope that all of those who must go unnamed, but who are certainly not forgotten, will accept my gratitude for making this volume so much better.

Lastly, and most importantly, I would like to thank my husband, Chris Beard, who was made to suffer every painful detail of the production of this book before, after, and often during his own work days, and who provided unlimited good judgment, intelligent solutions, and calm stability throughout.

—Sandra L. Olsen

About the Authors

David W. Anthony, Associate Professor, Department of Anthropology, Hartwick College, Oneonta, NY 13820

Dr. Anthony has a Ph.D. in anthropology and is an archaeologist specializing in Russian prehistory. Special topics of interest include the origins of Indo-European culture and the earliest evidence for horse domestication. Dr. Anthony has published numerous articles on horse domestication, focusing on the earliest occurrences of bit wear on the teeth of prehistoric horses. He has performed innovative experiments with modern horses to study the formation of bit wear, using a variety of materials.

Juliet Clutton-Brock, Principal Scientific Officer (retired), Department of Zoology, The Natural History Museum, Cromwell Road, London, UK SW7 5BD

Dr. Clutton-Brock, who holds a D.Sc. degree, has studied mammalian osteology and the history of domesticated mammals over the last thirty years. She has more than eighty publications in this field, including *Horse Power: A History of the Horse and Donkey in Human Societies*. Although retired from her official post, she retains research facilities at the museum.

Richard C. Hulbert, Jr., Assistant Professor, Department of Geology and Geography, Georgia Southern University, Statesboro, GA 30460

Dr. Hulbert has a Ph.D. in vertebrate paleontology and specializes in the evolution and paleoecology of late Cenozoic animals. He is currently describing new Miocene species and analyzing several late Miocene and Pliocene faunas from Alabama and Florida that include numerous horses. He is also conducting a detailed study of the first hipparionine horse found north of the Arctic Circle, in Canada.

Sandra L. Olsen, Associate Curator of Anthropology, Carnegie Museum of Natural History, 4400 Forbes Avenue, Pittsburgh, PA 15213

Dr. Olsen has a Ph.D. in archaeology and specializes in the field of zooarchaeology, the study of the roles of animals in ancient societies. Her research has taken her to the American Southwest, Britain, France, Greece, Cyprus, Kenya, Russia, and Kazakstan. Recently her primary focus has been on horses in prehistory, ranging from wild-horse hunting in the French Paleolithic to the earliest stages of horse domestication in Kazakstan. She has spent the past several years investigating Kazak horse pastoralism in China and Kazakstan.

Patricia Rice, Associate Professor, Department of Sociology and Anthropology, West Virginia University, Morgantown, WV 26506

Ms. Rice, who has an M.A. in anthropology, wrote her thesis on the influence of shifting political tides on Kazak economy. She is also an authority on animal images in European Paleolithic cave and mobile art and has published three articles comparing these images with the frequencies of species in archaeological collections of animal remains.

Victor Shnirelman, Senior Researcher, Institute of Ethnology and Anthropology, Russian Academy of Sciences, 32-A Leninsky Prospect, Moscow, Russia 117334

Dr. Shnirelman has a Ph.D. in history and is a leading researcher in both archaeology and ethnology. He is the author of several books and over 130 articles dealing with traditional economic systems, the origins of food-producing economies, and war and peace in traditional societies. Dr. Shnirelman has held appointments as a visiting researcher or professor at many highly respected North American and European institutions.

D. Phillip Sponenberg, Professor of Pathology and Genetics, Virginia-Maryland Regional College of Veterinary Medicine, Virginia Polytechnic Institute and State University, Blacksburg, VA 24061

Dr. Sponenberg, who holds both a D.V.M. and a Ph.D., specializes in diagnostic pathology, the genetics of coat color and morphological characteristics, and the development and interrelationships of breeds of domestic livestock. He is Technical Director of the American Livestock Breeds Conservancy, the only organization in the United States working to save rare breeds of livestock from extinction. Of special interest are breeds developed during colonial times that are now near extinction.

Corinne Raphel Sweeney, Associate Professor of Medicine and Vice Chair, Department of Clinical Studies, University of Pennsylvania School of Veterinary Medicine, New Bolton Center, Kennett Square, PA 19348

Dr. Sweeney holds a D.V.M. and specializes in equine internal medicine with clinical and research interests in respiratory problems. Her research investigations have focused on diagnostic testing for lung conditions, streptococcal respiratory infections, exercise-induced pulmonary hemorrhages in racehorses, and control of equine airways and pulmonary vasculature. She also has an interest in equine ophthalmology.

Susan L. Woodward, Associate Professor of Geography, Radford University, Radford, VA 24142

Dr. Woodward has a Ph.D. in geography and teaches biogeography, human ecology, and environmental studies. Her research focuses on Pleistocene faunal and floral changes, the domestication of plants and animals, and the ecology of exotic species. Her doctoral dissertation was on the natural history of feral burros in the Lower Colorado River Valley.

HORSES
Through Time

INTRODUCTION

SANDRA L. OLSEN

A horse! A horse! My kingdom for a horse!
—Shakespeare, *Richard III*, act 5, sc. 4

*I*n the history of humankind there has never been an animal that has made a greater impact on societies than the horse. Other animals were hunted much more or domesticated earlier, but the horse changed the world in innumerable ways with its tremendous swiftness. While asses, camels, elephants, yaks, and other animals were ridden by people, the horse provided the first source of "rapid transit." Prior to horseback riding, most people traveled on foot, carrying all their cargo on their shoulders, or they were restricted to using boats along rivers and coastlines. Other animals were slow, limited in how much weight they could carry, or were more restricted in their geographic distribution. Horses were swift of foot, could easily support one or two human passengers, could carry heavy loads, and, like asses, could survive, if necessary, on very poor quality vegetation or fodder.

Because of the obvious advantage of ease of transport, horses expanded the range that people could travel from their homelands. This provided the means to widen trade circles and increase communication among diverse cultures. The advantages of trade expansion and diffusion of technological innovations from one group of people to the next through increased long-distance travel were immeasurable.

The impact of horseback riding was not all positive, however. Along with domestication of the horse came a new way to move armies. The military advantage fell dramatically to those who were the quickest to gain access to and adopt the horse into their life-styles. This was as true in the New World as it was in Europe and Asia.

In our highly industrialized society we may tend to forget the enormous impact that horses have had on our history. In some areas of the world that impact may have dwindled but is still quite evident. There are other cultures, however, that continue to center many of their traditions and activities around the horse. And, should we become overconfident with our mechanized civilization, we should look at countries in the former Soviet Union that have reverted back to the highly reliable horsepower in the face of fuel crises and machinery breakdowns (figure 1). The time may come in our own future when an intermediate technology that includes horses may become advantageous over costly high-tech solutions.

The horse continues to serve another role beyond its purely utilitarian one, that of entertainment. Although leisure time seems to be shrinking in industrial societies, many people spend much of their free time in the company of

Facing page, 1. A woman drives a horse-drawn wagon hauling fodder in Samara, Russia. (Photo by Sandra Olsen)

3

horses. Their activities range from riding their own horses and pony trekking on vacation to sports requiring more proficiency like dressage (figure 2), hunts, show jumping, rodeos, and polo.

Equine Maxims Abound

To put the role of the horse in human history in perspective, we can look at many terms and phrases still prevalent in the English language that harken back to a time not so long ago when horses were of extreme importance to our society. Many phrases, like *stubborn as a mule, beating a dead horse, horseplay, horsing around,* and *horse laugh* are self-evident and require no explanation. Others have origins that are obscured in the past and lost to most of us. Some, like the humorous reference to an automobile as a *horseless carriage,* have survived longer than many would have anticipated. Although we rarely stop to look at their literal meanings, many of these linguistic phrases embody useful information about equine behavior or the care and treatment of horses. Everyone is acquainted with the sayings *You can lead a horse to water, but you can't make it drink,* which was cited as a proverb as early as 1546, and *That's a horse of a different color,* which probably originated in Shakespeare's *Twelfth Night* in 1601. But, what about the Old English rhyme:

> *One white foot—buy him;*
> *Two white feet—try him;*
> *Three white feet—look well about him;*
> *Four white feet—go without him.*

The origin of this message seems to lie in the fact that white hooves are weaker than others and split more readily because the pigment that colors a dark hoof also makes it tougher.

The familiar old phrase *Don't look a gift horse in the mouth* refers to the practice of horse traders determining the age of a horse by its anterior teeth, or incisors. Horses, like humans, have a set of temporary or milk teeth that erupt soon after birth. These include incisors, canine teeth in males, and premolars. Because it is easiest to look at the lower incisors of a living horse, these are used most frequently as a means of determining the age of the horse. The incisors erupt and wear down according to a fairly consistent schedule through the life of the horse. Wear is caused by the abrasive nature of the grasses and other food plants ingested by the horse. As the incisors wear down, the chewing surface changes in appearance, exposing more and more of the infundibulum, a natural concavity in the anterior teeth. By looking at the lower incisors to see which permanent teeth have erupted and their stage of wear, knowledgeable horse traders can estimate fairly accurately the age of the horse. Since older horses are less useful for heavy work, determining the age helps to evaluate a horse's worth. Hence, looking a gift horse in the mouth is the equivalent of asking someone how much they paid for a gift they have just given you and then complaining that it was not expensive enough. Getting information *straight from the horse's mouth* is also probably derived from the fact that a smart horse trader would look into a horse's mouth for himself to determine its age, rather than trusting the word of the seller.

Eating like a horse originates from the fact that horses spend much of their time consuming large quantities of food. Among livestock the equine digestive system is unusual. Compare, for example, other grazers, like cattle, sheep, and goats, all of which have four-chambered stomachs and rather slow digestive systems. The horse, on the other hand, has just one chamber in its stomach, and most of the fermentation occurs farther on in the cecum. In terms of its proportion to the total body weight, the horse's digestive system is only about one third the size of that of a cow. This fact means that food passes through a horse much faster than it does through a cow or other ruminant, so the horse requires more food in order to obtain sufficient nutrients. Therefore, under natural circumstances, equids must have large ranges in which to feed. Although their basic intake is necessarily quite high, horses can digest very low-quality food that other grazers would reject. As a result equids can occupy a vast range of habitats, some of which are severe in temperature and extremely arid.

Good old common horse sense most likely refers to the accumulation of knowledge about horses acquired by humans, not to the intelligence of horses. In order to buy, care for, train, handle, breed, and work with horses, an equestrian must know a great deal about them. The appreciation for the acquisition of knowledge about horses was evident even by the fourth century B.C., when the Greek writer Xenophon wrote his treatise *The Art of Horsemanship*. This early work covered such topics as how to avoid being cheated when buying a horse and how to train, groom, mount, ride, and stable a horse. It is easy, then, to see why someone is described as a good "horse trader" if he or she is shrewd at bargaining for any sort of commodity or deal.

The reason *horse sense* probably does not refer to the intelligence of horses is that they are, unfortunately, rather limited in this regard. Relative to their body

2. Margie Goldstein on Land of Kings in the Victory Parade after winning the Grand Prix, Upperville Horse Show, Virginia. This horse show is the oldest in the country. (Photo by Janet Hitchen)

size, horses have very small brains. Their behavior is linked primarily to instincts rather than to innate intelligence. Their strongest qualities relate to their instincts to flee from dangerous predators, to eat and drink regularly, to seek security in numbers, and to mate successfully. The training of horses relies, therefore, on repetition and the development of conditioned reflexes through reward or punishment. The most successful training takes into account the natural instincts of the horse and capitalizes on them. Thus, for example, young horses are enticed to jump over fences by having adult horses jumping ahead. The foal will concentrate on staying with the group and will leap over obstacles that it would otherwise avoid. As with folks who have dogs and cats, horse owners may tend to anthropomorphize horses, that is, to attribute human qualities to their animals' behaviors.

Horses are known for two things when it comes to locomotion, power and speed. *Horsepower* is a term still used today as a standard measure for engines and other machines, but what exactly is it? Does it refer to what a pony or a large draft horse can do? Actually, the unit of measure referred to as *horsepower* is standardized as the power to lift seventy-five kilograms (165 lb) one meter high (39 in. high) in one second. The average horse is actually ten to thirteen times stronger than that, meaning that one horse normally is capable of producing ten to thirteen units of horsepower. Horses have been used to pull a number of vehicles, including carts, wagons, carriages, chariots, and sleighs, hence the phrase *to work like a horse*.

The phrase *putting the cart before the horse* is probably ancient, because it first appeared in print in 1520 in Robert Whitinton's *Vulgaria*. I might add that before horses could be used to pull heavy loads, special yokes had to be designed, because the typical ox yoke would have applied too much pressure to the windpipe of a horse, cutting off its supply of oxygen.

Many phrases are linked to riding skills, dressage, and racing. During the Age of Chivalry, a knight was chivalrous if he was adept at riding a horse in full armor, not easy when the armor and rider together weighed in at around 200 kilograms (440 lb) (figure 3). *Chivalry* is a word derived from the French word for horse, *cheval*. Because of the code of gallantry, which knights were required to know well, *chivalry* eventually came to be associated with the ideal behavior for noblemen, above and beyond merely equine-related subjects. To be *cavalier* can mean to behave either aristocratically or in a dismissive manner but originates in the term assigned to gentlemen who rode for the military. Telling someone to *get off his high horse* probably originated from the fact that knights had to ride specially bred large horses because of the enormous weight of their armor. Nobles would ride through town quite literally looking down on others from their tall horses. Later on, politicians paraded in ceremonial processions on unusually large horses. A Scottish proverb incorporating a reference to one's "high horse" was cited by James Kelly in 1721. The phrase *Come off it* is also supposed to be derived from this saying.

Putting on airs may come from a term used in dressage to indicate a movement in which the horse's legs are off the ground. The various "airs" above ground are executed chiefly by horses trained in haute école (classical equitation), as performed, for example, at the Spanish Riding School of Vienna, and by the French Cavalry at the School in Saumur. These exercises include the capriole, courbette,

levade, pesade, ballotade, and croupade (see chapter 6). To *put on airs*, then, would be to show off a talent that is shared only with the most elite.

The lovely phrase *tilting at windmills*, which refers to attempting the ludicrous or impossible, is based on an episode in Cervantes' seventeenth-century classic *Don Quixote*, in which the hero believes the windmills are monsters that he intends to take on in mortal combat. Tilting is the competition in medieval jousting tournaments in which one contestant tries to knock the other off his horse (see chapter 6). Shakespeare was one of the first to write about charging ahead at *full tilt*, a phrase that came to refer to proceeding with determination as quickly as possible in a particular endeavor.

Horse racing is an extremely fruitful source of clichés. *Starting from scratch* first implied that someone was being honest in a horse race by making sure that his horse's front feet were just behind a line drawn in the dirt road that marked where the race was to commence. Although the phrase *up to scratch* was first published in reference to boxing 160 years ago, it may have been used earlier in horse races. A *dark horse candidate* is one about whom little is known. In 1831 Benjamin Disraeli wrote in *The Young Duke*, "A dark horse, which had never been thought of . . . , rushed past the grand stand in sweeping triumph." This is all the more ironic given that Disraeli himself was quite a dark horse in British politics. The idea comes from cases in which the public is either intentionally or accidentally kept in the dark regarding certain facts about an equine contestant that may possess the necessary qualities to win the race. The horse's lack of a reputation can put those betting on it at an advantage. *They're off and running* is a phrase, uttered by many racetrack announcers, that has come to refer to any situation in which the participants have made a strong beginning, especially in politics. *Beating a dead horse* was first applied to politics when Richard Cobden, a member of Parliament, was accused of this deed in 1887 when he kept pressing to reduce the budget. *Giving someone a leg up* literally refers to helping him or her onto a horse or a wall, whereas *going on a wild goose chase* makes reference to an equestrian sport started in Ireland.

3. A modern knight poses on his horse in front of Warwick Castle, England. (Photo by Sandra Olsen)

Some equine words and phrases are taken from horse tackle rather than from the horse itself. The origin of the phrase *bits and pieces* may have come from parts of a bridle. The bit fits into the mouth of the horse and rests on the gum between the incisors and the cheekteeth. It assists in controlling the pace and direction of the horse, as well as the position in which the animal holds its head. The cheekpieces are the parts of the bridle that connect the bit and the headstall. Today they are usually metal, but the earliest known ones, dating to the Bronze Age in Europe, were made of antler tines. Bits and pieces were collected and piled together in a barn or stable, hence the use of *bits and pieces* as a collective term for many small and varied objects.

Champing at the bit refers to the nervous behavior of a horse in response to the restraint of wearing a metal bit in its mouth. The horse chews or gnashes on the bit, particularly if it is uncomfortable. In humans the phrase implies frustration caused by restraint or delay, but this emotion can be reflected in any number of ways. Champing in wild horses is actually a submissive behavior in which the mouth is opened and closed rapidly with the lips drawn back at the corners and held away from the teeth. This conveys to another horse the recognition of its superior social ranking over the horse that is doing the champing.

Giving free rein to someone means that you are relinquishing any power over his or her behavior, whereas *reining them in* and *tightening the reins* have the opposite connotation. A person can also be *spurred on* or *spurred into action.* To *take the bit in one's teeth* refers to proceeding in a bold and confident manner and first appeared in print back in 1589. Going ahead *hell for leather* originally meant that a person who was riding as fast and hard as possible would put a lot of wear and tear on his leather saddle, bridle, and stirrups. Rudyard Kipling may have been the first to coin the phrase in 1899 when he wrote "The Story of the Gadsbys." *Riding roughshod over someone* is to disregard the person's physical and mental welfare. A horse is roughshod when the nails are left protruding out of its shoes so that the animal does not slip and fall. Consequently, being ridden over by a roughshod horse would be quite agonizing. In 1790 Robert Burns wrote about "a rough-shod troop o'Hell," and Thomas Moore used the term in its modern metaphorical sense in his 1813 *Intercepted Letters* when he wrote, "'Tis a scheme of the Romanists, so help me God! To ride over Your Most Royal Highness roughshod."

One very surprising word with equine origins is *crinoline,* our name for a full petticoat or a stiff type of cotton cloth used for interlinings. *Crinoline* originally referred to a loose-weave horsehair cloth used as a stiff lining for hats and lapels and as fabric for petticoats that helped skirts to stand out and look full. The word is derived from the Latin words *crinis,* meaning "hair," and *linum,* meaning "thread."

The incorporation of horse terms and phrases in our daily language does not stop there, because little girls wear *ponytails,* and when it is time to settle your account, you need to *pony up.* While *the old gray mare ain't what she used to be* and *nightmares* may not conjure up very positive connotations for female horses, a man who is referred to as a *stallion* certainly has a reputation to live up to. *Finding a horseshoe may bring luck to the finder,* but probably signifies misfortune for the horse and its owner who lost it. *Backing the wrong horse,* either literally or figuratively, is likewise disadvantageous, as is *changing horses in midstream.*

These are just a few of the ways horses have impacted our language. The persistence of these familiar old quotes in our daily speech registers in some small way just how horses have influenced our history and led us to our place in the modern world. If ever we doubt the impact that horses have had on our society, all we need to do is think about the frequency with which these horse-related maxims appear in our language.

Horses Through Time Addresses Important Equine Topics

This volume presents new information on a wide range of equine-related topics in a way that illustrates the significance of this species to humans as well as its place in the natural world. The book takes a largely historical perspective and in so doing demonstrates the important roles that horses have played throughout time.

Chapter 2, "The Ancestry of the Horse," sets the stage by documenting and deciphering the evidence for the whole evolution of equids. As one of the world's foremost authorities on horse evolution, author Richard C. Hulbert, Jr. provides an up-to-date picture of the varied and complex nature of the fossil record, leading from the tiny "dawn horse" of fifty-seven million years ago to the development of modern horses. His chapter not only informs those interested in the paleontology of horses, but also helps explain why modern horses have certain physical characteristics and behave the way they do. It is, therefore, useful to anyone interested in the anatomy, physical capabilities, diet, and behavioral aspects of horses.

Chapter 3, "Horse Hunters of the Ice Age," introduces readers to the wide range of evidence used by archaeologists to reconstruct the early relationships between humans and horses. At a time before domestication, early European hunters had a perspective on horses very different from that of modern humans, and yet these people captured the beauty, strength, and grace of horses in their cave art and horse effigies. Their art adds immeasurably to the physical evidence such as horse bones that archaeologists pore over as they study the roles of horses in the lives of Ice Age hunter-gatherers.

Several chapters deal directly or indirectly with the history of control, domestication, and breeding of horses by humans to suit their particular needs. Chapter 4, "Bridling Horse Power: The Domestication of the Horse," wrestles with the various theories for the origin of horse domestication at least 6,000 years ago. Author David W. Anthony's and Dory Brown's ongoing research on the topic is breaking new ground in documenting the earliest examples of riding based on tooth wear caused by wearing a bridle found in the archaeological record in Ukraine, Russia, Kazakstan, and elsewhere in the Eurasian steppes.

Chapter 5, "Horses in History," presents a concise review of significant events and developments in world history involving horses. Author Juliet Clutton-Brock is well known for her entertaining but highly informative popular books on domestic animals in prehistoric and historic times. Her chapter begins where Anthony's leaves off with some of the earliest historical accounts of horses and covers a range of topics from warfare to sports to the introduction of domestic horses into the New World.

Chapter 6, "In the Winner's Circle: The History of Equestrian Sports," complements Clutton-Brock's overview by supplying additional detail about the origin, development, and historical highlights of equestrian sports. This chapter offers the reader a glimpse of the wide variety of events performed in the past and demonstrates the great antiquity of many modern sports.

Chapter 7, "Hooves Across the Steppes: The Kazak Life-Style," by Victor Shnirelman, Sandra L. Olsen, and Patricia Rice, tells the story of how intertwined the lives of the nomadic Kazak pastoralists are with their herds. At the same time that we look back nostalgically at the horse in America, many cultures continue to rely heavily on horses for transportation, agriculture, haulage, and even meat and milk. Despite increasing stress, the Kazaks of Kazakstan, Mongolia, and northwest China still maintain a herding economy with a heritage centered around horses. This chapter recounts the numerous ways in which horses figure into the Kazak belief system and permeate nearly all their traditions.

Chapter 8, "The Proliferation of Horse Breeds," provides a generous out-pouring of information of interest especially to anyone who raises horses or is thinking about selecting a particular breed. Author D. Phillip Sponenberg discusses key characteristics of numerous breeds and explores their historical development. An important aspect of this chapter is the way in which it frames relationships among similar breeds with shared ancestry to explain their common heritage. The prevalence of certain traits in modern breeds is linked back to the horses' original uses in the past, whether it be for hauling, riding, or other purposes.

Chapter 9, "The Advancement of Equine Medicine," brings us from early historical accounts of rudimentary veterinary practices to the present state-of-the-art application of medical technology to horses. Author Corinne Raphel Sweeney uses as a modern case study the well-equipped University of Pennsylvania School of Veterinary Medicine New Bolton Center to demonstrate how medical techniques originally developed for humans are adapted to the treatment of horses. She also discusses the development of apparatuses specifically designed for treating horses and the great progress that has been made in improving fertility and neonatal survival rates.

Chapter 10, "The Living Relatives of the Horse," traces the distribution and characteristics of the horse's close relatives in the equid family, including zebras, asses, and onagers. Author Susan L. Woodward has studied feral asses in North America and knows much about the behavior and ecology of wild equids. This chapter is a fitting subject on which to close since it helps to put horses in their proper place among other equids in the animal kingdom and harkens back to a time when horses themselves were truly wild.

Reading List

Clutton-Brock, J. *Horse Power: A History of the Horse and the Donkey in Human Societies.* Cambridge, MA: Harvard University Press, 1992.

Dossenbach, H. D., and M. Dossenbach. *The Noble Horse.* New York: Portland House, 1985.

Edwards, E. H. *Horses: The Visual Guide to Over One Hundred Horse Breeds from Around the World.* New York: Dorling Kindersley, 1993.

Edwards, E. H., editor. *Encyclopedia of the Horse.* New York: Crescent Books, 1990.

Hendricks, B. L. *International Encyclopedia of Horse Breeds.* Norman: University of Oklahoma Press, 1995.

Rogers, J. *The Dictionary of Cliches.* New York: Ballantine Books, 1985.

Sponenberg, D. P., and B. V. Beaver. *Horse Color.* College Station: Texas A&M University Press, 1983.

THE ANCESTRY
OF THE HORSE

RICHARD C. HULBERT, JR.

Among mammals horses are classified with the ungulates, the great group of large-bodied herbivores (plant-eaters). Other living ungulates include the rhinoceroses, camels, deer, antelope, cattle, elephants, and manatees. The combination of ungulates' large, sturdy bones and teeth and their great abundance in most faunas leads to their having an excellent and relatively complete fossil record. The horse family, Equidae, is no exception to this generalization. Many tens of thousands of specimens of equid fossils have been discovered in North America, Eurasia, Africa, and, to a lesser degree, South America. These range from very rare complete skeletons to isolated bones and teeth, the most common finds.

Paleontologists have been analyzing the equid fossil record for well over 150 years, continually making new discoveries, describing new species, reinterpreting old data, and in general learning more about the evolution, anatomy, and ecology of this group. For example, paleontologists named an average of three new species of fossil horses per year between 1973 and 1987. Many paleontologic interpretations are controversial, with contending or alternative hypotheses and theories held by different specialists. As new specimens are found and more data accumulate, some of these ideas are proven unlikely, whereas others are corroborated or totally new hypotheses are proposed. By this method paleontologists progressively gain greater understanding of the evolutionary history of the horse, as well as other organisms.

The fossil record of the horse has an important role in the history of science, in particular the study of biologic evolution. In the late 1800s horses became the first group of mammals that paleontologists could place in a reasonably plausible sequence of ancestors and descendants from a living species back to the beginning of the Age of Mammals, 65 million years ago. Although we now know this sequence was grossly oversimplified, incomplete, and in places simply wrong, it was still an important achievement for the time. With the wide availability of fossil specimens, most natural history museums had the resources to display an exhibit on the evolution of the horse and scores of biology and geology textbooks used the horse as an example for an evolutionary sequence.

Horse evolution became popular because of several factors. First, horses were still in wide use as a means of transportation in the late 1800s. Second, the newly opened American West proved to have a relatively complete sequence of rocks containing fossils that spanned the entire history of the horse. Third, many

Facing page, see figure 9.

13

of the horse's evolutionary changes, such as increase in size and loss of toes, were very obvious. One did not have to be a skilled anatomist to observe them. Fourth, these same changes could be (and were) interpreted as a progressive series of improvements through geologic time to ever-more-advanced, more highly specialized forms. This simplistic interpretation of evolution as progress is incorrect in many ways, but accorded well with then-prevailing evolutionary theories. Finally, the fact that most horse evolution had taken place in North America and not the Old World, which is the native home of living equids (chapter 3), gave the story an additional interesting twist.

Through the course of the twentieth century, the portrayal of horse evolution has followed a two-track system. While professional paleontologists uncovered and unraveled an increasingly complex evolutionary history, museum displays and general textbooks resisted change and sacrificed accuracy for simplicity. Thus today's college biology textbook incorporates the latest findings about molecular structures of enzymes, the intricacies of DNA synthesis, and the workings of the immune system, while presenting a forty-year-old depiction of horse evolution. The great vertebrate paleontologist and evolutionary theorist George Gaylord Simpson bridged this gap in 1951 with his book simply entitled *Horses*. It popularized the then current view of horse evolution proposed by Reuben A. Stirton and his students at the University of California. This book, although now outdated in many respects, remains a good general review of the ancestry of the horse. Bruce MacFadden's *Fossil Horses*, the first book in English devoted to equine paleontology since Simpson's, provides an updated, but more technical reference.

Throughout this essay the word *horse* is used in its general sense, to refer to any member of the family Equidae. This usage is common among paleontologists who, for example, routinely refer to "Eocene horses" or "three-toed horses of the Miocene" (figure 1). Other authors in this volume use the same word in a more restricted sense, to refer only to that species with the scientific name *Equus caballus*, the domestic horse, and the closely related Mongolian wild horse, *Equus przewalskii*. (The Appendix includes the scientific classification of *Equus caballus*.)

Origin of the Family Equidae

The horse family, Equidae, like that of many other mammals, first appeared at the beginning of the Eocene epoch, about 57 million years ago (figure 1). The world was then a far different place. The general climate was much warmer, with subtropical plants and animals living at the Arctic Circle. The landscape was predominantly forested, with little of today's wide-open grasslands, steppes, and savannas. The continents of Europe and North America were much closer together (they have since drifted apart, widening the Atlantic Ocean), and a high-latitude land bridge connected them via Scandinavia, Greenland, and the northern islands of Canada. This connection allowed extensive interchange of land animals between the two continents, so their faunas were very similar.

The extinction of the dinosaurs and other animals at the end of the Cretaceous Period (the last period of the Mesozoic Era), 65 million years ago, had created several ecological vacuums, among them niches for medium- to large-sized herbivores. Most Cretaceous mammals were small, generally no bigger than a rabbit. Small, active herbivores find it difficult to extract enough energy by consum-

Epoch	MYA	Events in Horse Evolution

CENOZOIC ERA

Recent

—— 0.01 — *Equus* extinct in NA and SA

Pleistocene

Last three-toed horses (AF)
—— 1.65 — Hipparionines extinct in NA *Equus* dispersal to SA
Equus dispersal to Old World *Hippidion* & *Onohippidum* dispersal to SA

Pliocene

—— 5.2 — Two mass extinction events for NA horses

First one-toed horses in NA Anchitheres extinct in NA
First hipparionine horses in Old World

Hipparionine diversity in NA

Merychippine diversity in NA; first hipparionines & equines

Miocene

—— 23.3 — Anchitheres appear in NA; dispersal to AS and EU

Oligocene

Palaeotheres extinct in EU

—— 35.4 — First three-toed horse, *Mesohippus* (NA)

Epihippus (NA)

Formation of Messel lake-bed deposits (Germany)

Eocene

—— 56.5 — Oldest known horses (NA,EU,AS)

Radinskya (China)

Paleocene

Tetraclaenodon (NA)

—— 65 — *Protungulatum*, oldest known ungulate (Montana)

MESOZOIC ERA

Cretaceous

NOTE 1: MYA=million years ago; NA=North America; SA=South America; AS=Asia; AF=Africa; EU=Europe.
NOTE 2: The Mesozoic Era is known as the Age of Dinosaurs; the Cenozoic Era, the Age of Mammals.

1. Major events in the evolution of the horse.

15

2. *Posterior upper teeth (left side) of* Radinskya *from the Paleocene of China. Note the* π*-pattern, most evident in* M_1 *and* M_2*. This pattern closely resembles the upper molar of the primitive equid* Hyracotherium, *discussed in the text. Because the* π*-pattern is basic to all perissodactyl molars, some paleontologists think* Radinskya *is more closely related to perissodactyls than the phenacodonts, which lack this pattern. (After McKenna et al., in Donald R. Prothero and Robert M. Schoch, 1989. Copyright © by Oxford University Press, Inc. Reprinted by permission.)*

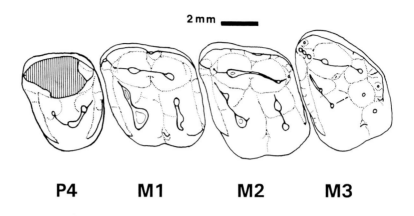

2mm

P4   **M1**   **M2**   **M3**

ing the leaves of plants alone. Instead they must eat the more nutritious parts of plants, such as buds, nuts, seeds, roots, and fruits. Larger mammals, with their more extensive intestines and relatively slower metabolisms, can more easily survive on a diet of leaves. They are also better able to counteract or withstand the poisonous chemicals many plants store in their leaves for defense. Following the dinosaurs' demise many types of medium and large mammals appeared. Studies of their teeth indicate that they had predominantly browsing (leaf-eating) diets. Most of these animals became extinct by the end of the Eocene (35 million years ago), with three very successful groups of survivors emerging from their ranks. These were the perissodactyls (horses, tapirs, rhinoceroses, and some extinct families), the artiodactyls (pigs, hippos, camels, deer, antelope, giraffes, and many others), and the proboscideans (elephants and their extinct kin).

There are currently two alternative hypotheses regarding the origin of perissodactyls. The traditional hypothesis argues for their origin in North or Central America from an extinct group of medium-sized herbivores, the phenacodonts, because many features of early perissodactyls resemble the Paleocene phenacodont *Tetraclaenodon*. A second hypothesis, supported by several recent investigations, considers perissodactyls to be more closely related to other ungulate groups, including the proboscideans, hyraxes, manatees, and extinct phenacolophids, than they are to phenacodonts. The fossil records of these groups suggest a likely common origin in either northern Africa or southern Asia. Recent attention has been focused on the phenacolophids, from the early Cenozoic of Asia. (Despite the similarity in names, these animals are not closely related to the phenacodonts.) Of particular importance to this hypothesis is the newly discovered Paleocene phenacolophid *Radinskya* from China. Its upper molar teeth have cusps forming a pattern similar to the Greek letter pi (π) (figure 2). This pattern forms the basic plan of the upper molars of all perissodactyls and is notably absent in phenacodonts. Although *Radinskya* is probably not the direct ancestor of perissodactyls, its discovery supports their Old World origin from a common stock with elephants and hyraxes. Further study, both of fossils and DNA-sequences of living forms, will be required to determine which, if either, of these two theories is more likely.

By what anatomical criteria is a mammal placed in the order Perissodactyla? Because the focus here is mostly on fossils, only skeletal features or those that can be inferred from bones are emphasized. Almost all authorities agree that perissodactyls include the living horses (family Equidae), tapirs (family Tapiridae and several extinct families), rhinos (Rhinocerotidae, plus two extinct families), and three major extinct groups, the palaeotheres, the chalicotheres, and the titanotheres (also known as brontotheres) (figure 3). These mammals all share a number of anatomical attributes that suggest their close relationship. Many of these are technical details of the ear region of the skull or the cusp pattern of the teeth, but some involve the feet. (The skeleton of the horse in the Appendix will help in this discussion.) In all perissodactyls the first digit (the equivalent of the human thumb or big toe) is absent on both the forefeet and the hindfeet, as is the fifth digit on the hindfoot. The third (central) digit is notably larger than the others. The perissodactyls are commonly referred to as the "odd-toed ungulates" because all or most of the weight is supported by either one or three digits. This is something of a misnomer because some perissodactyls (including the living tapir) have four digits on the forefoot, and there are ungulates other than perissodactyls with an odd number of digits. The bones forming the feet, especially the metapodials, in perissodactyls are elongated. Another important perissodactyl innovation is in the ankle joint, specifically in the bone called the astragalus (or the talus in humans). The perissodactyl astragalus has two raised parallel ridges on the surface where it articulates with the lower leg bone, or tibia. These permit efficient rotational movement in a fore-and-aft direction, but limit lateral movement at the ankle joint. All of these and other features suggest that from the very beginning perissodactyls had adapted to running at fast speeds over long distances. It is important to note that one of the other successful ungulate groups, the artiodactyls, also rapidly evolved characteristics of running mammals, in some ways even more advanced than those of perissodactyls. It is tempting to credit the suc-

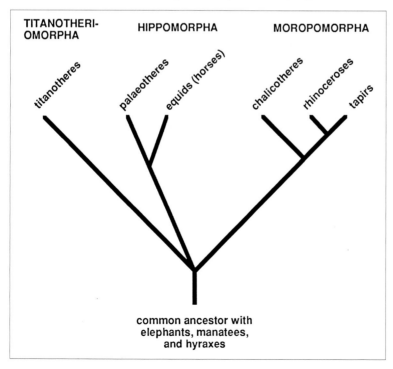

3. *Hypothesized evolutionary relationships among the major groups of perissodactyls. Note the three primary subdivisions. Only the equids, rhinos, and tapirs are still living; the others are known only from fossils. (After Prothero and Schoch, 1989)*

cess of these two groups to these innovations for running, as opposed to their many slower Eocene competitors that became extinct.

It is now known that the earliest perissodactyls had a second advantage over their Eocene contemporaries: a larger, more advanced brain. This advanced brain could have conveyed competitive advantages over other Eocene herbivores in ways like more complex social behavior and better recognition and evasion of predators.

Regardless of their place of origin and their particular ancestral stock, the first perissodactyls diversified rapidly into three major groups, with the horse included in the hippomorphs (figure 3). Fossils of the earliest members of these three groups are found in early Eocene rocks in Asia, Europe, and North America. In America the states of Wyoming, Colorado, and New Mexico have produced the most important specimens. Because Eocene perissodactyls all shared a fairly recent common ancestor, it is not surprising that the earliest members of each group generally resemble one another. Therefore, only relatively complete, well-preserved fossils can be definitively identified to family. Paleontologists who study these

4. Evolutionary relationships among early Cenozoic horses from North America. Note that equid evolution is always a series of branching lineages, never a simple progression of genera.

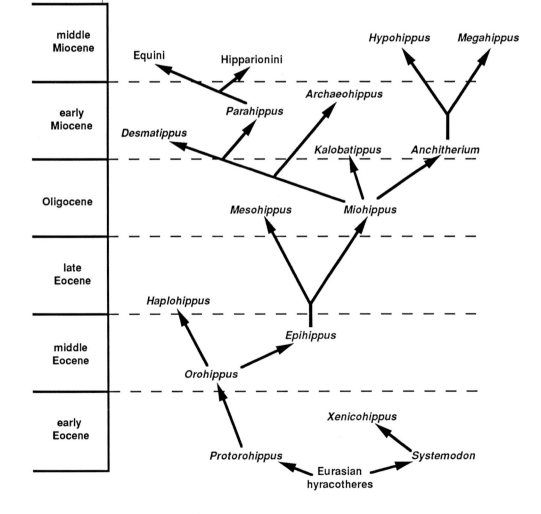

early perissodactyls do not agree on their classification; thus, a species one worker calls an equid might be placed in the titanotheres by another and the chalicotheres by a third. Such disagreements should be expected, given that many species are known only from fragmentary fossils and that they closely resemble one another at this stage of their evolution. Exactly which of these early species are members of the horse family Equidae and which are instead members of closely related, collateral lineages is an area of ongoing research and is still controversial.

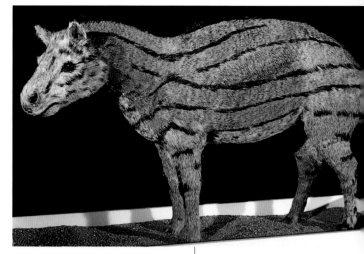

5. *Reconstructed* Hyracotherium. *This genus lived in the early Eocene, about 57 million years ago. (Carnegie Museum of Natural History, photo by Melinda McNaugher)*

This problem has unfortunate consequences in determining what name to apply to the oldest horses. For many years the genus *Hyracotherium* has been widely used and generally regarded as the first true horse (that is, of the family Equidae) (figure 4). The first named species, however, *Hyracotherium leporinum* from England, is now placed in a separate family, Palaeotheriidae, while many other species of *Hyracotherium* in North America are considered closely related to true equids. Those that fall in the family Equidae should eventually be given a different genus name. Until paleontologists sort out all the relationships, many continue to lump this group together. For simplicity all early Eocene members of the Hippomorpha are informally referred to here as "hyracotheres."

The Dawn Horses of the Eocene

At the beginning of the Eocene epoch, about 57 million years ago, hyracotheres, the tiny "dawn horses" of the Eocene, appeared in the faunas of North America and Eurasia. They were slender-legged, relatively small (about 4-11 kgs or 9-25 lbs), browsing herbivores (figures 5-7). All were similar in appearance and presumably in their ecology, differing only in body size and very subtle details of their teeth. The best clues as to how the hyracotheres actually lived and what they ate come from two widely separated fossil localities, Costillo Pocket in south-central Colorado and the Messel lake-bed deposits near Frankfurt, Germany.

6. Hyracotherium *skeleton. (Carnegie Museum of Natural History, photo by Melinda McNaugher)*

Costillo Pocket preserves the partial remains of thirty-two individuals representing two hyracothere species: a less-common smaller form (eight specimens) and a more-common larger species (twenty-four specimens). The sample of the large species is important as it represents the best census of a hyracothere population yet discovered, and it allows paleontologists to statistically analyze the differences between individuals. These in turn allow the extrapolation of ecological information based on comparisons with living mammals and other fossil samples. The most important

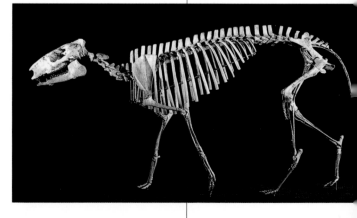

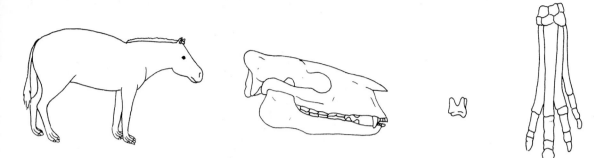

7. Hyracotherium *with its skull, upper molar, and forelimb. Note the four toes on the forelimb and three on the hindlimb. (Drawing by Linda Witt Fries)*

8. *Lateral (top) and ventral views of skulls of* Systemodon *(or* Hyracotherium) tapirinum *from Costillo Pocket, Colorado. The male skull is larger, more robust, and has larger canines. This shows a much greater degree of sexual dimorphism than is observed in living horses. (After Gingerich, 1981; used by permission)*

result of the analysis of the Costillo Pocket hyracothere is that males and females of the same species showed many significant differences (figure 8). The individuals presumed to be males were on average about 15 percent larger in size, had more robust skulls, and had much larger canine teeth (by about 40 percent). The term sexual dimorphism is used by biologists to describe species with significant differences (exclusive of the reproductive organs) between males and females. Modern horses have a very low degree of sexual dimorphism, with almost equal body size in males and females of the same breed. The size of the canine teeth is the only significant sexually dimorphic character in living horses. Males have large canines that are used in fights between each other for dominance and control of harems, and females either have greatly reduced canine teeth or lack them altogether. All fossil horse populations that have been studied show sexual dimorphism for canine size. This factor has obviously been constant throughout their history.

The degree of sexual dimorphism in body size in the Costillo Pocket hyracothere is one of the greatest known for any perissodactyl. Philip Gingerich, who studied this sample, inferred from this that females lived together in small permanent groups, and that there was extensive competition among males for the right to breed with these groups. This in turn led to selective pressure for larger

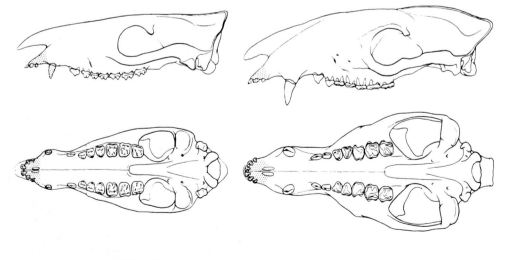

FEMALE　　　　　**MALE**

body size and canine teeth. In North America early Eocene hyracotheres replaced similarly sized, primitive ungulates, which did not have pronounced sexual dimorphism. Gingerich noted that this transition coincided in western North America with a climatic and environmental shift from a fully forested habitat to more open woodlands. He concluded that, instead of the traditional view of hyracotheres as forest dwellers, at least in North America they lived predominantly in the more open glades. These were covered by herbaceous plants, shrubs, and dry-adapted ferns, but not grasses. This view was based on observations of their adaptation for running (a skill of more value for herbivores in open habitats), their marked sexual dimorphism, and their larger and more complex brains, as well as on paleobotanical data.

The second fossil locality that provides major insights into hyracothere ecology is the famous Messel site in Germany. Messel consists of fine-grained sediments deposited at the bottom of a stagnant lake and is one of those rare places where more than just the skeletons of fossil animals are preserved. The chemistry of the lake waters prevented the complete destruction of organic tissues by bacteria, and the lack of strong currents and scavengers kept most skeletons intact and articulated. Many specimens preserve not only the whole skeleton, but also the original outline of the body. Traces of hair, skin, internal organs, and stomach contents are also found. Fish make up the majority of the fauna, but about thirty-five species of mammals have been found, including two species of the hyracothere *Propalaeotherium* (figure 9). Experts are divided on whether this genus is a true horse (equid) or a palaeothere. While the diet of hyracotheres has long been inferred on the basis of their teeth, the stomach contents of the Messel *Propalaeotherium* provide the first direct evidence (figure 10). As was long suspected, leaves of trees and shrubs were the major component, but more surprising was the presence of grapes in one individual. Whether fruit was a common element of the diet of all hyracotheres remains to be established.

A number of changes occurred at the end of the early Eocene. Because of continental drift, the direct connection between North America and Europe was severed, and Europe was also periodically separated from Asia by shallow seas. Global climates remained warm but became more seasonal, with yearly dry seasons.

9. Articulated skeleton of Propalaeotherium parvulum *from Messel, Germany. This species lived in the middle Eocene, about 49 million years ago. (Original in Senckenberg Museum, photo of cast in Carnegie Museum of Natural History by Melinda McNaugher)*

10. Leaf cuticle (lower side of leaf) from the stomach contents of Propalaeotherium hassiacum *from Messel, Germany. This discovery supports the hypothesis that* Propalaeotherium *was a leaf-eating browser rather than a grazer. (Courtesy of Senckenberg Museum, photo by Jens Franzen)*

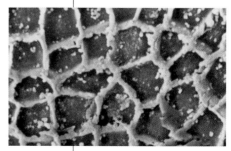

This led to increased openness in the vegetation, a trend that continued through the Oligocene and Miocene, and culminated in widespread savannas. After the early Eocene European hyracotheres diversified, with as many as seven species known from one locality in Spain. Some European lineages became large-bodied, with proportions resembling the modern tapir. They tended to retain the basic foot structure of the original hyracotheres, while other groups of European herbivores, including tapirs and rhinos, evolved further adaptations for running. One can presume that the hyracotheres remained in or near forested regions, while the runners opted for more open spaces. With historical hindsight it is obvious that those species that sought the open ranges were more successful, because the diversity of European palaeotheres and equids declined in the late Eocene. Only a few persisted until the middle Oligocene (about 30 million years ago), when they became extinct in Europe. Asia always differed from Europe and North America in the Eocene, as neither equids nor palaeotheres formed an important percentage of its herbivore fauna. Instead, titanotheres and small, fast-running rhinos and tapirs were more common. Equids and palaeotheres became extinct in Asia in the early Oligocene, slightly before their extinction in Europe.

Unlike their Eurasian cousins, North American horses took a different course in their evolutionary history and became increasingly adapted for living in open habitats and for running. Throughout the middle Eocene (between 50 and 39 million years ago), there was no trend to increase body size, nor any significant advance in limb or foot structure. The main change was in the dentition. In early Eocene horses the last three teeth in the jaw (the molars) were adapted for chewing leaves and other soft vegetation. The four teeth preceding the molars, the premolars, were not, having more triangular or blade-like shapes. During the Eocene the last three premolars acquired the same shape and function as the molars in a sequential process from back to front. This resulted in a doubling of the surface area for chewing (from three molars to three molars plus three molar-like premolars); that in turn allowed them to process food more efficiently. The first premolar remained small, and was sometimes lost in later horses. The middle Eocene horses that had one molar-like premolar are assigned to the genus *Orohippus*; those with two, to *Epihippus* (figure 4). During the transition from *Hyracotherium* to *Orohippus* to *Epihippus*, the structure of the grinding surface of the chewing teeth changed modestly. The individual bumps or cusps on the teeth of early Eocene hyracotheres were distinctly separated from each other, with just a hint of ridge development. In *Orohippus* and even more so in *Epihippus*, these cusps became connected to one another by a series of low ridges across the surface of the tooth. These ridges were later modified in the course of horse evolution to form the distinctive patterns found on the chewing teeth. The teeth of early and middle Eocene horses had very low crowns, similar to those of humans. Such teeth are suitable for processing relatively soft vegetation like leaves of trees and shrubs, but would wear down rapidly with a coarse diet of grasses or gritty plant matter. Like the early Eocene horses, those of the middle Eocene are best known from western North America, including Wyoming, Utah, New Mexico, and western-most Texas.

The Rise of the Three-toed Horses

At the start of the late Eocene, about 37 million years ago, three new types of horses appeared in North America. These are the genera *Haplohippus*, *Mesohippus* (figure 11), and *Miohippus*. *Haplohippus* differed only slightly from *Orohippus*,

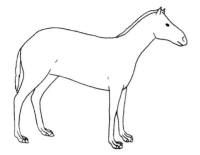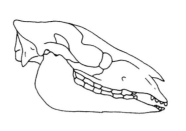

but the other two were much more advanced. *Mesohippus* and *Miohippus* are among the best known of the fossil horses, thanks to the incredibly fossiliferous rocks of late Eocene and Oligocene age in South Dakota and adjacent states. Many whole or nearly whole skulls and a number of skeletons have been found weathering out of heavily eroded sediments forming badlands. These horses are known from western Texas, Florida, and Oregon, in addition to the Great Plains of the United States and Canada.

In facial and body proportions, *Mesohippus* and *Miohippus* definitely had much more classic horselike features than older genera. When compared with *Epihippus* and *Orohippus*, they had the following new features. The fifth digit of the forefoot was lost, leaving three toes (digits two, three, and four) on both the forefoot and the hindfoot. Body weight was still partially supported by fleshy pads behind the toes (as in modern dogs). Although the smaller species of *Mesohippus* and *Miohippus* were similar in size to the larger species of *Epihippus*, there were also larger species up to seventy-five centimeters (2.5 ft.) tall and weighing about fifty-five kilograms (121 lbs). The muzzle of the skull was lengthened, and there was a longer gap between the anterior nipping teeth (the incisors) and the posterior chewing teeth. A distinct depression or pit (called a facial fossa) was present on the side of the skull in front of the opening for the eye. These facial fossae, found in many fossil horses, are not present in living horses, and thus their function has been much debated. Those who classify fossil horses also debate how much emphasis should be given to the differences in size, shape, location, and depth of the facial fossae.

The teeth of *Mesohippus* and *Miohippus* also differed in many respects from those of *Epihippus*. The incisors were larger, and the uppers bore cup-like depressions (found in all horses thereafter). The second upper premolars were completely molar-like, giving them a total of six grinding teeth per jaw. The system of ridges connecting the cusps was fully developed, and ridge height was increased for more efficient chewing.

Miohippus differed from *Mesohippus* by having a relatively longer skull, a deeper facial fossa, and in the hindfoot there was a broadening and strengthening of the central digit at the expense of the side toes. According to a recent review by Donald Prothero and Neil Shubin, as many as five or six species of *Mesohippus* and *Miohippus* coexisted at various times between 34 and 29 million years ago.

Originating from late Oligocene *Miohippus*, two main lines of descent are recognized from the early Miocene of North America (figure 4). One line, the anchitheres, retained the low-crowned, relatively simple teeth and padded feet of *Miohippus*, but grew to very large size, comparable to modern *Equus*. Their body weights are estimated to have ranged between 200 and 400 kilograms (441–882

11. Mesohippus *with its skull, upper molar, and forelimb. This genus lived in the late Eocene and the Oligocene, about 35 million years ago. (Drawing by Linda Witt Fries)*

lbs). The anchitheres were not merely overgrown *Miohippus* but had their own specializations. One species had very long, slender legs (other anchitheres tended to be more stout), while another had peculiarly enlarged, spoon-like lower incisors. Anchitheres were widespread in North America (they are known from Florida to California). One species of *Anchitherium* entered Asia across the Bering Strait in the early Miocene. All horses or horse-like palaeotheres in the Old World had been extinct since the middle Oligocene, a period of about four million years. *Anchitherium* filled that gap as it spread throughout Eurasia, diversifying into several species of various sizes. Anchitheres in both North America and Eurasia became extinct in the late Miocene, about 9 million years ago. Because of their simple, low-crowned teeth, the diet of anchitheres is thought to have been predominantly soft vegetation, particularly leaves. Unfortunately, no Miocene equivalent of the site of Messel has yet provided direct evidence of this. Their extinction is thought to be linked to global climatic change (increased aridity) that led to the loss of forested habitat and the spread of savannas and grasslands. Many browsing herbivores became extinct at this time.

The second line, the Equinae, contained distinctly different types of horses. The first of their major innovations concerned the foot and was related to an increasing need to run faster and more efficiently. The fleshy pads behind the toes were lost, and during normal movement on hard surfaces all body weight was supported only by the hoof of the third digit. A series of strong ligaments ran from the central metapodial to the rear of the lengthened toe bones. These provided support and a spring-like action to the foot. The two side digits were reduced but (at this stage) retained small toe bones complete with tiny hooves. The side digits came into play only when traveling on soft ground, during rapid starts and lateral movements, and when moving at maximum speeds. Other modifications to the limbs related to greater running abilities included reduction of the shaft of the ulna, the smaller bone in the lower foreleg, and the fibula in the lower hindleg.

Early Miocene members of the Equinae can be divided into two groups, the diminutive *Archaeohippus* and a diverse group of medium-sized species, the parahippines (figure 4). In its skull and teeth, *Archaeohippus* showed little difference from the anchitheres; indeed, for that reason it was long classified with that subfamily instead of with the Equinae. *Archaeohippus* provides a good counter example to the general observation that horses increased in size over the course of their evolution. This genus is one of at least four instances of dramatic size reduction in North American horses during the Miocene. *Archaeohippus* was similar in size to a small *Mesohippus*, with very slender limbs. Although originally described from specimens found in Oregon, it was most abundant in the Gulf Coast region, with records from Texas, Florida, and Panama.

Most of the remaining horses of the early Miocene form the parahippine species-complex, which in many accounts are grouped together in a single genus, *Parahippus*. Although it is evident that actually several genera are represented, there has never been a comprehensive, critical study of the parahippines, so even the number of valid species is not known. Parahippines differed from *Miohippus, Archaeohippus,* and anchitheres in having two additional ridges on the crown surface of the upper teeth. In some there was a modest but significant

24

increase in the height of the crown, indicating that there was heavy wear on the teeth due to the abrasive nature of the diet. Grass is generally much more abrasive than the leaves of trees and shrubs, so these animals were probably relying more on grass than their predecessors. Because these animals had teeth that could continue to push up through the gums as they wore down, their life spans could be maintained or increased. Once other herbivores' teeth are worn down to the gum, they can no longer feed and survive. The second innovation was the addition of a third component to the tooth. In mammals with low-crowned teeth, such as humans, hyracotheres, and anchitheres, the crown of the tooth consists of an outer layer of shiny, very hard enamel with an inner core of dentine. Mammals with high-crowned teeth, including the modern horse, have a third substance that covers the enamel and fills in depressions on the crown surface or the valleys between the ridges. This substance is called cement, because it acts as a glue to bind the roots of the teeth firmly in the bony sockets of the jaws. Only in species with high-crowned teeth does the cement cover the enamel of the crown. Certain advanced species of parahippines were the first horses to have cement on their crowns. But the cement layer on the crown was fairly thin and not found on the milk (temporary) teeth.

Parahippine skulls had long muzzles, like modern horses, and there was a complete bar of bone at the rear of the eye socket to better absorb forces generated by stronger chewing. Advanced parahippines were probably the first horses to add a significant amount of grass to their diets, although they still ate leaves as well. Such herbivores are called "mixed-feeders" to separate them from those that eat predominantly leaves (browsers) or grasses (grazers).

About 17 million years ago, late in the early Miocene, parahippine species declined in abundance (although they continued on for another four million years), as another group took center stage. This group, the merychippine species-complex, dominated North American equid faunas for the next three million years or so. As was the case with the parahippines, the merychippines were long classified as a single genus (*Merychippus* [figure 12]) when in fact they represent many separate lineages. The merychippines, however, have been studied in recent years by several paleontologists and their complex evolutionary history is no longer such a mystery. The term merychippines is used here informally to collectively refer to a group of fossil species of North American horses that includes early members of both the tribes Equini and Hipparionini (figure 13) and that are all at a similar evolutionary stage. While a number of differences in the skull and teeth separate the merychippines as a group from the parahippines, these are most-

12. Merychippus *with its skull, upper molar, and forelimb. This genus lived in the Miocene, about 17 to 11 million years ago. (Drawing by Linda Witt Fries)*

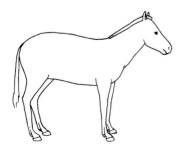

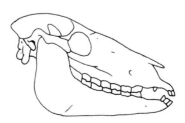

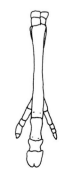

13. Evolutionary relationships of late Cenozoic North American horse genera in the tribes Hipparionini (right) and Equini. The two tribes diverged from each other about 18 million years ago, and each diversified in the middle Miocene. Species in both tribes that lived between 17 and 14 million years ago are informally called the merychippine horses. The middle to late Miocene (15 to 6 million years ago) witnessed the acme of generic diversity of North American horses. Note the decline in diversity in the Pliocene, until only Equus remained in the Pleistocene. It, too, became extinct in North America about 11,000 years ago.

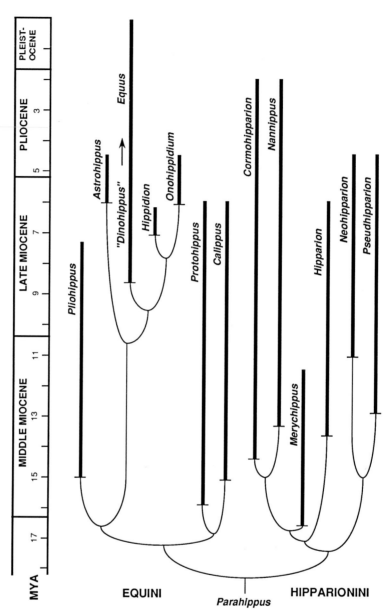

ly relatively minor and technical in nature. In general, the trends listed above for parahippine chewing teeth were continued. Merychippine teeth have a thicker coating of cement, a more complex series of folds and ridges, and taller crowns (some exceeding 2.5 cm or 1 in. in height) than those of parahippines. The merychippines were still mixed-feeders, but were eating proportionally more grass than their parahippine contemporaries.

The great diversification of horses in the Miocene originated from the merychippines (figure 13). Whereas there had always been several species of horses coexisting in North America at any one time since the Eocene, from the latter half of the middle Miocene to the late Miocene (between about 14 and 6 million years ago), there was an unprecedented number of coexisting species (anywhere

from eight to twelve or more). Paleontologists long wondered how so many similar species could coexist. Their great numbers appeared to violate the general ecological axiom that two (much less eight) coexisting species could not occupy the
same niche, because one would outcompete the other and drive it to extinction. A
number of observations, both on the fossils themselves and on modern grazing
herbivores, have solved this dilemma. First, not all Miocene horses with high-
crowned teeth were pure grazers like the modern horses; some remained mixed-
feeders. Even those that were grazers did not necessarily eat the same types of
grasses or the same parts of the grass plant. Detailed studies of the ecology of
modern grazers living in African savannas have revealed a complex partitioning of
resources. Those factors that are important in ecologically separating modern
African grazers, such as differing combinations of body size and relative muzzle
width and length, are also found in Miocene grazing horses.

The Heyday and Passing of Three-toed Horses

Evolving from a common ancestor, three-toed hipparionine and equine
horses diversified rapidly between 18 and 15 million years ago and spread across
North America. For many millions of years, hipparionine horses dominated
North American faunas and spread throughout the Old World as well. Because the
modern horse *Equus* is a member of the equines, the hipparionines are disregarded as an unimportant side branch in many general accounts of the evolutionary
history of horses. One reason for this is that despite their numerical superiority in
the fossil record, hipparionines all retained a three-toed foot, giving them a more
primitive appearance. In factors related to the dentition, however, various hipparionines were the most advanced horses ever to have existed, or were at the very least
equal to living *Equus*.

Hipparionine and equine horses both have high-crowned, cement-covered
chewing teeth. As the high-crowned teeth were worn, a pattern of enamel lines was
exposed on the chewing surface. Although there was much variation in the
details of this pattern, both as an animal grew older and between individuals of
the same species, genera and species can usually be identified on the basis of
their own particular enamel pattern. One fairly reliable characteristic that dis-
tinguishes hipparionine teeth from those of equines relates to a structure called
the protocone, a round, oval, or bean-shaped enamel feature found on the inner
half of the chewing surface of the upper teeth (figure 14). The protocone can be
either connected or isolated. The former is characteristic of most equines; the latter, of hipparionines. Another general feature is that in hipparionines the two
internal enamel lakes on the upper teeth have complex borders with intricate

*14. Right upper molars of repre-
sentative members of the tribes
Equini (*Protohippus *on the
left) and *Hipparionini
(Cormohipparion), *showing
the characteristic differences in the
upper teeth between the two tribes.*

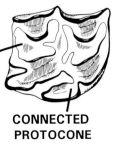

SIMPLE
FOSSETTES

CONNECTED
PROTOCONE

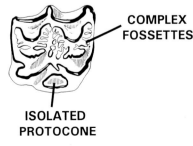

COMPLEX
FOSSETTES

ISOLATED
PROTOCONE

folds and wrinkles (figure 14). Most equines have much simpler lakes.

From the late middle Miocene to the early Pliocene (from 14 to 3 million years ago), there were more species of hipparionine horses present in North America than equines. Rich deposits of this age are well known from the Great Plains (especially Nebraska), the Texas Panhandle, California, and Florida, although much of the continent except the Northeast is represented. The southernmost hipparionines are found in Honduras; they apparently never entered South America. Six hipparionine lineages were present in North America and are recognized by most specialists as distinct genera (figure 13). All had slender, gracile legs compared with living *Equus*. Most species of four of these genera were about the size of a deer or pony, but two lineages, *Nannippus* and *Pseudhipparion*, were dwarfs. *Pseudhipparion* and the larger *Cormohipparion* were the two most abundant horse genera in most faunas east of the Rocky Mountains between 13 and 9 million years ago. Along the West Coast, *Hipparion* and *Cormohipparion* were the common horses. Skulls and teeth of typical hipparionines are shown in figure 15.

Hipparionine horses appeared for the first time in the Old World about 11 million years ago, the start of the late Miocene, and coexisted for a time with resident anchitheres. The first hipparionine to disperse was a member of the North American *Cormohipparion* lineage. It crossed the Bering land bridge (once located where the Bering Strait is today) from North America to Asia and rapidly spread to Europe and northern Africa. Shortly afterwards the Indian subcontinent and southern Africa were colonized. Just as in North America, Old World hipparionines diversified into many species throughout the late Miocene and into the early Pliocene. Research on them is perhaps the liveliest topic in equid paleontology, with many scientific papers published each year by specialists with differing viewpoints.

Global climates began to change drastically very late in the Miocene as the Earth entered a new climatic phase, culminating in the cyclic glacial/interglacial ages that have alternated for the last 3 million years. The very species-rich savannas were replaced with less-diverse pure grasslands. This is manifested in the North American fossil record by numerous extinctions near the end of the Miocene (about 6 million years ago) and again in the early Pliocene (about 4.5 million years ago). Three-toed horses, rhinoceroses, and mastodonts were especially hard hit. The first extinction event resulted in the loss of four genera and ten species of horses, while four more genera and six species became extinct during the second event. Only three horse species survived. Two of these were three-toed hipparionines—one species each of *Nannippus* and *Cormohipparion*. Both lasted until about 2 million years ago (late Pliocene), when these last three-toed horses in North America became extinct.

A fairly similar pattern is seen in the Old World. Following maximum diversity in the late Miocene, hipparionine numbers declined, especially in Europe. A very

15. Skulls of North American Miohippus *and three representative hipparionine horses: A,* Miohippus obliquidens, *South Dakota, Oligocene (after Osborn, 1918); B,* Merychippus insignis, *South Dakota, Miocene (after Skinner and Taylor, 1967); C,* Cormohipparion sphenodus, *Nebraska, Miocene (after MacFadden, 1992); and D,* Pseudhipparion retrusum, *Nebraska, Miocene. (Drawings by Linda Witt Fries)*

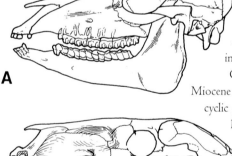

A

B

C

D

advanced hipparionine lineage appeared early in the Pliocene, apparently evolving in China. This group of species shared a number of specialized features in its chewing teeth and feet with *Equus* and *Neohipparion* (the dentally most-advanced North American hipparionine). Some even believe that these Chinese species were derived directly from *Neohipparion* of North America, but most likely their similarities resulted from convergent evolution. Presumably these specialized hipparionines, like *Equus*, were well suited for arid habitats and a diet of dry grasses. Offshoots of this Asiatic lineage spread to Europe and Africa and for a while successfully competed with *Equus*. These, the last hipparionines, became extinct in the late Pliocene in Europe, the early Pleistocene in Asia, and the middle Pleistocene in Africa (about 400,000 years ago).

The Fossil History of Equus and Other One-toed Horses

The equines appeared late in the early Miocene at the same time as the hipparionines, about 17 million years ago (figure 13). The early equines were all three-toed, like their parahippine ancestors, and two genera, *Protohippus* and *Calippus*, always retained this condition. *Calippus* (figure 16A) included some very small species. With the exception of the medium-sized *Astrohippus*, all other equines tended to be large, especially when compared with the average hipparionine. In one branch of the equines, the side toes were reduced in size and presumably had little function. They were eventually lost in the late Miocene. The condition of having one digit per foot, called monodactyly, probably evolved twice within the Equini, once in the genus *Pliohippus* (figure 17), and once in the lineage that includes *Astrohippus* and *Equus* (figure 18). Although monodactyl horses are widely portrayed as superior runners to those with three digits per foot, acquisition of this character did not immediately gain them superiority in terms of numbers.

Geography played an important role in the evolution of the equines and thus of the modern horse. For example, *Pliohippus* (figure 16B), *Calippus*, and *Protohippus* were common in the East, from the plains to Florida, but were absent in the West. Early in the late Miocene, about 10 million years ago, several interesting equine species were present in California and Utah. They apparently represent the oldest members of the *Astrohippus-Equus* lineage. Their foot structure has not been described, but some were probably monodactyl. At this time the intermontane basins of the West were much more arid than the plains. It seems plausible that many of the adaptations of *Equus*, including monodactyly and very high-crowned teeth (to eat dry grass covered with grit), were the result of this type of environment. To this day

16. Skulls of four representative members of the tribe Equini: A, Calippus regulus, *Nebraska, Miocene;* B, Pliohippus pernix, *Nebraska, Miocene (after Webb, 1969);* C, Equus conversidens, *Arizona, Pleistocene (after Skinner, 1942);* D, Hippidion neogeus, *Argentina, Pleistocene; note the very deep nasal notch (after Burmeister, 1875). (Drawings by Linda Witt Fries).*

most living members of the genus *Equus* are anatomically, ecologically, and physiologically well adapted to very dry habitats. *Equus* did not evolve from either *Pliohippus* or *Protohippus*, as is still sometimes stated, although they all are closely related.

There is some controversy over how to define the genus *Equus* and which fossil species to refer to it. This author defines *Equus* as those equine species that form the side branch to those that make up the genera *Hippidion* and *Onohippidium* (figure 13). Others prefer to arbitrarily exclude the older members of this group, those older than 4.5 million years ago, and regard them as a separate genus, *Dinohippus*. Under this latter scheme, *Equus* first appeared 4.5 million years ago, having evolved from its ancestor *Dinohippus mexicanus*. Using this author's definition of *Equus*, the genus appeared about 7 to 8 million years ago, in the late Miocene. The difference in classification is not in the age of the pertinent fossils, but into which genus they are assigned.

Equus (including *Dinohippus*), *Onohippidium*, and *Hippidion* all were large, monodactyl equids. The last two differed from *Equus* (figure 16C) in the configuration of the nasal bones in the skull, which were widely separated from the premaxilla by a very deep notch (figure 16D). The patterns of facial fossae also distinguished them. *Onohippidium* and *Hippidion* were originally described from the late Pliocene and Pleistocene of South America. Although their North American origin was widely recognized, it was not until 1979 that actual fossils of these genera were identified from North America. A species of *Onohippidium* was described from the early Pliocene of New Mexico, and a late Miocene mandible from Texas was referred to *Hippidion*. These two genera were among the first wave of mammals to disperse into South America after the formation of the Panamanian land bridge about 2.5 million years ago. They were the first horses on that continent, preceding *Equus* by about a million years.

Early *Equus* (the *Dinohippus* of most other authors) spread rapidly eastward in the late Miocene. It was present in Florida shortly after its earliest-known appearance in Oregon. The Florida fossils, ironically, were found during construction of a practice racetrack in Marion County near Ocala, a region now renowned for breeding and training thoroughbred racehorses. *Equus* remained uncommon in North America until very late in the Miocene, when the hipparionines and three-toed equines experienced heavy extinction. The monodactyl equines, usually *Equus* and *Astrohippus*, came to dominate most faunas after 6 million years ago. During the early Pliocene, at about 4.5 million years ago, all equines with the exception of *Equus* became extinct. A single, widespread species known as *Equus simplicidens* is recognized across North America between 4.5 and 2.5 million years ago. Idaho has produced the best samples of this species. Although once placed in its own genus, *Plesippus*, modern authorities classify it as a member of *Equus*, and some regard it as especially close to the living Grevy's zebra. *Equus* truly began to diversify in the late Pliocene, when a number of species, perhaps four, coexisted in North America.

If ever a fossil group can be said to have overwhelmed paleontologists with too many specimens and too much data, it is *Equus*. Literally hundreds of species have been named, including about sixty from North America. The vast majority of these were based on such incomplete specimens that they never should

have been described in the first place. Whereas all experts in the field would agree with this last statement, they do not agree on which of these species are the truly valid ones; nor is there uniform agreement as to what constitutes the limits of a "good species" of *Equus*. Also, while several authorities have analyzed the relationships of fossil and living *Equus*, their results show a depressing lack of congruence. Some believe that almost every living species can be traced back to separate North American ancestors, while others contend that there were fewer dispersal events between the continents and more convergent evolution. Note that this is a common conundrum for vertebrate paleontologists (similar debates were noted with hipparionine horses) and not limited to equids.

Without getting into details, which are murky to begin with, starting in the very late Pliocene, about 2.5 million years ago, most North American fossil faunas contained two to four species of *Equus*. Often there was a small, pony-sized type coexisting with a larger form, both with relatively stout limbs. An additional, very slender-legged, usually medium-sized species probably related to the Asiatic asses was occasionally present as well, especially in the early and middle Pleistocene. There are more Pleistocene fossil localities than from any other age, because this period is the most recent, and *Equus* is common in almost every locality that contains large mammals. This situation continued until near the end of the Pleistocene, about 11,000 years ago, when many North American mammals became extinct over a short period of time. Victims of this mass extinction event included mammoths, mastodons, ground sloths, camels, tapirs, and horses among the large herbivores as well as the large carnivores that preyed upon them, such as lions, saber-toothed cats, and dire wolves. There is an ongoing controversy as to the immediate cause of this event, with rapid climatic and ensuing vegetational change, and overhunting by humans being the two opposing views. In either case the 57-million-year history of the horse in North America came to an end, at least until the introduction of domesticated horses and donkeys by European explorers and colonists.

North American *Equus* also dispersed to other continents. It first appeared in South America in the middle Pleistocene and successfully spread throughout that continent. There it coexisted with *Hippidion* and *Onohippidium* until the end of the Pleistocene. Then, as in North America, all South American horses became extinct.

17. Pliohippus with its skull, upper molar, and forelimb. This genus lived in the middle and late Miocene, about 15 to 7 million years ago. (Drawing by Linda Witt Fries)

18. Equus with its skull, upper molar, and forelimb. The genus of modern horses, asses, and zebras first appeared in the early Pliocene about 4 million years ago at various locations in the western United States. The largest known early Pliocene sample was found in southern Idaho. (Drawing by Linda Witt Fries)

Eurasia and Africa also proved receptive to *Equus*. The following account is based on recent research by Augusto Azzaroli of Italy, Vera Eisenmann of France, and Ann Forsten of Finland. The oldest well-documented Eurasian *Equus* is late Pliocene in age, about 2.5 million years ago, although there are a few slightly older, more questionable records. It is very similar to the North American *Equus simplicidens* in most features, including a slight facial fossa, but it had longer leg bones. This species, *Equus livenzovensis*, is known from southern Russia, Italy, and Spain. It was replaced slightly later in the Pliocene by a similar-sized species with more complex teeth, a fainter facial fossa, and a deeper nasal notch (although not nearly so deep as *Hippidion*). This important species, *Equus stenonis*, is well known throughout the latest Pliocene and early Pleistocene of Europe, northern Asia, and China, with many recognized subspecies. *Equus stenonis* is widely regarded as the starting point for the first great diversification of Old World *Equus*. Its possible descendants include *Equus bressanus* from the early Pleistocene of western Europe, the largest-ever Old World horse; *Equus namadicus* and related species from the Indian subcontinent; and *Equus numidicus* and *Equus mauritanicus* from the late Pliocene of northern Africa. These last two are considered the likely progenitors of modern zebras. *Equus numidicus* led to a group of sub-Saharan Pleistocene species that includes Grevy's zebra, *Equus grevyi*, and, according to V. Eisenmann, the mountain zebra, *Equus zebra*. *Equus mauritanicus* is related to the living plains zebra, *Equus burchelli*, the recently extinct quagga of southern Africa, and, according to some, the mountain zebra as well.

The two remaining groups of *Equus*, the asses and the true or "caballine" horses, both probably originated in North America. Representatives of each are known by at least the early Pleistocene, by about 1.5 million years ago. They first appeared in Eurasia somewhat later, about 900,000 years ago. Species of the slender-legged Asiatic ass group were present in Europe through the late Pleistocene, but are now limited to mountainous regions of central Asia and the Middle East. The origins of the African ass, *Equus africanus*, and its domesticated offshoot, the donkey, are less clear. They might have a separate North American ancestry. In the Old World good records start in the late Pleistocene of Africa and southern Europe.

Caballine horses, the group that includes the living *Equus caballus* (the modern domestic horse) and *Equus przewalskii* (the wild Asiatic horse), dispersed to Asia from North America very late in the early Pleistocene. This group proved to be very successful in northern Eurasia, where it largely replaced the resident *Equus stenonis* and its descendants. *Equus caballus* ranged widely in the late Pleistocene, with fossils known from England and Spain east to Japan. Siberian individuals crossed over into Alaska in the Pleistocene, probably the first instance of an Old World horse dispersing into North America since the Eocene hyracotheres.

Summary

This essay has traced, through fossils, the ancestry of modern horses from the family's beginning to the recent past and the origin of the living species. Clearly horses were once much more widely distributed than they are today and

more important in large-mammal faunas. The fossil record of horses has traditionally been interpreted as displaying a series of gradually changing trends, such
as increasing body size, loss of side toes, and increasing tooth crown height. This
interpretation is faulty for several reasons. When viewed as a whole, the fossil
record of horses reveals a complex pattern of branching lineages, much of which
researchers are only beginning to understand. There is no simple progression of
ancestors and descendants at the level of either the species or the genus. When
viewed in detail, most species persisted for one to four million years, without
showing gradual changes for important characters. The apparent "trends" have
been driven principally by climatic change at a global level and its effect on vegetation. Species that prior to a change were limited to marginal habitats found
themselves in a transformed world much better suited to their particular way of
life and then became more abundant. The rise of *Equus* serves as a good example.
Early in the late Miocene, many types of three-toed horses flourished in North
America, and several anchitheres were still present. By the end of the Miocene the
anchitheres were extinct, the three-toed horses in decline, and the formerly limited
monodactyl horses were dominant. This last group was the best adapted to handle
the pronounced change in climate, in this case increased aridity. One can easily
imagine that if the climatic change had been in the opposite direction, to a moister
climate reminiscent of the Eocene, then the forest-adapted anchitheres might have
prevailed instead of the equines.

Most nontechnical surveys of horse evolution present the story as if it
were a series of established facts. In reality it is a web of hypotheses and theories,
with many points of contention and controversy. No two paleontologists interpret
the fossil record exactly alike, and this is certainly true in the case of horses. It is,
however, only through this competitive process that scientists arrive at an increasingly accurate account of horse evolution.

The future holds many promising avenues for research on fossil equids.
First and foremost, new fossil sites are continuously being discovered, so geographic
and chronological gaps in the fossil record continue to be eliminated. Research on
specimens from these and pre-existing localities will continue at the most fundamental level, the recognition of species and determination of their evolutionary
relationships. This most basic aspect of paleontologic research is still needed at
numerous points in the history of horses, among the Eocene hyracotheres and the
Miocene parahippines to name just two. Ecological studies of fossil horses will
become increasingly sophisticated, especially in the interpretation of diet and
behavior, as will studies of their functional anatomy. The fossil record of horses is
no longer prominent in providing data for the study of evolutionary processes.
Instead, equids are now just one of many groups that a researcher can use as examples. Nevertheless, because of our long-term relationship with horses, their fossil
record will always have special significance.

Reading List

Azzaroli, A. "The Genus *Equus* in Europe," in *European Neogene Mammal Chronology,* ed. by E. H. Lindsay, V. Fahlbusch, and P. Mein. New York: Plenum Press, 1990. Pp. 339-56.

Bernor, R. L.; H. Tobien; and M. O. Woodburne. "Patterns of Old World Hipparionine Evolutionary Diversification and Biogeographic Extension," in *European Neogene Mammal Chronology,* ed. by E. H. Lindsay, V. Fahlbusch, and P. Mein. New York: Plenum Press, 1990. Pp. 263-319.

Burmeister, H. *Die fossilen Pferde der Pampasformation.* Buenos Aires: La Tribuna, 1875.

Carroll, R. L. *Vertebrate Paleontology and Evolution.* New York: W. H. Freeman and Co., 1988.

Colbert, E. H., and M. Morales. *Evolution of the Vertebrates,* 4th ed. New York: Wiley-Liss, 1991.

Eisenmann, V. "Family Equidae," in *Koobi Fora Research Project.* Vol. 2, *The Fossil Ungulates: Proboscidea, Perissodactyla, and Suidae,* ed. by J. M. Harris. Oxford: Oxford University Press, 1983.

Forsten, A. "Horse Diversity Through the Ages." *Biological Reviews* 64 (1989), 279-304.

Gingerich, P. D. "Variation, Sexual Dimorphism, and Social Structure in the Early Eocene Horse *Hyracotherium* (Mammalia, Perissodactyla)." *Paleobiology* 7 (1981), 443-55.

Hulbert, R. C. "Taxonomic Evolution in North American Neogene Horses (Subfamily Equinae): the Rise and Fall of an Adaptive Radiation." *Paleobiology* 19 (1993), 216-34.

Hulbert, R. C., and B. J. MacFadden. "Morphological Transformation and Cladogenesis at the Base of the Adaptive Radiation of Miocene Hypsodont Horses." *American Museum Novitates* 3000 (1991), 1-61.

MacFadden, B. J. *Fossil Horses: Systematics, Paleobiology, and Evolution of the Family Equidae.* New York: Cambridge University Press, 1992.

MacFadden, B. J., and M. F. Skinner. "Diversification and Biogeography of the One-Toed Horses *Onohippidium* and *Hippidion*." *Postilla* 175 (1979), 1-10.

Osborn, H. F. "Equidae of the Oligocene, Miocene, and Pliocene of North America." *Memoirs of the American Museum of Natural History* 2 (1918), 1-331.

Prothero, D. R., and R. M. Schoch, editors. *The Evolution of Perissodactyls.* New York: Oxford University Press, 1989.

Radinsky, L. "The Adaptive Radiation of the Phenacodontid Condylarths and the Origin of the Perissodactyla." *Evolution* 20 (1966), 408-17.

_____ "The Early Evolution of the Perissodactyla." *Evolution* 23 (1969), 308-28.

Simpson, G. G. *Horses.* New York: Oxford University Press, 1951.

Skinner, M. F. "The Fauna of Papago Springs Cave, Arizona, and a Study of *Stockoceros*." *Bulletin of the American Museum of Natural History* 80(6) (1942), 143-220.

Skinner, M. F., and B. E. Taylor. "A Revision of the Geology and Paleontology of the Bijou Hills, South Dakota." *American Museum Novitates* 2300 (1967), 1-53.

Webb, S. D. "The Burge and Minnechaduza Clarendonian Mammalian Faunas of North-Central Nebraska." *University of California Publications in Geological Sciences* 78 (1969), 1-191.

HORSE HUNTERS
OF THE ICE AGE

SANDRA L. OLSEN

Most of our knowledge about the earliest
interactions between humans and horses comes from the late Pleistocene (the geologic epoch commonly referred to as the Ice Age), from approximately 125,000 to
10,000 years before the present (B.P.). To reconstruct a picture of the horses that
humans first encountered, scientists can examine data from three sources: frozen
carcasses of horses in Siberia and North America that may have had no contact
with humans; horse bones from archaeological sites in Europe, Asia, and America;
and artistic representations of horses made by hunters living in Western Europe.

The fossil record for horses during the Pleistocene[1] of Europe and Asia
is somewhat confusing because of the wide variation in the size of horses and
because of the fragmentary nature of the fossils. In addition, the paleontological
classification is cluttered with old names of species and revision is sorely needed.
Instead of referring to all the old names, some of which are undoubtedly invalid,
it is best to consider Pleistocene horses as a group, recognizing that there is considerable variation in size and proportions through time and over large distances
that may represent distinct species in some cases and mere grades of the same
species in others.

Distribution of Horses in the Ice Age

Pleistocene fossil horses have been found from eastern Siberia,
Mongolia, and China through Eurasia, including Russia, Hungary, the Czech
Republic, Italy, Germany, France, Spain, and even England, but not so far west
as Ireland. Based on their prevalence in the fossil record, horse populations
were relatively high in Eurasia during the Pleistocene.

In the New World the range of horses extended from Alaska to
southern Mexico and from California to Florida during the late Pleistocene.
The distribution of horses, as well as mammoths, in Alaska during this time
was primarily on floodplains. R. D. Guthrie has calculated that the proportions of
horses in the total fauna of Alaska were about 32.7 percent of the individuals and
17 percent of the biomass, but horses may not have been nearly so numerous in
the rest of North America. Their greatest frequencies in that continent occurred
between 10,000 and 15,000 years ago.

Most researchers agree that ancient horses preferred open grasslands but
were often associated with forest steppes as well. They seem to have been primarily grazers that also depended in a minor way on browsing woody plants.
According to Guthrie, New World horses and mammoths preferred fiber-rich
medium-to-tall grasses growing near rivers and to a lesser extent, sedges and minor
amounts of brush. Bison, on the other hand, opted for short grasses in drier areas.

Facing page, see figure 5.

---

1. For the epochs in the Cenozoic and their dates, see chapter 2, figure 1.

Frozen Horse Carcasses from Siberia and North America

New discoveries of frozen bodies of enormous mammoths are usually well-publicized in the media. In the last hundred years there have been numerous examples in both Siberia and North America. It is not so well known that many Pleistocene horse carcasses have also been discovered in the Arctic permafrost. These remains provide valuable documentation regarding the coat, soft tissue, and diet of these Ice Age beasts.

According to paleontologists, at least three species have been identified from the remains in Siberia. All of these horses bear a close resemblance to the surviving wild Asiatic horse *(Equus przewalskii)* in terms of their stature, appearance, and habitat. One of the best documented examples is the Chersky horse *(Equus lenensis)*, which lived in the late Pleistocene in northeastern Siberia, from Taimyr to the Chukchi Peninsula. It is unknown whether this species lived on into the Holocene (Recent) epoch (10,000 B.P. to present), but it could be the direct ancestor of the present-day Przewalski horse. One particularly well-preserved stallion, dating to around 34,000-39,000 years B.P., was found near the Selerikan River, in the Indigirka Basin. This adult male, found in 1968, reveals much about the Chersky horses. It stood about 134-136 centimeters (13.4-13.6 hands[2]) at the withers and was heavily built, being somewhere between a draft and a racehorse in robustness. Its hooves were unusually large and extremely worn. The thick coat of the Selerikan stallion was coffee brown with a dark dorsal stripe and black mane and tail. Its stomach contents included 90 percent herbaceous plants such as grasses and sedges, 5-7 percent woody plants like willow and dwarf birch twigs, and 1-2 percent mosses including *Sphagnum*. The preferred habitat of the Chersky horse was probably open steppe with nearby forests, much like the environment wild Przewalski horses once inhabited. A pregnant mare was also found in the Indigirka Basin.

In 1993 a frozen horse carcass was found along the Last Chance Creek near Dawson City, Yukon, Canada (figure 1). Dated by radiocarbon to about 26,000 B.P., it is considerably younger than the Selerikan specimen. The Last Chance horse has been identified as *Equus lambei*, which is known from skeletal remains elsewhere in the North American Arctic region. The pelt from ear to tail, the right foreleg, and the gut contents were preserved. Its coat varies from a blackish-brown just above the hoof through chestnut on the upper arm to a paler color on the body. The mane and tail hair are blond. Stiff white body hairs seem to indicate that the animal had a winter coat at the time of death.

1. Ice Age horse skin found washing out of the permafrost at Last Chance Creek, Yukon. It dates to approximately 26,000 years ago. (Photo by Stephen Mooney)

2. A hand is a unit of measure equal to ten centimeters (4 in.).

Horse Remains in Archeological Sites
Horse Scavenging and Hunting in the Middle Paleolithic

The importance of wild horses to humans in the late Pleistocene is well documented in the collections of animal bones from prehistoric campsites across Europe. The period of human development examined here is the Paleolithic, or Old Stone Age (table 1). The Middle Paleolithic (approximately 125,000-35,000 B.P.) was the era when Neandertals (*Homo sapiens neanderthalensis*) lived. These people had strongly built, but fully modern bodies with brains as large as present-day humans. Experts disagree about the extent to which their language abilities and symbolic thought were developed. In Europe and the Near East, Neandertals often inhabited rockshelters and caves, where the bones of the animals that they consumed accumulated.

Their technology was somewhat limited, especially when compared with the following period, the Upper Paleolithic. The Neandertals had stone tools, but there is little evidence that they could attach them to wooden shafts or handles, so it is not certain that they had proper spears. Their hunting equipment may have been restricted primarily to a large pointed stick, a club, hand-thrown rocks, hand-held axes or knives, and fire. Hunting of large game must have been more direct and simpler than the strategies employed by modern humans to dispatch their

Table 1. Time Scale for Western European Early Prehistoric Periods

YEARS AGO	GEOLOGIC EPOCH	CULTURAL PHASE	SPECIES OF HUMAN
8,000-10,000	Holocene (Recent)	Mesolithic	*Homo sapiens sapiens*
10,000-35,000	Late Pleistocene	Upper Paleolithic	*Homo sapiens sapiens*
35,000-125,000	Late Pleistocene	Middle Paleolithic	*Homo s. neanderthalensis*
125,000-800,000	Middle Pleistocene	Lower Paleolithic	*Homo erectus*

prey. Archaeologist Mary Stiner has recently provided strong evidence that Middle Paleolithic people in Italy, and, therefore, possibly most of western Europe, relied on collecting small animals and scavenging large game like horse and deer. Although there is less concrete evidence, they almost certainly also foraged edible plants. As support of the theory that Neandertals were largely scavengers, Stiner recorded a high percentage of skulls of large game in Middle Paleolithic sites. High frequencies of skulls may be interpreted as an indication that the people were collecting body parts from animals that had already been attacked by predators like hyenas, wolves, bears, and cats. The skull is difficult for many predators to crack open, but humans, with their ability to use hammerstones and other tools, could easily access the nutritious brains of the prey. Animals found in the archaeological deposits also tended to be within the age range of those most frequently killed by wild predators, that is, the older, more feeble game. Stiner noticed a shift away from these trends at around 55,000 years ago. After this time more limb bones, ribs, and vertebrae were represented in caves and rockshelters occupied by Neandertals, indicating that these people had access to meat on the whole carcass, not just the heads. Also, more game animals of prime reproductive age were represented in the archaeological fauna. These changes indicate that Neandertals were shifting away from scavenging toward hunting large game for themselves. Unfortunately, there is no evidence for a marked change in weaponry at 55,000 years ago that would explain how people were able to hunt larger animals. The important introduction of stone projectile points for spears did not occur until 20,000 years later, at the beginning of the Upper Paleolithic.

The development of large-game hunting made an enormous impact on other aspects of life. The departure from depending on fortuitous scavenging of leftovers from carnivores' kills gained humans much-needed independence and security. It may have allowed human bands to expand in size, since communal hunting was probably more successful than stalking with such limited weaponry. Communal hunts could produce numerous kills during one episode, providing enough food for the whole community. Whereas scavenging is highly risky and unpredictable, hunting puts more control in the hands of the participants.

Horses were part of a group of large herbivores that occupied Europe during the late Pleistocene and were utilized as important food sources by humans of the Middle and Upper Paleolithic. Chief among these other animals were rein-

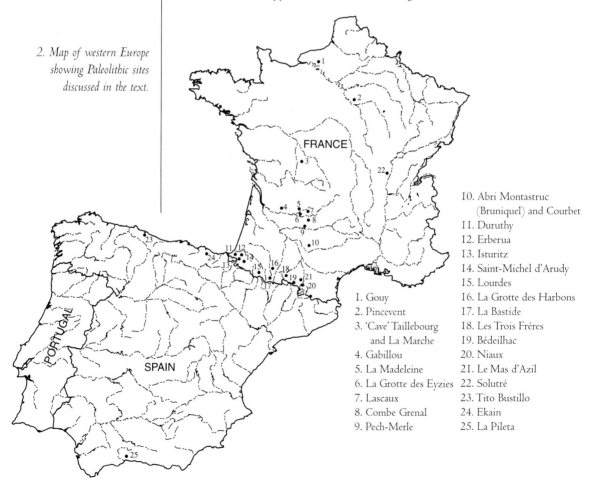

2. Map of western Europe showing Paleolithic sites discussed in the text.

1. Gouy
2. Pincevent
3. 'Cave' Taillebourg and La Marche
4. Gabillou
5. La Madeleine
6. La Grotte des Eyzies
7. Lascaux
8. Combe Grenal
9. Pech-Merle
10. Abri Montastruc (Bruniquel) and Courbet
11. Duruthy
12. Erberua
13. Isturitz
14. Saint-Michel d'Arudy
15. Lourdes
16. La Grotte des Harbons
17. La Bastide
18. Les Trois Fréres
19. Bédeilhac
20. Niaux
21. Le Mas d'Azil
22. Solutré
23. Tito Bustillo
24. Ekain
25. La Pileta

deer, red deer, bison, aurochs or wild cattle, ibex, saiga antelope, and mammoths. The horse is represented in the collections of animal bones in most Middle to Upper Paleolithic sites to a minor extent, but is the dominant species in only certain areas. During the late Pleistocene there were major climatic fluctuations that altered vegetation patterns and shifted the population frequencies of these different herbivores, causing the numbers of horses to rise or fall in relation to other species through time. For example, at the Middle Paleolithic site of Combe Grenal, a cave located on the Dordogne River in southwest France (figure 2), red deer were most prevalent in the lower levels, reindeer in the middle levels, and horses and asses in the upper, more recent levels. The climatic shift to a cold, dry phase corresponds closely with the increase in equids.

Certain geographic regions seem to have been more suitable for horses over the long term. These areas were well watered by large rivers and supported vast open grasslands, although forests were often present in the margins. During the Middle Paleolithic the region richest in horses was the Upper Danube Valley and its surrounds, directly north of the Alps and the Bodensee. A variety of sites in the Upper Danube region of southern Germany show a heavy bias toward horses in their game species. Mammoths and rhinoceroses may have actually contributed more meat by weight in all of these sites, but were killed less often.

The European Middle Paleolithic people exploited horses in much the same way as they did any other large game. Archaeologists can observe the locations of cut marks inflicted by stone butchering tools on bones and, based on the animal's anatomy and current experimental butchery, can reconstruct what the Paleolithic people planned to do with the carcass. In the case of the horse, there is evidence that they cut out the tongue (which would have been a valued piece of meat), skinned and eviscerated the animal, disarticulated the body at the joints to prepare it or parcel it out to people, and sometimes filleted or deboned the meat. Horses were apparently treated no differently from any other game animal in terms of consumption.

Upper Paleolithic Horse Hunters

Most of our knowledge of Ice Age horse hunters comes from the next cultural period, the Upper Paleolithic (approximately 35,000-10,000 B.P.). This era saw the arrival of fully modern humans (*Homo sapiens sapiens*) in Europe. These people undoubtedly had developed considerable linguistic skill, as well as tailored clothing, musical instruments, personal ornamentation, and remarkable artistic abilities.

Upper Paleolithic hunters developed more complex weaponry, including stone, antler, and bone spear points that were clearly designed to be hafted onto wooden shafts, in addition to spear-throwers and antler harpoons. The earliest spear points were made of antler and date to the early Upper Paleolithic. These were simple points without barbs, but with split bases to fit onto the spear shaft. Stone spear points, which appeared slightly later in western Europe, have a stemmed base for hafting. From this time forward a variety of antler, stone, and bone projectile points were developed. It is also likely that hunters of this time had some form of traps and snares since cordage was known, but these have not thus far been recovered from the archaeological record.

Southern France and northern Spain are probably the best-known and most-publicized regions for the Upper Paleolithic, primarily because of their magnificent cave paintings depicting Pleistocene animals. For the most part the collections of animal bones in the caves and rockshelters that were occupied by these modern humans are dominated by reindeer, but horse bones were usually present in large numbers.

Katherine Boyle has conducted a large survey of the animal remains from Upper Paleolithic sites in southwest France. Her findings reveal that while reindeer generally outnumber all other herbivores in the central part of this region, horses and reindeer are present in about equal proportions in the northern part, and horses and saiga antelopes are tied for greatest frequency in the western part. It has become clear that the fauna in a particular region at a particular time was responding to the topography, climate, and vegetation and that the Upper Paleolithic hunters responded likewise by taking what was available. Certain other criteria, such as seasonal migration, congregation, and dispersal of herds of different species undoubtedly played a role.

The dangers and risks involved in killing some species also came into play. Mammoths, for example, provided masses of meat and other raw materials like ivory, but would have been incredibly dangerous to bring down. Horses themselves would not have been easy prey. They were not like our feral horses that carry genes selected through hundreds of generations of domestication to make them more mild tempered. Truly wild horses, like the Przewalski horse, can be fierce and aggressive, as well as agile. Chasing down and killing horses when the hunter was on foot and armed only with a spear must have been a serious challenge.

It is interesting to look at the ways in which horses were exploited and revered during the French Upper Paleolithic. Horses, like other game, were butchered so that their skin, meat, and bone marrow could be utilized. Horse skulls and teeth were sometimes treated with special reverence. In the deep recesses of the caves of La Bastide and Erberua in the Pyrenees, and at the open-air site of Pincevent, near Paris, horse teeth and bones were set beside hearths, perhaps as offerings. At the Grotte des Eyzies the palette of a horse had been scraped to remove the thin skin of the roof of the mouth. In this case, because the palette is fragmentary, it is unclear whether the people were simply eating every morsel or cleaning the skull to put it in a shrine. At the sites of La Madeleine and the Grotte des Eyzies, horse remains were not common, but the last phalanges, or toe bones, bear stone tool cut marks on their bottom surfaces, showing that the hooves were removed by hunters. Hooves may have been boiled in water to make a glue that would have had many uses for prehistoric hunters, but they could have also served as small containers, been made into ornaments or rattles, shaped into small objects, or eaten as a source of protein.

The final chapter of the Ice Age, known as the Magdalenian period (15,000-12,000 B.P.), is the best documented in the western European Paleolithic. There are large numbers of archaeological sites containing animal bones from this period, and some of the best artistic depictions of animals in rockshelters and portable art date to this time. One of the most important regions where horses were the predominant prey species was central Germany, an area bounded by the

Thuringian Forest uplands to the south and the Elbe Valley to the north. Here, on the southern edge of the North European Plateau, the environment consisted of open steppe. Most of the sites from this period were open-air camps ranging from small to large, but typically representing only one habitation of a few months or less. Many of the larger settlements had hearths and areas paved with stone that are thought to represent house structures. Two large sites were located in caves. The steppe vegetation was apparently ideal for horses, but reindeer, mammoths, woolly rhinoceroses, saiga antelopes, and elk (moose, according to American terminology) were also found in smaller numbers in these animal remains. All the sites are located on the steppes at between 200 and 500 meters (656-1,640 ft.), where the vegetation would have been richest. The people from this time chose to avoid the higher Alpine tundra of the Thuringian Forest and the damp Elbe Valley lowlands. What is perhaps most interesting is that these horse hunters did not seem to be highly nomadic. The small camps, thought to be summer occupations, are interspersed with larger ones, probably inhabited in the winter. Stone tools were made from material collected mainly in the immediate vicinity and rarely from over 100 kilometers (62 mi.) away.

In a survey conducted by Olga Soffer, horses were found at 50 percent (seven out of fourteen) of Upper Paleolithic sites located in the northern part of the central Russian plain and 43 percent (three out of seven) of sites in the south. Horse teeth (incisors) at these sites were apparently used for decoration. These had a groove around the root or were pierced so that they could be either suspended from a string as a pendant or sewn onto clothing.

The Horse Hunting Site of Solutré: A Natural Corral

It is during the Upper Paleolithic that evidence for communal hunting becomes identifiable. The site of Solutré (figure 3), in east-central France, provides a well-documented example of recurrent communal horse hunts over 20,000 years (32,000-12,000 B.P.). Although this horse-kill site has Middle Paleolithic deposits at its base, most of what is known about communal hunting comes from the thicker overlying levels dating to the Upper Paleolithic.

3. The Paleolithic horse-kill site of Solutré, France, dating to approximately 32,000 to 12,000 years ago. The arrow marks the location of the site. (Photo by Sandra Olsen)

Solutré is located ten kilometers (6.2 mi.) west of the modern city of Mâcon. It is situated in a small valley formed between two limestone ridges, Mont Pouilly and the Roche de Solutré. The valley forms a corridor linking the vast floodplain of the Saône River and the eastern edge of the Massif Central, a large group of mountains in central France (figure 4). The site, which covers about a hectare (2.47 acres) and contains deposits over nine meters (29.5 ft.) deep, rests on the talus slope of the south face of the Roche de Solutré. Realistic estimates of the number of horses killed there range from 32,000 to 100,000 individuals. In the densest areas of deposit, there are bones of about eleven and a half horses per cubic meter (1.31 cu. yd.).

Solutré was discovered in 1866 by Adrien Arcelin, a local archivist and paleogeographer, when he noticed stone tools and horse bones washing out of the talus slope of the cliff. He and others excavated deep pits and trenches in the site to try to reconstruct how it was formed. In a popular novel *Solutré, ou les Chaseurs de Rennes de la France Centrale* (1872), Arcelin speculated that Solutré was the result of hunters driving horses off the top of the cliff to plummet to their death on the rocks below. This concept was probably borrowed from the accounts of French explorers in North America who had seen Plains Indians drive hundreds or even thousands of bison off cliffs in large-scale communal hunts. Several artists of the time had portrayed the dramatic scene of horses tumbling off the sharp precipice at the western end of the Roche (figure 5), creating an image that stuck in the minds of all who saw their artwork. That idea persisted even with prehistorians until fairly recently, when a few researchers challenged that interpretation.

The way to reconstruct what really happened at the great horse-kill site of Solutré is to look at a wide range of evidence, including the regional topography, the available weapon technology, the behavior of wild horses, the ages of the horses, the seasons of death, and how the horses were butchered and utilized.

First, the location of the site is not at the base of the steep precipice at the western end of the limestone ridge, but rather on the south slope, which is more broken and gradual. No animal bones or stone tools were ever found at the western end, despite extensive surveys. This evidence demonstrates that every horse would have had to be carried around to the south side to be butchered, even though it would clearly be easier to remove the meat at the point where these heavy animals died. Further, since no spear points were found at the base of the western cliff, it appears that none were ever abandoned there in the midst of killing individuals that had survived the fall. In sharp contrast spear points are plentiful at the site on the south side of the Roche. This evidence strongly suggests that the animals were killed at the location where their carcasses were

4. Topographic map of the region around Solutré showing the cul-de-sac, cliff face, proposed migration route, and short drive route to the location of the site.

Key:
Clear arrows: Arcelin's hypothesized drive route
Black arrows: Seasonal migration route
Small arrows: Diversion into cul-de-sac

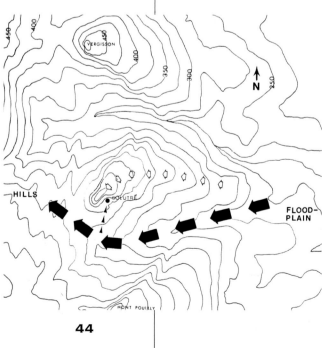

butchered. The terrain around the site would not be conducive to driving horses off the top, since it does not have a clean vertical drop, but it would be suitable for a natural corral. The cul-de-sac in the cliff face forms a niche into which horses could be driven and surrounded either by humanly constructed barriers or by spear-wielding hunters. Although the horses might have been able to clamber partially up the rugged slope, their travel would have been considerably hampered, allowing the hunters to attack them.

Although the Upper Paleolithic hunters may have been armed only with spears, they could have employed a number of tactics to assist them in the hunt. Upper Paleolithic hunters knew how to create fire, so they could have either set controlled brushfires or carried torches to frighten and direct the fleeing horses. They could have formed a drive lane, an artificial construct that funnels herds toward the kill point. Plains Indians and other cultures that conducted communal drives of large game made drive lanes by constructing piles of stones at intervals a few meters apart in two converging lines. Sometimes they used skins stretched on frames or piles of brush as barricades for the drive lane. Animals will naturally take the path of least resistance and will avoid going between closely spaced obstacles. Even low, poorly constructed walls of brush will deter them if a more open route is evident. The only kind of drive lane that would be likely to survive would be one consisting of piles of stone, but near Solutré the local villagers have been scavenging stone to build their houses and other buildings for over a thousand years. Besides, much of the lane would now be located under presently standing structures.

Wild horses, as far as can be reconstructed, would have behaved very differently from bison, so the analogy with North American bison jumps is not strictly applicable to Solutré. At certain times of the year, American bison would congregate in herds numbering thousands, even hundreds of thousands of individuals. During this time it was possible for hunters on foot or horseback to drive the bison to a predetermined point, where the animals could be coerced off a cliff. The ideal situation was a vertical drop of at least ten meters (33 ft.) at the edge of a plateau. (If the bison were already on the plateau, they were driven over level ground by a large number of people with the aid of a drive lane, fire, yelling, or other noise.) By instinct, the bison herds always followed the lead of the dominant females. When the leading edge of the herd reached the cliff and tried to turn away, the momentum of the herd following close behind pushed them over the edge or caused them to be trampled to death on top. It is only when the herds were large, over 100 or more individuals, for example, that this technique could be applied successfully. When the bison dropped over the edge of the cliff, most

5. Emile Bayard's romantic nineteenth-century depiction of horses leaping off the steep precipice at the west end of the Roche de Solutré. No bones were found at the base of this cliff, and it is highly unlikely that horses could have been forced by prehistoric hunters to jump to their deaths in large numbers.

45

would perish from the fall, but others had to be finished off by hunters with spears or bows and arrows located down at the bottom of the cliff.

Horses, on the other hand, have a very different social structure. By studying feral horses, that is, those that were turned loose or escaped domestic herds and their descendants, it is possible to reconstruct how Ice Age horses may have behaved. Both wild and feral horses form two types of social groups: the family or harem band that consists of a dominant stallion, his mares and their offspring, and a bachelor group that is a weakly formed association of lower-ranking males. Both groups are generally small: the family bands often incorporate fewer than eighteen individuals; the bachelor groups only two to five males. It would be nearly impossible to drive such small groups off a cliff, since the individuals could turn away abruptly in the face of danger without a huge herd trampling over them. Furthermore, horses flee from predators or other dangers in single file if in a band or by scattering in different directions if in a bachelor group.

In summary, then, the combination of the topography at Solutré and horse behavior makes the original hypothesis of Arcelin unlikely. If the horses did not go over the cliff, however, why was this particular location singled out for use in slaughtering horses for over 20,000 years? The site does not contain artifacts and features that indicate prolonged habitation by the prehistoric people, except perhaps in its uppermost level. The presence of numerous skulls, articulated limbs, backbones, and feet supports the idea that this was a kill and butchery site rather than a base camp. The most likely explanation for the continuous use of the site is that its natural features served it well for the capturing and killing of horses.

Whereas the topography does not support the horse jump hypothesis, it does provide a better explanation. The valley in which Solutré is located could have functioned as a corridor for horses migrating from the Saône floodplain, where they would have wintered, to the foothills of the Massif Central in the

6. Engraving of a horse on the wall of the Cave of Gabillou in the Dordogne region of France. (Photo courtesy of Jean Gaussen)

spring and summer. There, the horses would find fresh pastures, as well as relief from the heat and biting insects. Seasonal melts provide plenty of springs in the mountains that are not available later on in the year. The horses would have likely moved down onto the floodplain before the first deep snowfall in the mountains so they could have access to drinking water at the river through the winter.

The season in which a mammal is killed can often be determined by looking at thin sections of the tooth roots with a polarizing microscope. Each summer and winter a band of cement is produced on the root to hold the tooth in its socket. The summer and winter bands differ in appearance: the summer band is broad and contains a lot of organic matter, while the winter band is narrow and is mostly mineral. Thin sections of the tooth roots show layering that resembles tree rings. The outermost band tells whether the animal died in the warm months or during the winter. At Solutré a small sample of teeth showed that most of the horses studied were killed during the warmer months, spring through autumn.

Few juvenile horses were recovered during excavations at Solutré. The fact that most were adults suggests that either the small carcasses of the young were carried away from the site whole to be butchered at the hunters' camp or the young were released unharmed to maintain the local population.

There were many cases in which whole vertebral columns or legs were found articulated at the site, and cut marks made on the bones with stone butchering tools were extremely rare. These two facts may indicate that more horses were killed than could be thoroughly butchered, so that much of the meat was left on the bone and spoiled before it could be used. If the temperature was warm and most of the horses in a band were killed at once, this could certainly be the case. Without the possibility of freezing the meat, the only way to preserve it was to cut it into thin strips and hang it up to be air-dried or smoked. At the Grotte des Eyzies, a site in southwest France that was contemporaneous with the last deposit at Solutré, there is good evidence that people did use a technique to debone or fillet reindeer carcasses in order to prepare the flesh for smoking or drying. This method does not appear to have been used at Solutré and may not have been known by the hunters there.

It is clear that Solutré provides a rare opportunity to understand Paleolithic hunters. It is also obvious that the only way to grasp how these hunters used this specific location over and over for a long period of time is to put together a wide range of information, including topographic, artifactual, skeletal, and equine behavioral studies.

Upper Paleolithic Art

What can be discerned about the human/animal relationships at this time in Europe is richer than for any previous era in human history and many subsequent periods before writing was established. This is because by the end of this time, humans had developed symbolic representation in the form of engravings (figure 6) and painted art on cave walls, as well as mobile art consisting of small effigies carved in antler, ivory, and bone and engraved on stone plaques. When this information is put together with that gleaned from actual animal bones, weapon technology, and site locations, valuable hypotheses can be proposed regarding how horses were hunted and their relative importance in the diet compared with other large game.

Cave Art

The vivid polychromatic portrayals of wild horses in the cave art of the French and Spanish Upper Paleolithic help scientists to put the "flesh back on the bones" of this extinct species. The resemblance to the extant Asiatic horse *(Equus przewalskii)* is quite evident in these early depictions. For example, like the Przewalski horse, the European wild horse typically had a dun coat with a white belly; a dark erect mane; a short, dark-colored brushy tail; a dorsal stripe down the back; cross stripes on the withers; sometimes zebra striping on the legs; and a large, pendulous belly. Many of these features are well illustrated in polychromatic paintings at Tito Bustillo and Ekain (figures 7 and 8), caves on the northern coast of Spain.

The heads in many of the more realistic depictions look oversized in relationship to the short body and legs, as do the heads of Przewalski horses. This fits with measurements of skulls and teeth of actual horses from Paleolithic sites. (In a sense, *our* mental template of a "typical" horse's stature and configuration is based on a generalized view of a *domestic* horse, which is quite different from the physical characteristics of the truly wild horses of Europe and Asia.) The large head housed enormous teeth, comparable to or even larger than those of much larger modern domestic horses. The swollen belly reflects the relatively big intestine. These two factors, the large teeth and intestine, are features resulting from the poor vegetation these animals consumed.

Zebra striping on the legs of horses in Paleolithic art was first found in 1968, when discovery of the Cave of Ekain in northern Spain revealed twenty-six paintings of horses. Since then it has been observed in several other cave paintings. Zebra striping restricted to the legs is not uncommon in Przewalski horses and occasionally occurs in domestic horses. In 1868 Darwin, in *The Origin of Species*,

7. Polychrome painting of a horse in the Cave of Tito Bustillo near Ribadesella, Asturias region, northwest Spain. (Photo courtesy of Alfonso Moure Romanillo)

documented the presence of striping on horses across the whole Eurasian continent. According to Darwin, hybrids of the various species of equids—the horse, donkey, onager, and even the quagga (see chapter 10)—were often more likely to show striping than any of the purebred animals. He noted that striping was most common on dun-colored horses, but occurred more rarely on darker horses that he referred to as chestnut and bay. The dun coloring, which is prevalent in the cave paintings, is close to the natural pelage of the donkey, onager, and Przewalski horse. There is a tendency for the stripes to be most visible in the foal and to fade as the animal matures. Darwin also observed that zebra striping on rare occasions is found on the cheek, forehead, and hindquarters of domestic foals. At Gouy, in the Seine Maritime, an unusual engraving of an equid has vertical stripes on the head, and down the neck and the whole body. Whether this depiction represents actual body striping or is just artistic license is difficult to determine, because the stripes do not closely mimic those seen on living zebras and the engraving is fairly crude. Given Darwin's findings, it may not be too outrageous to believe that Paleolithic people may have seen horses with stripes all over their bodies. In fact, the equids that preceded modern horses in Eurasia had teeth that classified them as "zebrine." However, the true horse that existed in the Eurasian Paleolithic originated in North America and migrated across the Bering Land Bridge into Asia. We can only speculate about whether some of these horses had stripes, barring the finding of well-preserved frozen carcasses possessing them.

Artists also portrayed some horses as solid black or with dark heads, as at Lascaux, in the Dordogne Valley, and at Pech-Merle, near Cabrerets, France. One at Lascaux has a dark rump and head, as well as five cross stripes at the withers. Two dark-headed horses at Pech-Merle also have spots on their torsos, but since some of the spots are outside the margins of their bodies, the spots may not reflect a piebald or Appaloosa type of pelage at all. Elsewhere spots have been

8. Polychrome wall painting of a horse at the Cave of Ekain in the Basque province of Guipuzcoa, Spain. Note that the appearance is much like that of a Przewalski horse, with an erect mane, dun coat, dorsal stripe, withers stripe, zebra stripes on the legs, and light-colored belly. (Photo courtesy of Jesus Altuna)

interpreted as wounds, demarcations for drive lanes, and symbols of some sort. Other images of horses, like a multicolored one at Lascaux, are more realistically described as dappled. Some horses at Lascaux are shown as bay.

At the Cave of Niaux, in Ariège, France, a horse's winter pelage was clearly depicted by its "beard," long coat, and feathering on the lower limbs. Other examples are also known. It has been suggested that winter coats may reflect overall changing climate, as well as individual seasons.

In a few cases behavior is illustrated. At the famous Cave of Lascaux, a band of horses is shown as if trotting along in single file, as they do when fleeing danger. In the Cave Taillebourg, at the site of Le Roc-aux-Sorciers, near the village of Angles-sur-l'Anglin, Vienne, France a fragment of a bas-relief sculpture of a horse has its head bent down as though grazing.

At La Pileta, Málaga, Spain, there are a total of fourteen horses depicted on the cave walls. One horse of particular interest is shown in black outline and has double dashes in red and black paint applied with fingers all over its body. These are thought to represent wounds. According to a study of the fingerprints, each pair of marks was made by a different person. Because the horse is a female and its belly is large, some art historians have speculated that the horse was supposed to be pregnant. European wild horses, like the Przewalski horse, probably had large abdomens, so it is better not to hypothesize about whether the artist intended for the animal to be pregnant.

What may be more useful is to determine the sex ratio. This information could shed light on the hunting strategies employed. If the hunters were stalking or driving the more-cohesive family bands, consisting of mares, their offspring, and one dominant stallion, there should be a higher ratio of females to males. If they were stalking the looser bachelor groups, then most or all should be male. The sex of a horse can be determined in the silhouette views that are standard in Paleolithic art. On male profiles the prepuce (sheath) is depicted just anterior to the thigh, whereas females have a smooth abdominal line. Although no thorough study has been performed, it appears, based on published cave paintings and engravings, that most of the depictions are female. It could, of course, be argued that the absence of the prepuce in some cases was an oversight, that the animal's sex was irrelevant to the artist, or that the prepuce would not always have been visible in profile. Unlike red deer, horses have no other obvious external sexual characteristics, so the prepuce must be included in the profile to indicate that the individual is a male.

Some interesting ideas have been presented to interpret ancillary symbols around the animals in cave art. These may help to explain how Paleolithic people hunted and also the meaning of the art itself. The fact that hunting is the most common identifiable action portrayed may imply that the artists were using their art as part of a ritual involving hunting magic, in order to improve their success rate. More rarely, courting or mating of animals is shown. Such depictions may portray a fertility rite to increase the numbers of the prey. These conclusions are speculative, of course, but are based on many studies of primitive art by present-day hunters and gatherers.

That the animals depicted were frequently the targets of hunters is shown by the association of weapons with the animal figure. Frequently, plain lines or lines with diagonal hatching are shown near or overlapping an animal's body. These appear to be spears piercing the body. The hatching could be a stylized way of showing barbs that are often found on antler projectile points, but these diagonal lines usually appear nearer what would be the base of the weapon instead of the tip. It is more likely that the diagonal lines represent feather fletching on the ends of the weapons' shafts. Spears sometimes have fletching, particularly if they are short and are hurled with a spear-thrower. Fletching was an important invention, because it stabilized the spear as it traveled through the air and caused it to spin, thereby increasing penetration when it struck its target. There is no evidence of bows and arrows until the end of the Pleistocene, but it is possible they existed earlier.

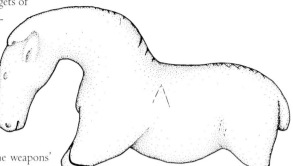

9. Tiny statuette of a horse carved in mammoth ivory from Vogelherd Cave, Württemberg, Germany. It is estimated to be about 30,000 years old and is 4.8 centimeters (1.9 in.) in length. Note the extremely arched neck. (Drawing by Sandra Olsen)

Thomas Kehoe has recently put forth an intriguing hypothesis that rows of dots on the walls of the Lascaux Cave symbolize drive lanes. The dots could represent small fires or piles of stones. Rectangular symbols may, at least in some cases, represent corrals, especially when they occur at the end of two converging lines of dots as they do in the artwork at Lascaux.

Most of the parietal art in caves is found in France, Spain, and to a lesser degree Portugal, but there are also several cases throughout Italy and Sicily. The farthest north such art has been found is the Cave of Gouy, near Rouen, France. Unfortunately, no caves with decorated walls have been found in Germany, where horse bones were most plentiful in archaeological sites.

One of the most remote examples of Paleolithic parietal art was found in 1959 at Kapovaia Cave in the southern Ural Mountains, on a tributary of the Belaia River in Russia. Two horses are represented in a red wash as part of a frieze of animals that includes eight mammoths, two rhinoceroses, and some schematic signs. The horses have arched necks with their noses down, similar to a small ivory sculpture from the site of Vogelherd (figure 9), in Germany, dating to about 30,000 B.P. Another horse image was found in the Cave of Ignatiev, just 100 kilometers (62 mi.) away from Kapovaia.

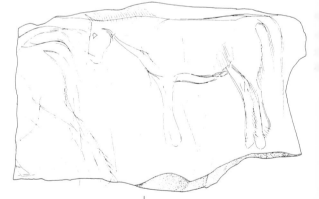

10. Stone plaque from Montestruc, Tarn-et-Garonne, France (British Museum collections, drawing by Ann Sieveking)

It is often difficult to date parietal art accurately, but where there are archaeological deposits from human occupation, it is sometimes possible. The one stylistic trend that has been documented is that heads of horses started out large and were reduced to unrealistically diminutive sizes toward the end of the Paleolithic.

Cave artists depicted one other species of equid only rarely. The extinct Pleistocene European ass (*Equus hydruntinus*) is shown in a painting in Lascaux and in two engravings in the Cave of Trois Frères. In artistic representations asses may

11. Hyoid bone carved to resemble a horse's head from Isturitz, in the Pyrenees, France. The large number of these pierced ornaments found in one group suggests that they were strung as a necklace. (Drawing by Sandra Olsen)

be distinguished from horses by their longer ears, elevated head position, and longer neck. The rarity of asses in Paleolithic art agrees with their low frequencies in the bone remains from archaeological sites in western Europe.

Mobile Art

Other kinds of Paleolithic art are mobile and come in a variety of forms. Stone plaques (figure 10) are portable, miniature versions of wall engravings that can appear in open-air sites as well as rockshelters. At the site of Gönnersdorf, Germany, the dominant animal portrayed on plaques was the horse. In this case sixty-one plaques with the images of seventy-four horses have been found. At La Marche, France, horses outnumbered all other animals depicted on plaques, with a total of ninety-one images on sixty-four stones. Occasionally, an animal rib, shoulder blade, or other flat bone is engraved like a plaque.

A tongue bone (hyoid) of a horse naturally resembles the profile of an animal head at one end, so Paleolithic artists were able to add a few details by engraving facial features on the bone to produce realistic effigies (figure 11). These *contours découpés*, as they are called by French archaeologists, come primarily from just four French sites, three of which are in the Pyrenees Mountains. A few have also recently turned up in the Spanish sites in Cantabria and Asturias. About two-thirds of the 150 known examples of animal heads are those of horses engraved on horse hyoids. Other animals on horse hyoids include the chamois and bison. Some of the engraved heads have a perforation representing the eye or nostril, while others have a small hole in the neck or just below the ear and were probably worn as pendants. The large number of horse-head pendants found at the rock-shelter of Isturitz, in Spanish Cantabria, suggest that they were worn together as a necklace.

North of Moscow, at the site of Sungir near the city of Vladimir, is an early Upper Paleolithic living site and cemetery that date to 25,000-28,000 years ago. Found at the site was a fine ivory pendant of a horse (figure 12) that was coated with red ocher and decorated with two rows of drilled pits filled with black pigment.

Another type of mobile art consists of three-dimensional sculptures in stone, ivory, antler, or bone. Although these could be quite large free-standing stone figures, many of the sculptures of animals were made on antler and bone tools, the most common of which were spear-throwers and objects known as *"bâtons de commandement"* (figure 13). There have been various interpretations of how *bâtons* were used, but they very likely were either shaft-straighteners, used in man-ufacturing wooden spear shafts, or thong-smoothers, through which damp hide thongs were pulled in order to stretch and straighten them. Ethnographic and his-torical examples of tools very similar to *bâtons* are known for Plains Indians, Inuit, and other cultures. Antler spear-throwers, clever tools that acted as an extension of the hunter's arm and greatly increased the distance a spear could be hurled, also were often carved to represent animals. Figure 14 shows one with a horse's head carved at the end. The forelock acts as a hook that holds the base of the spear in the proper position just prior to throwing. The shaft of the spear-thrower is carved to represent a horse's leg.

Many of these carvings of horses are remarkably realistic representations that sometimes show that the artist was very aware of animal anatomy and behavior. A spear-thrower from Bruniquel, France, has a carving of a horse that appears to be jumping. Another horse from Mas d'Azil seems to be neighing. One of the finest examples of horse sculptures comes from the German cave site of Vogelherd (figure 9) and is about 30,000 years old. This exquisite figurine, with its dramatically arched neck and lowered head, was carved in mammoth ivory and was found with five other ivory statuettes (including two mammoths, and two or three lions or other felines). The Cave of Lourdes also produced a well-known ivory horse. At Mas d'Azil and Bédeilhac horse teeth were carved into human figurines.

At Duruthy, France, a so-called "horse sanctuary" contained horses carved in sandstone, limestone, and ivory. The largest, made in sandstone, was found kneeling against two real horse skulls and on top of a horse jaw. Three small horse head pendants were found nearby. The shrine dates to the fourteenth millennium B.P.

Analysis of Paleolithic Art

Pat Rice and Ann Paterson have compared the prevalence of different species of animals in the bones excavated at 151 French and 61 Spanish Upper Paleolithic sites with the frequencies of the same animals in the three forms of art: cave paintings and engravings, plaques, and effigies on bone and antler artifacts. These researchers found some differences but also some strong similarities. Horses were less common in the skeletal remains than deer, but in art horses outnumbered every other group of animals. The irony is that modern artistic depictions usually show Cro-Magnon hunters slaying an enormous mammoth. In reality, and even in the art of their own time, Paleolithic people were far more likely to have focused on horses, deer, bison or wild cattle, and ibex than on the rare and formidable mammoths.

12. Horse pendant from Sungir, an early Upper Paleolithic site north of Moscow dating to 25,000-28,000 years ago. (Photo by Randall White)

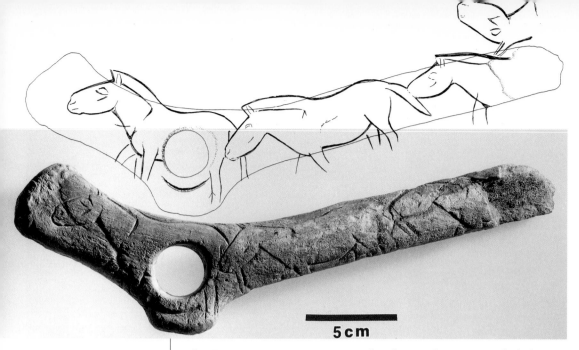

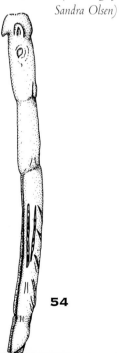

13. "Bâton de commande-ment," or shaft-straightener, incised with a line of horses. The artifact is made on reindeer antler and comes from the site of La Madeleine, France. (Copyright ©British Museum, drawing by Ann Sieveking)

14. Antler spear-thrower made to resemble a horse, from Courbet, France. (Drawing by Sandra Olsen)

54

The Controversy Over Horse Husbandry in the Upper Paleolithic

A model was recently put forth by Paul Bahn arguing that Upper Paleolithic people may have exercised some form of herd control, an intermediate step leading to domestication. Bahn presented the idea that Paleolithic people may have ridden horses, or used them for pack animals or to pull loads. Several authors, including most notably Randall White and Mary Littauer, have countered Bahn's arguments with other plausible explanations.

The strongest evidence presented for the control of horses at this early date consists of depictions of what Bahn interprets as bridles on the heads of horses in wall engravings and effigies carved in stone or antler. These artistic renderings display lines encircling the nose and running from the nose back toward the ear (figure 15). At first glance these lines could be interpreted as part of a bridle, including the nose band, chin strap, and cheekpieces. On closer inspection, however, it is clear that these lines represent natural features on the heads of the Pleistocene horses. The wild Asiatic (Przewalski) horse, which is colored like many of the prehistoric depictions of the European Ice Age horses, has what is known as a mealy muzzle, or pale cream-colored ring around the end of the snout (figure 16). This is one of the characteristics of what is today called a Pangaré coat pattern on horses (see the Appendix). Although there are no clear examples of a mealy muzzle in cave paintings, it is possible that some of the engravings with lines around the nose are meant to portray this change in coloration around the tip of the muzzle. The horizontal lines running from the nose back toward the neck probably represent natural contours of the horse's head. Curved lines are often incised to represent the contours of the large masseter muscle at the back of the lower jaw, and some lines indicate changes in fur patterns. Similar lines are seen on engravings of bison and other animals, although their positions are slightly different, but no one has suggested that bison were domesticated.

Bahn had also argued that some of the manes and tails portrayed in Paleolithic art appear to have been trimmed, but all wild equids (not feral horses) have short, erect manes and most have brushier tails than domestic horses. This is because they shed their manes and tail hair regularly every spring. Domestic horses lose their hairs one at a time, just as humans do.

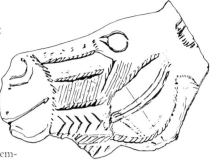

The spots on horses in the paintings at Pech-Merle are sometimes thought to represent piebald coats, known only in domestic animals, but the spots extend outside the margins of the horse and probably symbolize something entirely different.

The remains of seven foals and two "very young" horses found at the Harpons site in France suggest possible husbandry to Bahn. The assemblage also includes nine young adults and one very old horse, a composition that may simply point to the mass slaughter of a family band. Newborn horses have been reported from other sites, like Isturitz, but because similar occurrences of very young or even fetal animals have been found for common wild species, like deer, in sites all over the world, caution must be exercised when assuming that this is evidence of herd control. Hunters may have opted to kill animals that had attained full growth and avoid pregnant individuals whenever possible, but if the survival of their own band was at risk, they would have taken anything that was available.

Bahn also believed that the Paleolithic *bâtons de commandement* were cheekpieces for a bridle. Although they bear a vague similarity to much-later Bronze Age antler cheekpieces, the *bâtons* are generally larger and heavier with only one very large perforation near one end. Bronge Age cheekpieces typically have two or three holes for the leather straps.

Further, Bahn presented examples of damage on incisors (the anterior teeth) of Paleolithic horses that he hypothesized was caused by the nervous habit of crib-biting. This practice has been observed in horses that get bored with being penned and begin to chew on their stalls. If this behavior occurs only in situations where the animal is enclosed by a human-made structure, then surely horses were being controlled in the Paleolithic. R. A. Rogers and L. A. Rogers have shown, however, that similar damage appears on horse incisors dating to the early and middle Pleistocene of North America, long before the arrival of humans. Littauer pointed out that such wear could have just as easily been formed when the animal browsed on the bark of trees.

As exciting as it would be to conclude that humans were taming, herding, and even breeding horses in the Paleolithic, it seems unlikely based on existing evidence. Not only is the evidence questionable, but horse populations diminished tremendously in Western Europe after the close of the Ice Age (10,000 years ago) until clearly domestic ones re-entered some 7,000 years later. If Paleolithic hunters had succeeded in controlling or domesticating horses, then why did the numbers of horses drop so dramatically in subsequent periods?

15. Carving of a horse head from Saint-Michel d'Arudy, France, showing facial lines that indicate the line demarcating the mealy muzzle and the natural contours of the face. These lines have been interpreted by Bahn to represent a bridle. (Drawing courtesy of Randall White)

16. A Przewalski horse showing the contours of the face and the sharp color demarcation around the muzzle depicted in figure 15. (Photo by Sandra Olsen)

Summary

The combined information from frozen horse carcasses, skeletal material from archaeological sites, and cave and mobile art provides a rich picture of the relationship between humans and horses during the Pleistocene Ice Age. Most researchers now agree that early Neandertals were scavenging the meat of horses and other large game rather than killing them. At some point, possibly in the second half of the Neandertals' reign, hunting was developed. Hunting undoubtedly led to many changes in human culture by giving people more control over the sources and quantity of their food. Beyond that, it surely changed the human/animal relationship by converting people into active, aggressive predators. Horses that might have previously felt comfortable lining up at a watering hole to drink in close proximity to Neandertals might have had to learn to flee or defend themselves against approaching hunters with spears. From that time forward, humans began their role of supremacy over horses, and the two were no longer neutral occupants of their environment.

Reading List

Bahn, P. "Crib-biting: Tethered Horses in the Palaeolithic?" *World Archaeology* 12 (1980), 212-17.

———. "Reply to 'Horse Sense, or Nonsense.'" *Antiquity* 54 (1980), 140-42.

Bahn, P. G., and J. Vertut. *Images of the Ice Age.* New York: Facts on File, 1988.

Bökönyi, S. *The Przevalsky Horse.* London: Souvenir Press, 1974.

Boyle, K. V. *Upper Palaeolithic Faunas from South-west France: A Zoogeographic Perspective.* International Series 557. Oxford: B.A.R., 1990.

Chase, P. G. *The Hunters of Combe Grenal: Approaches to Middle Paleolithic Subsistence in Europe.* International Series 286. Oxford: B.A.R., 1986.

Groves, C. "The Taxonomy, Distribution, and Adaptations of Recent Equids," in *Equids in the Ancient World,* ed. by R. H. Meadow and H.-P. Uerpmann. Wiesbaden: Dr. Ludwig Reichert Verlag, 1986. Pp. 11-65.

Guthrie, R. D. "Paleoecology of Large Mammal Communities in Alaska." *American Midland Naturalist* 79 (1968), 346-63.

Kehoe, T. "Corralling Life." *Wisconsin Academy Review,* March (1987), 45-48.

Littauer, M. "Horse Sense, or Nonsense?" *Antiquity* 54 (1980), 139-40.

Mohr, E. *The Asiatic Wild Horse.* London: J.A. Allen, 1971.

Olsen, S. L. "Solutré: A Theoretical Approach to the Reconstruction of Upper Paleolithic Hunting Strategies." *Journal of Human Evolution* 18 (1989), 295-327.

———. "Pleistocene Horse-Hunting at Solutré: Why Bison Jump Analogies Fail," in *Ancient Peoples and Landscapes,* ed. by E. Johnson. Lubbock: Texas Tech University Press, 1995. Pp. 65-75.

Rice, P. C., and A. L. Paterson. "Cave Art and Bones: Exploring the Interrelationships." *American Anthropologist* 87 (1985), 94-100.

———. "Validating the Cave Art-Archeofaunal Relationship in Cantabrian Spain." *American Anthropologist* 88 (3) (1986), 658-67.

Rogers, R. A., and L. A. Rogers. "Notching and Anterior Beveling on Fossil Horse Incisors: Indicators of Domestication?" *Quaternary Research* 29 (1988), 72-74.

Soffer, O. *The Upper Paleolithic of the Central Russian Plain.* San Diego: Academic Press, 1985.

Stiner, M. *Honor Among Thieves: A Zooarchaeological Study of Neandertal Ecology.* Princeton: Princeton University Press, 1994.

Weniger, G.-C. "Magdalenian Settlement Pattern and Subsistence in Central Europe: The Southwestern and Central German Cases," in *The Pleistocene Old World, Regional Perspectives,* ed. by O. Soffer. New York: Plenum Press, 1987. Pp. 201-15.

White, R. *Dark Caves, Bright Visions: Life in Ice Age Europe.* New York: The American Museum of Natural History, 1986.

———. "Husbandry and Herd Control in the Upper Paleolithic: A Critical Review of the Evidence." *Current Anthropology* 30(5) (1989), 609-16.

Four

BRIDLING
HORSE POWER

*The Domestication of
the Horse*

DAVID W. ANTHONY

Hast thou given the horse strength?
Hast thou clothed his neck with thunder?
Hast thou made him leap as a locust?[1]
The glory of his nostrils is terrible.
He paweth in the valley,
And rejoiceth in his strength;
He goeth on to meet the armed men.
He mocketh at fear, and is not afraid;
Neither turneth he back from the sword. . . .
He swalloweth the ground with fierceness and rage. . . .
He saith among the trumpets: ha, ha!
And he smelleth the battle afar off,
The thunder of the captains,
And the shouting.

Job 39:19-25 *(King James Version)*

*H*orses almost certainly were first domesticated for use as food animals, like cattle or pigs, but it is as instruments of transport that they have made their impact on human history. Until the invention of the steam engine (and for a good many years after), there was no means of transport faster than a rider on horseback. Before the invention of firearms, well-trained cavalries repeatedly overwhelmed pedestrian military forces, recharting the course of ancient history at Issus and Adrianople (figure 1), and on the barren plains of Asia. Horses changed the way people hunted and made war, altered concepts of distance, extended interregional trade, brought previously isolated cultures into contact, provided new standards of wealth, opened the world's grasslands to efficient human exploitation, and redefined the cultural identities of those societies that became equestrian. Horseback riding and horse-drawn chariots may have also played a role in the initial spread of the Indo-European languages, a language family that ultimately gave birth to English, French, Russian, Hindi, Persian, and many other tongues.

This momentous history began when horses were first exploited for their strength and speed, rather than for their flesh and hides. Wild horses must have been tamed and may have been fully domesticated before they were useful as transport animals. When and where this occurred, whether it occurred many times or just once, and which prehistoric culture was the first beneficiary of the speediest form of animal transport are questions that have generated intense debate.

Facing page, see figure 5.

---

1. The King James Version incorrectly translates "leap as a locust" as "afraid as a grasshopper." The Revised Standard Version (1953) and other later versions corrected this error. The correct translation is substituted here.

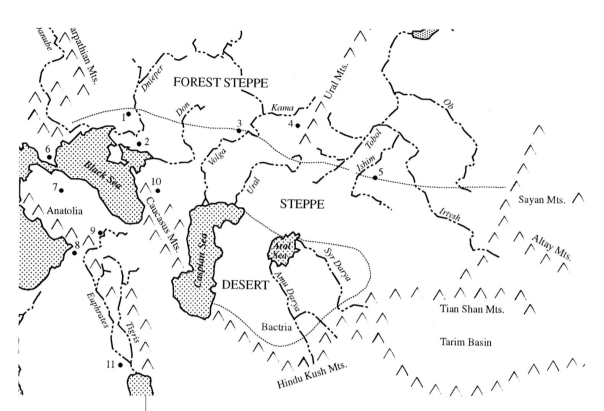

1. Map of Eurasia showing the locations of important sites. The dotted lines indicate the boundaries of the ecozones.

Key

1. Dereivka
2. Kamennaya Mogila
3. Khvalynsk
4. Mullino II
5. Botai
6. Adrianople
7. Demircihöyök
8. Issus
9. Malatya
10. Maikop
11. Ur

Zoologists, archaeologists, and historians have failed to agree on answers to the basic questions, When and where were horses first domesticated? When and where did horseback riding begin? And how does one distinguish wild horses from domesticated ones?

It is very likely that the first riders lived in the grasslands that extend 4,500 miles across the center of the Eurasian continent, from the European foothills of the Carpathians on the west to the arid Mongolian plateau in the east. Since the beginning of recorded history, the peoples of this vast steppe zone have been warlike nomadic herders who virtually lived on horseback. The Greek historian Herodotus penned a vivid description of Eurasian pastoral nomads when he portrayed the Scythians in 450 B.C.:

> A people without fortified towns, living, as the Scythians do, in wagons which they take with them wherever they go, accustomed, one and all, to fight on horseback with bows and arrows, and dependent for their food not upon agriculture but upon their cattle: how can such a people fail to defeat the attempt of an invader not only to subdue them, but even to make contact with them?
>
> The Histories, IV, 46-47

The Scythians trotted into the light of history about 670 B.C., when Assyrian documents mentioned them as troublesome intruders in the affairs of the kingdoms of western Iran and the Caucasus Mountains. Distinctive Scythian ornamental styles and horse trappings have been found by archaeologists in graves dated two centuries earlier in central Asia, particularly in sites in Kazakstan and the Altay-Sayan Mountains. However, the Scythians were not the earliest mounted nomads. Similar societies had existed in the steppes long before.

In the grasslands north of the Black Sea, the predecessors of the Scythians were pastoral nomads called Cimmerians (Conan the Barbarian of literary and screen fame was supposedly a Cimmerian). Tales of these tribes drifted south through the Caucasus Mountains or were carried out of the Black Sea by sailors and picked up in the Near East. The Assyrians called these people Gimirrai; and the Biblical "Gomer," one of the offspring of Japheth in Genesis, may have been a Cimmerian. In the Aegean the Odyssey of Homer, composed about 700 B.C., referred to Cimmerian mare-milkers who lived in a land of perpetual darkness far to the north. King Midas, an Anatolian despot whose name still connotes fabulous wealth, lost his kingdom to Cimmerian raiders who had been expelled from the grasslands north of the Black Sea by the arrival of the Scythians.

The way of life practiced by the Scythians and Cimmerians was impossible without mounts. When and where did this way of life begin? An historian's approach to this question would be to go back to the literate societies of Iran and the Near East, where the early documents might cast at least a dim light on events among the nonliterate peoples off to the north. If we can determine when riding appeared in the ancient civilized world, we might obtain an approximate date for riding in the steppes. Although this approach is disturbingly indirect, it has dominated Western studies because the archaeological evidence from the steppes has been uncertain and difficult to evaluate until quite recently.

Riding in the Ancient Near East: Putting the Cart Before the Horse

Horses became extinct in the Near East prior to the end of the Pleistocene (10,000 B.C.) except in Turkey, where they survived only into the early Holocene (Recent) epoch.[2] Other equids, probably asses and ass-onager hybrids, were used to pull primitive war wagons in conflicts between the city-states of Sumer (southern Mesopotamia) as far back as the Early Dynastic III Period (about 2550 B.C.). Horses reappeared in domesticated form in Anatolia (Turkey) before 3050 B.C. Towns in Anatolia began engaging in trade with the merchants of lowland Mesopotamia at about the same time (the Uruk IV Period, 3300-3100 B.C.). Horses could have been brought to Mesopotamia during this period, but the earliest horse remains and depictions that have been found in the lowland cities occurred in archaeological deposits dated to the Akkadian Period, about 2350 B.C. It was only after 2150 B.C. (during the Ur III Period) that horses became widespread in the Near East.

Awkward-looking horseback riders, perhaps grooms or messengers, were portrayed in minor Near Eastern artworks as early as the Akkadian Period (figure 2), but horseback riding was not important in war or in the leisure pursuits of the urban elite until 1,500 years later. Cavalry forces were not used in battle in the Near East until about 850 B.C. In the archives of the city of Mari there was a now-famous letter from the palace prefect to King Zimri-Lim (1782-1759 B.C.) advising him that the preservation of his dignity required that he should ride in a chariot or even on a mule, but not on horseback. Perhaps, as Mary Littauer has suggested, horse sweat was considered so disagreeable that horseback riding was avoided by the elite.

On the other hand written records and pictorial evidence make it clear that horses were used to pull chariots in Anatolia and the Near East as early as 1900 B.C. Large

---

2. See chapter 2, figure I for the dates of geologic time periods mentioned in this chapter.

2. The depiction of a horseback rider on an Ur III seal (dated to 2150 B.C.) is important for establishing that horses were being ridden in Mesopotamia by this time. (Photo courtesy of David Owen)

units of horse-drawn chariots were an innovation that became important in Near Eastern warfare after about 1600 B.C. It seems clear that in the "civilized" world, horses were first used to pull chariots. Horseback riding was adopted by the military and the elites in the Near East only after centuries of chariot warfare. Many writers have thought that the Near Eastern evidence could be extended to the rest of the ancient world: horse draft preceded horseback riding.

It has long been assumed that effective horseback riding began among the "barbarian" tribes living north of the civilized world, in the Eurasian grasslands beyond the walled towns of northern Iran and Afghanistan. Contact with these tribes is presumed to have inspired the Assyrian use of mounted troops after 900 B.C. Sculptures portraying riders on horseback have been looted from sites dated to around 1500 B.C. in Afghanistan. Others have been excavated from a site of the same period, called Pirak, in neighboring Baluchistan. Seal impressions of riders have been recovered by Russian archaeologists from graves dated to about 1600 B.C. on the upper Amu Darya River (the ancient Oxus), in Afghanistan (figure 3). These portrayals of riders seem to reflect the commencement of effective horseback riding in the northern hinterlands of Iran and Afghanistan some time between about 2000 and 1500 B.C.

This date for the inception of riding and the priority of the chariot seem to be supported by linguistic and archaeological evidence from the cultures of the Eurasian grasslands themselves. Archaeologists recognize a cluster of new customs that appeared across the western Eurasian steppes in Russia and Kazakstan at about 1300 B.C. These changes suggest to some an important transition from an economy based on small-scale farming and herding to one more like that of the later Scythians, based almost exclusively on mobile nomadic herding, a way of life called pastoral nomadism (see chapter 7). In Kazakstan and eastward to the Altay-Sayan Mountains, this shift is seen archaeologically as the change from the late Andronovo to the Karasuk cultures. The development of effective horseback riding has been advanced by some as an explanation for the evolution of pastoral nomadism as a new way of life in the steppes. If pastoral nomadism appeared relatively recently, then by this argument riding should also be a recent innovation. If the appearance of horseback riding was not responsible for this shift, then what was?

Another argument for the priority of the chariot and the lateness of riding lies in linguistics. The Scythians and their ancestors in the steppes north of Iran and Afghanistan were speakers of Iranian languages. The ancient Persians of Iran also spoke Iranian languages, so the ancestors of the Persians were related in some way to the ancestors of the nomadic Scythians. It is likely that early Iranian speakers invaded Iran from the steppes between about 1700 and 1200 B.C. and established the ancestral Persian and Median communities, the progenitors of the later Persian state. Ancient Iranian was also closely related to the Indic languages of the Vedic epics of north India and Pakistan. The horse-worshiping heroes of the Rig-Veda text seem to have fought and boasted their way into the Indian sub-continent during the same 1700-1200 B.C. period. Both the Indic-speakers and the Iranian-speakers called themselves Aryans, from which the name Iran is derived. In the oldest Aryan poems and texts, which arguably refer to events that occurred before 1200 B.C., warrior-gods and heroes are usually described as drivers of chariots but only rarely as cavalrymen. This fact provides another hint that driving might have preceded riding, and riding might have developed relatively late.

There have always been dissenters who have argued for a much earlier beginning for riding, particularly among Russian and Ukrainian archaeologists. These voices are now supported by recent studies of bit wear on the teeth of horses from Dereivka in Ukraine that suggest that riding began by 4000 B.C. in the Ukrainian steppes (see discussions below). (The bit is an apparatus of metal or other strong material that is connected to the bridle and fits in the horse's mouth to control the position of its head and to assist in managing the direction and pace of the horse's progress.) If the bit wear evidence from Dereivka is valid, horseback riding began in the steppes about 3,000 years before it became widespread in the civilized Near East. It is possible then that riding began not long after horses were domesticated.

At least one conclusion emerges clearly from the documentary evidence: the city dwellers of the ancient Near East acquired horses from nonliterate peoples who occupied the mountains and steppes off to the north. Horses were first domesticated and ridden far from the eye of the historian. To understand the beginning of the horse-human partnership then, we must rely on the testimony of archaeology and zooarchaeology (the zoological and cultural study of animal remains from archaeological sites).

The Lineage of the Domesticated Horse

Most discussions of the genetic origin of domesticated horses refer to three primitive wild races or subspecies that might have been ancestral to modern domesticates: the tarpan of the Pontic-Caspian steppes of eastern Europe and Russia; the Przewalski horse of the Mongolian plateau; and a coldblood[3] western European forest horse of a large, heavy build, supposedly descended from the Pleistocene equids of Europe. Based on archaeological skeletal remains, however, there is little or no support for the existence of these three distinct wild populations prior to domestication.

3. *Coldblood* is a term that is applied to large European horses that are well adapted to cold climates and have a calmer temperament than do hotbloods like Arabians.

3. Horse and rider portrayed in a seal impression from a cylinder seal found in a grave in southern Bactria, on the Amu Darya River, Afghanistan. Based on its style and mythological themes, this seal is dated to about 1800-1600 B.C. (After V. I. Sarianidi, "Mesopotamia and Bactria in the Second Millennium B.C.," Sovietskaya Arkheologiia 1986 [2]*). Drawing by Sandra Olsen)*

The tarpan is a horse that has defining characteristics based on medieval and historic travelers' descriptions, not on systematic biological classification. It is, in essence, the historic-period wild or feral horse of the Pontic-Caspian steppes. Many of the loose horses of that region, regardless of their origin, could have been called tarpans. Only two skeletal specimens of animals identified as tarpans survive. Both individuals died in captivity, the last one in Moscow in 1884, when tarpans became extinct.

The tarpan was said to be distinguished by its mouse-dun color (see the Appendix), an erect mane, and a relatively short head, but since the extant sample consists of only two skeletons, little is known about the range of variation in the physical characteristics of tarpans. The wild horses of the historic-period Pontic-Caspian steppes had certainly interbred with domestic stock, since there are numerous reports of tarpan stallions abducting domesticated mares, and there is a very long history of escaped domestic stock in the region. The tarpan is, therefore, an historic-period, regional folk type with very little taxonomic validity. The statement that modern horses are descended from tarpans is taxonomically meaningless and historically inaccurate. Tarpans have attained their taxonomic status as the ancestor of modern domesticates only through a process of elimination.

The other good candidate for the ancestor of the domesticated horse is the Przewalski horse (*Equus przewalskii*), the wild horse of Mongolia. The Przewalski was hunted to extinction in the wild between 1880, when Captain Nikolai Przewalski first observed the wild horses of the Dzungarian region of western Mongolia, and 1969, when the last wild sighting occurred. Przewalski horses survive in zoos, however, and have been well studied. Chromosome differences between Przewalski's and modern domesticated horses have convinced many that modern domesticates could not have descended from Przewalski's.

All modern Przewalskis are descended from just eleven captives that were removed within the last 100 years from an isolated upland region situated at least 1,000 miles east of the steppes, where domestication probably occurred 6,000 years ago. This small founding population for modern Przewalski horses represents a severe genetic bottleneck that could influence the outcome of genetic studies and cause problems when trying to reconstruct how much the ancestors of domestic horses and the ancestors of Przewalski horses differed. Przewalski horses have sixty-six chromosomes, whereas all domestic breeds have just sixty-four. The Przewalski condition is probably the primitive one, because geneticists believe that the change could have derived from something called "Robertsonian fusion" of two chromosomes in one or more individuals. Following that genetic change, interbreeding among descendants that had just sixty-four chromosomes occurred, establishing a separate lineage either in the wild ancestor of the horse or in the earliest domesticated individuals. Modern horses could, then, have descended from primitive horses with sixty-six chromosomes. Crosses between domestic horses and Przewalskis are perfectly viable.

Studies of mitochondrial DNA by M. George and O. Ryder suggest that the ancestors of the modern Przewalski became separated from the ancestors of modern domesticated horses long before domestication occurred. This again would seem to rule out the possibility that Przewalski horses were the ancestors of domestic horses. However, the DNA data are not supported by studies of blood. Blood-typing (based on serological and blood-protein markers) shows that the two groups are very close. Given the current status of the genetic studies, it is likely that the first domesticated horses looked very much like the Przewalskis that we see in today's zoos, but that modern Przewalskis are at best a sister group of domesticated horses.

The third commonly cited ancestral type, the coldblood heavy horse of Europe, is a relatively modern group of breeds with no prehistoric taxonomic status, as Sandor Bökönyi has shown. In fact the Holocene (Recent) prehistoric horses of western Europe tended to be smaller and more gracile than the horses of the steppes to the east. The Bronze Age horses of Germany were even smaller than those of the Neolithic. European horses of the Roman era were, as a rule, quite a bit smaller than ordinary modern riding horses. Those that were above pony size (notably the horses of Thrace and Thessaly) probably owed their stature to eastern stock with which they were bred. The large, heavy, coldblood horses of western Europe are derived from a medieval breed, and are not an ancestor.

Modern domesticated horses are probably descended primarily from a wild ancestral population that roamed the Eurasian grasslands about 5000-4000 B.C., often referred to as *Equus ferus*, or the wild European horse. No "pure" representative of these ancestral animals survives today. It is fruitless to attempt to link modern breeds to wild regional types that predated domestication. There simply is not sufficient skeletal evidence to document the existence of well-defined types within the Eurasian grasslands prior to 4000 B.C., although steppe horses of that era can sometimes be distinguished from European forest horses on the basis of size. In appearance early Postglacial horses probably resembled the modern Przewalski—large-headed, thick-legged, stocky animals with shaggy coats and stiff manes. The most realistic preserved portrayal of a Copper Age horse was engraved on a silver vase from the Maikop "chieftain's grave" in the North Caucasus Mountains, dated to about 3000-2700 B.C. (figure 4). It looks very much like a Przewalski.

Domesticated or Wild?

How does one distinguish the bones of a domesticated horse from those of its wild cousins? What evidence demonstrates that domestication has occurred?

There are two standard ways to approach the study of animal domestication—zoological and archaeological. In the zoological approach the analyst identifies modifications in prehistoric animal anatomy (skeletal in most archaeological cases); posits changes in diet, breeding, or activity that might account for the observed anatomical traits; and suggests (if only implicitly) a set of human control behaviors that might have led to the observed changes (such as penning, foddering, restricting movement, and breeding for particular genetic traits). For example, a reduction in size might follow domestication if the domesticates were penned and fed a poorer diet than their wild cousins, or human manipulation of

4. Mythological scene impressed on a silver vase from the "chieftain's grave" at Maikop (dated to between 3000-2700 B.C.), showing a realistic portrayal of a steppe horse with an erect mane. (After M. Gimbutas, The Prehistory of Eastern Europe, *vol. I in* American School of Prehistoric Research, Harvard University, *Bulletin 20, 1956). (Drawings by Dorcus Brown)*

a domesticated herd might result in more anatomical diversity than would be seen in a wild population. In some cases no serious attempt is made to explain an anatomical change in terms of diet or behavior; a new morphological trait (flattened horn cores in sheep, for example) is recognized as a useful identifier of domesticated forms, although it has no known function. Of course, if the domestication process did not initially involve significant changes in diet or activity of the affected animals, then the zoological approach will not work.

Zoological analyses of animal domestication rest upon a complex methodology. The measurements and statistical tests that might validate a claim of significant anatomical change can be moderately elaborate, and zoological analysis has gone beyond simple bone measurements to consider changes in bone density, internal bone structure, angles of articulation between long bones, microscopic tooth wear, and even changes in protein structure. Allan Gilbert has recently developed tests that can distinguish the bones of different equid species or hybrids based on the constituent proteins preserved in bone albumin.

The limitations of the zoological approach are illustrated by the study of size reduction. In horses, as in people, stature is an extremely plastic trait, meaning that it can change rapidly from one generation to the next depending on diet and nutrition. Size reductions can occur naturally among feral horse populations if they are forced into peripheral ranges or if their diet is depleted by climatic or ecological changes, including changes caused by the activities of nearby human populations. The feral island ponies of Assateague Island, Maryland, are a case in point: though they rarely reach thirteen hands[4] in height in the wild, they are descended from full-sized horses, and if a colt is removed and fed a higher-protein diet, it will grow to normal horse size. Their small stature is a reversible condition caused by a protein-poor diet in an ecologically peripheral range. Moreover, the Assateague ponies have been forced into such an inferior range by human activity. The lesson here is that small wild horse populations occupying ecologically restricted ranges might be forced by neighboring humans into even worse ranges—resulting in a decline in stature—in the absence of any attempt at domestication.

The second approach is archaeological. Archaeologists study past human behavior. Animal bones can be examined as the patterned remains of particular types of human activities. Because humans do not exploit animals randomly, different strategies of animal exploitation should be detectable through a careful analysis of the species, ages, and sexes of the animals slaughtered by humans at a given site. To give a simple example, a high percentage of the males in a herd kept primarily for meat should be slaughtered quite young, as soon as approximate adult weight is attained, while most of the females, kept primarily for breeding and dairying, should be slaughtered late in life, after the best milking years are past.

Documenting the age and sex characteristics of the animals killed at a particular archaeological site can be difficult, given the problems caused by poor preservation, small sample sizes, and the paucity of sex criteria in osteological remains. There are several methods for calculating an animal's age at death. Molar crown heights and stages of tooth eruption and wear are important for horses. The sex of horses can be determined if the mandible is recovered because canine teeth are normally present in male horses, but occur only rarely in females. Horse teeth contain very important clues to age and sex, and they preserve well.

4. A hand is a unit of measure equal to ten centimeters (4 in.).

Of course, the ideal analysis considers both zoological and archaeological data. In the case of the domestication of the horse, however, neither zoology nor archaeology has produced conclusive results. There is no confirmed evidence that the earliest domesticated horses differed zoologically in any systematic way from their wild cousins, at least not in skeletal traits. It is possible that the earliest domesticated populations were not as a rule bred, stalled, penned, or foddered in ways that led to consistent physical changes.

Before reviewing some of the major studies of horse domestication, it should be acknowledged that domestication was a long, drawn-out process, not a single event. No one can expect to discover a sudden, dramatic change in horse anatomy reflecting the "moment" of domestication. One might, on the other hand, expect to find a more rapid change in the age and sex characteristics of horses slaughtered for food. However, any observed changes should be related to an explicit hypothesis describing why domestication occurred. Horses were apparently domesticated long after the other major Western herd animals (sheep, goats, cattle, and pigs). The people who first domesticated horses probably already had other domesticated animals, and they were able to hunt and fish for other sources of protein. Why did they bother with horses?

Why Were Horses Domesticated?

Many of the most profound changes in human organization and social behavior have come about as the unintended consequences of relatively small, intentional acts. Both the shift from hunting and gathering to farming and the development of cities from medium-sized tribal villages can be described in this way. Humans are blessed with sufficient intelligence and foresight to analyze the myriad problems they face and to act in their own self-interest—but they seldom understand the ultimate implications of their actions.

Horse domestication almost certainly should be understood in this way. It is doubtful that any prehistoric genius foresaw the potential capabilities of the wild steppe horse as a transport animal. Wild horses are alert, suspicious, large, powerful animals, and stallions attack both predators and rival stallions. The so-called "wild" horses we know today, such as the mustangs of western North America, are feral animals descended from domesticated populations that were bred for ease of handling for thousands of years. The truly wild horses of the Copper Age probably were more aggressive and tougher than any modern horse. Even in zoos and game preserves, Przewalski horses have a reputation for being difficult to manage and almost impossible to train as mounts (though it has been done). Riding probably began only after horses had been domesticated and people were familiar with them as animals that could be controlled. It is likely that the original purpose for domesticating wild horses was simply to acquire a plentiful and relatively low-maintenance source of meat.

Americans are not accustomed to thinking of horses as low-maintenance sources of meat only because they treat them as companions and performers. The Copper Age peoples of the Ukraine, however, saw animals in a more practical light. They obtained the meat in their diet from herds of domesticated animals as well as from the hunting of wild game, including wild horses. Their domesticated stock—cattle, sheep, and pigs—needed fodder over the winter or they would starve. In a snowy field sheep and cattle use their noses to push aside the snow in order to eat the dead grass beneath (see chapter 7). When these animals are left alone during long snows, their noses become raw and bloody. If they are not fed, they will stand and starve in a few inches of snow in a field full of winter grass.

Horses, on the other hand, are well adapted to surviving in cold weather. They use their hooves to scrape snow away from the grass beneath and can, therefore, feed themselves without human assistance. After horses were reintroduced into North America, for example, the Plains Indians very rarely provided any winter fodder or shelter for even their most prized horses. Horses were probably first domesticated in the Eurasian steppes because they were native to the grasslands, unlike cattle and sheep, which were imported from the south. Horses could survive the steppe winters without labor-intensive foddering and watering by river-valley farmers who themselves had to strain to survive the severe climate. For people who already kept cattle, the process of learning to control and domesticate horses might have been relatively easy, since horses and cattle share some behaviors and can be controlled in similar ways. Both have dominant males who need to be controlled, and the females of both species observe a system of social ranking. In both horse bands and cattle herds high-ranking females lead in most of the daily movements. The clever cowherd who already knew that the key to the cattle herd was the lead cow ("Bossy") would have quickly seen that the key to managing horses was in some ways similar.

Understanding these reasons for domesticating horses leads to considering the kinds of ancient sites that could contain the bones of the earliest domesticated horses. Thus, the next step is to look carefully at societies that already kept domesticated cattle and hunted wild horses for a regular part of their diet.

Where Were Horses Domesticated?

Domestication, like marriage, secures permanence for a preexisting relationship of some importance. Humans do not attempt to domesticate unfamiliar animals. They would have no motive to do so, and they would lack critical knowledge of the animals' habits and behaviors. To find the people who first domesticated horses, one should look for societies that interacted regularly with wild horses.

It was only in the Eurasian steppes or along the steppe borderlands that wild horses were sufficiently plentiful to play a significant long-term role in the economies of human societies after the Ice Age. The steppe belt runs across the middle of Eurasia from the Carpathian foothills of Ukraine to Mongolia. Postglacial hunter-gatherers regularly hunted wild horses throughout this vast region, establishing the kinds of human-horse economic relationships that must have preceded domestication. This consideration alone would draw our attention to the Eurasian steppes and steppe borderlands. Other locales, however, have also been advanced as potential places of origin for the domesticated horse. They are, broadly, the forest zone of Europe and the uplands of Anatolia and Iran.

The sections that follow briefly review the competing archaeological hypotheses for early domestication. Most of them are based on observed changes in equine skeletal anatomy. Changes in horse-human interactive behaviors, which were the crucial element in the process that led to domestication, have not been considered by researchers to the same extent as skeletal anatomy, except in a few cases.

Reindeer Herders in Northern Eurasia

It was once thought that reindeer riding (like that practiced by the Yakuts of Siberia) was older than, and provided the model for, horseback riding. Unfortunately, specialized reindeer herding of the type associated with riding did not develop until the sixteenth and seventeenth centuries A.D., millennia after the horse was domesticated. Research by the Soviet ethnographer S. Vainshtein has established that reindeer saddles were modeled after earlier medieval horse saddles rather than the other way around. While the reindeer transport traditions of northern Eurasia undoubtedly inspired Santa Claus, they did not inspire the first horseback riders.

The European Paleolithic

Some scholars, notably Paul Bahn, have suggested that horses were at least managed and perhaps domesticated 20,000 years ago by Ice Age hunter-gatherers who created the cave paintings, ornaments, and mobile art of the Upper Paleolithic (see chapter 3). This idea has been widely popularized by Jean Auel in her best-selling fiction books beginning with *Clan of the Cave Bear*.

Stocky, thick-legged, large-headed horses living throughout Europe during the Pleistocene Ice Ages were depicted magnificently in cave paintings and sculpted bone objects by Upper Paleolithic artists, particularly in southwest France and northern Spain. Some of these depictions seem to show rope halters around horse heads (see chapter 3, figure 15). This interpretation is convincing at first. However, the shaggy winter coat of the modern Przewalski horse often sports a line of tufted hair running down the cheek and around the nose in exactly the positions marked by the "halter" lines in Paleolithic art. The "winter coat" interpretation of these lines is simpler and more likely than an interpretation based on bridling.

Some Upper Paleolithic horse teeth exhibit odd wear that Bahn has suggested resembles the wear caused by crib-biting, a vice associated with stalled or penned horses. However, similar wear has been found on the teeth of Early Pleistocene equid fossils from America, animals that could not possibly have been domesticated because they predate the evolution of both modern humans and horses (see chapter 3). There has never been a controlled study that reliably identifies the diagnostic traits of cribbing wear on equid teeth so that it can be positively distinguished from natural wear or incidental damage to the incisors. The crib-biting suggestion remains untested and inherently unlikely. It would require not only domestication but long-term stalling of horses by Paleolithic hunters.

On the whole there is little archaeological evidence even for herd management and no convincing support for domestication associated with the Ice Age horses of the European Upper Paleolithic.

The Western and Central European Neolithic

After about 8000 B.C., as the postglacial climate warmed and forests spread northward, large herds of horses survived only in the eastern European and central Asian grasslands. Scattered populations of wild horses continued to live in the forests of western and central Europe, but by about 6000 B.C. there were only a few localities outside the steppes where wild horses were numerous enough to be selected as prey by human hunters. Even in these localities horses appeared only sporadically in the post-Pleistocene diet. A small species of ass, *Equus hydruntinus*, was eaten in the Balkans and Spain during the Neolithic, but appears to have become extinct during the Copper Age.

None of these central or western European equid populations was systematically hunted over large regions for long periods of time. Equids simply do not appear in the animal bone samples in the majority of Neolithic and Early Copper Age sites—sites occupied before 3000 B.C.—in central, western, and northern Europe. In sites that do contain horse bones, they typically occur as a very low percentage (less than 5 percent) of the total dietary animal bones. Red deer, roe deer, wild pig, aurochs (wild cattle), beaver, fish, and water birds were the important game animals; and cattle, pigs, and sheep were the mainstays of the domestic economy.

A few small populations of wild forest horses were occasionally hunted by early farmers or stockbreeders in the estuarine marshes of northern Europe, in the mountain meadows of Southern Germany and Poland, and in the dry uplands of southern Iberia. At some Late Neolithic and Copper Age[5] sites in these regions, horse bones account for more than 5 or even 10 percent of the skeletal remains. However, after the end of the Pleistocene (10,000 B.C.) and before 3000 B.C., there was no region in central, western, or northern Europe where humans depended on horses for a significant portion of their annual diet on a regular and continuing basis.

Recently, H.P. Uerpmann published an exhaustive study comparing measurements of the lower leg bones (metapodials) of Late Neolithic and Copper Age horses from western and central Europe. On the basis of this study, he suggested that horses were domesticated independently from local wild stock in a number of places in Europe. N. Benecke has come to the same conclusions concerning local domestication even earlier. These studies have documented significant decreases in mean size and increases in variability among Late Neolithic or Copper Age horses (3000-2500 B.C.) in many parts of Europe, trends that certainly suggest domestication. Uerpmann categorized the steppe horses of Dereivka, an important site in Ukraine (see below), as probably wild, partially because of their large size.

Uerpmann studied the Copper Age horses of Spain particularly closely. He suggested that the smaller, more variable horses of the Copper Age Bell Beaker culture (about 3000-2500) B.C.) were the domesticated descendants of local wild horses. Domestication occurred, he asserted, because the Copper Age Iberians wanted riding animals. They were inspired by the example of the civilizations of the Near East, where asses and ass-onager hybrids were used to pull military and elite wheeled vehicles. Uerpmann thought that a trans-Mediterranean trade in copper might have been the link through which the Iberian Bell Beaker culture learned of the Near Eastern use of equids for draft.

Although Uerpmann was probably correct in his conclusion that the Bell Beaker horses of Spain were domesticated, he was probably wrong in his

5. The Late Neolithic in northern Europe, the Copper Age in Spain and the Early Bronze Age in the Near East were contemporaneous (ca. 3000-2500 B.C).

explanation of why domestication occurred. The question of whether Near Eastern merchant sailors made contact with Copper Age Iberia has been debated for a long time, and the current consensus is that the evidence for contact is slim to nonexistent. There is no direct evidence for equid riding or draft in Bell Beaker Iberia. Horses were eaten, but they were not a dominant element in the Bell Beaker diet. Pre-Bell Beaker Iberians seem also to have eaten horses—presumably wild ones—only occasionally. If domestication is the culmination of a long process of economic dependence and close interaction, then the conditions for independent horse domestication were not clearly present in Iberia. In fact it is difficult to explain the appearance of domesticated horses in Iberia without appealing to some outside influence, as Uerpmann did. That influence might have been the Bell Beaker culture itself.

Bell Beakers were decorated ceramic drinking cups of a particular form and style. They occurred across central and western Europe about 3000-2500 B.C., probably as part of the paraphernalia of social drinking among competing local elites. Horses generally considered to be imported domesticates appeared with the Bell Beaker cultures in the British Isles and in other parts of Europe. The Bell Beaker cultures have traditionally been interpreted as a network of cultural interaction through which domesticated horses from the east were introduced to much of central and western Europe. It is clear that small herds of wild horses already occupied many parts of Europe before the Bell Beaker period, but it is difficult to determine the role that these local wild horses played in later domesticated populations.

Perhaps in Spain and southern Germany, where earlier wild horses were at least sporadically eaten, local wild horses began to be captured for domestication after knowledge of riding had diffused from the eastern European steppe societies. In southern Germany, where M. Glass has studied the horses of the Cham culture (also 3000-2500 B.C.), it seems likely that larger eastern horses were added to the smaller native wild horse population during the earliest phase of domestication. In other regions perhaps only local wild horses were domesticated.

This question of local versus imported domesticates is interesting in view of the genetic data. If many genetically distinct local wild horse populations contributed to the gene pool of modern domesticates, all of their ancestors must have had sixty-four chromosomes, given that all modern domesticated horses have that number. If the sixty-four-chromosome count is the result of a mutation from a primitive sixty-six-chromosome count (see page 65 above), then that mutation occurred long before domestication and was widespread among wild European horses.

Anatolia and the Caucasus

It is not likely that horses were domesticated in the Near East. The native postglacial equids of north Africa were asses and zebras, and the native equid of northern Syria, Iraq, and Iran was the onager, *Equus hemionus*. There is debate over whether wild horses were present in the uplands of eastern Anatolia (modern Turkey) and the Caucasus.

Wild horses might have survived in the Caucasus uplands after the end of the Pleistocene, but this is uncertain. Horse bones have been recovered in very small percentages from Copper Age sites (Arukhlo and Tsopi) in Georgia in the central Caucasus near Tbilisi dated to 5500-4000 B.C. Only in the dry plains of the lower Kura drainage in Azerbaijan are they found in any numbers at this early period—at only one site, Alimeklek-tepesi, where only 7.5 percent of the animal bones were derived from horses. These early Caucasian horses might have been a local mountain race or alternatively might have been introduced as domesticates from the steppes to the north. In either case there were very few of them.

In later antiquity, Anatolia was famous as a horse-breeding region, but horses probably were not native there. Horses do not appear in archaeological sites in Anatolia until the late Chalcolithic, or Copper Age. They initially appear sporadically in Chalcolithic levels at a cluster of sites in southeast Anatolia, near Malatya and Elazig, between 3300-3000 B.C. Horses were present also at Demircihöyök in northwestern Anatolia in levels dated to the same period. There is disagreement about whether these early Anatolian horses were wild or domesticated. The absence of horses from a great many well-studied earlier sites in Anatolia suggests that horses were not present as part of the natural wild fauna. Sandor Bökönyi has concluded that the Chalcolithic horses of Anatolia were introduced as domesticates from the Caucasus and/or from southeastern Europe.

Dereivka, a Copper Age Site in Ukraine

Dereivka is located on the west bank of the Dnieper River near the ecological boundary between the forest-steppe zone to the northwest and the true steppe to the southeast. The Copper Age occupation is radiocarbon dated to 4200-3800 B.C. Excavations conducted there by D. Telegin between 1959-1967 yielded 2,412 identifiable horse bones, representing a minimum of fifty-two animals (probably many more). The horse remains were mixed with those of cattle, sheep or goats, pigs, red deer, otter, fish, and freshwater shellfish in extensive trash middens. Telegin's excavations revealed the floors of two dwellings with interior hearths, ancillary buildings, a pottery-making work area, and a variety of trash and storage pits. Dereivka is a settlement of the Sredni Stog culture (4500-3500 B.C.), which is now known from smaller excavations at almost 200 sites in the steppe zone of Ukraine. The percentage of horse bones from Sredni Stog sites is about three times higher than the average for earlier Copper Age sites in the same region. It is safe to say that there was a significant increase in the exploitation of horses during the Sredni Stog Period in the steppes of Ukraine. This increase in usage might signal the beginnings of domestication.

One horse from Dereivka, a seven- to eight-year-old stallion, has become the focus of intense debate. Its bones were found with those of two dogs near the edge of the settlement. The horse was represented only by the skull, the lower jaw, and the articulated bones of the left forefoot. The dogs were similar: the remains of one dog consisted of a skull, lower jaw, and the bones of both forelegs; the other dog was represented by a skull, lower jaw, and an articulated vertebral column. It is possible that the bones of the horse and the first dog were originally attached to skins suspended on poles to mark a sacred location or to serve as a part of a ritual. Horse head-and-hoof displays of this kind have been used to mark sacred locations throughout the Eurasian grasslands from the Copper Age to the present (figures 5 and 6). Dog pelts were not treated this way in historically documented rituals from this area, and one of the dogs (the one with the backbone) looks more like it was butchered for consumption. However, other dog rituals did occur on the site—for example, a whole dog was buried beneath the threshold of one of the Dereivka dwellings. The "cult stallion," as this horse can be called, was the principal subject of the early zoological studies of the Dereivka horses. Just recently it has been shown to have worn a bit in its mouth.

The Dereivka horse bones were studied in the 1960s and 1970s by V. I. Bibikova, whose analysis relied largely on cranial measurements, and by G. Nobis, who used a wider array of measurements. On the basis of these studies, Dereivka is today widely cited as the earliest-known archaeological site with domesticated horses.

5. Reconstruction of a horse sacrifice based both on Oirot Mongol rituals performed in this century and on archaeological head-and-hoof burials. The bones are left in the head, tail, and feet to maintain the form of the horse and to help it to hang properly. (Drawing by Nancy J. Perkins)

There are, however, many who doubt the Dereivka evidence. The zoological analyses were less conclusive than many had initially hoped. Bibikova's principal study, published in a Russian biological journal in 1967, relied on one skull and mandible. Bibikova compared the horse skull with those of modern Przewalski and domesticated horses, and with skulls from a variety of archaeological horses, both domesticated and wild. The results of the cranial comparison were not (indeed, could not be) conclusive. Today, archaeologists prefer not to base a determination of domestication on a single skull, particularly if the skull is derived from a unique ritual deposit. The animal chosen for such a ritual might well have been atypical, compared with the horse population as a whole.

Bibikova felt, however, that several traits of the cult stallion were strongly suggestive of a domesticated status. These were a large but lightly built cranium; a very long nasal portion (muzzle), a short tooth row, and a wide occiput (the back portion of the skull). Nobis's later study utilized more of the available sample of Dereivka horse bones, which he found to be highly variable in measurements of bone robustness. This anatomical diversity was suggestive of a domesticated population. Diversity, however, is only an indirect indicator.

The studies of Bibikova and Nobis underscore how difficult it is to identify skeletal traits that can reliably distinguish the earliest domesticated horses from their wild cousins. It might be more productive to analyze the Dereivka horse bones as artifacts of human behavior, rather than as purely zoological specimens. Recently Marsha Levine has reassessed the Dereivka horses from this point of view.

Levine used measurements of molar crown heights to obtain age-at-death statistics for the horses of Dereivka. Horse premolars and molars grow and are worn down continually, so their heights should correlate with their age. Therefore, a young horse should have tall teeth (high crowns), and an old horse should have short teeth that ultimately are worn down to the gum line (low crowns). About half of the original sample of horse bones from Dereivka had unfortunately been discarded because of a lack of storage space in Kiev before Levine arrived in 1988. Nevertheless, she was able to locate 151 molar and premolar teeth from a minimum of sixteen individual animals for her crown-height analysis. According to her findings, almost 60

6. Head-and-hoof deposit containing the remains of two horses in a Bronze Age human burial chamber at the site of Utyёvka VI, near Samara, Russia. Buried were two horse skins, each of which was probably first hung over a pole during a funerary ceremony. The bones left behind after the skin deteriorated include the cranium, mandible, caudal (tail) vertebrae, and fore- and hindfoot bones. (Photo by David Anthony)

percent of these teeth were from animals killed between five and eight years of age. Moreover, nine of the ten tooth rows for which sex could be determined were from males. The horses slaughtered at Dereivka, therefore, appeared to have been primarily males between five and eight years old.

This mortality profile did not correspond to one expected for domesticated horses. Domesticates should have been killed at a younger age if they were kept only for meat, and been quite a bit older if they were used for riding. Stockbreeders who were attempting to manage a domesticated herd might well have culled males, since only a few stallions are needed for reproduction, but presumably they would have culled males at two to three years, as soon as they attained adult meat weight. Levine concluded that the mortality profile best corresponded to a pattern of hunting wild horses by stalking. Young adult stallions, five to eight years old, might have been consistently killed as they challenged stalking hunters. Levine suggested that most of the horses eaten at Dereivka were wild, although a few might have been tamed and ridden.

Levine's interpretation of the Dereivka horse remains is attractive but not definitive. The crown-height aging technique is not particularly accurate. Recent studies of the method suggest that it cannot provide age-at-death statistics more precise than about ±1.5 years (a three-year span) from the molar teeth of a mature individual in animals that live as long as horses. Levine's mortality peak between five and eight years does not represent an actual count of individual horses that can be identified as having been butchered between five and eight years of age; rather it represents an area of statistical overlap in age estimates that are much broader. The Dereivka age-at-death statistics are not, then, as precise as they might seem.

It is important to remember that all of the Dereivka age estimates are based on teeth. Teeth are part of the head, and heads may receive special treatment. Dereivka contains at least one horse head, that of the cult stallion, that was used in a ritual or cult activity. This animal's death might not have been linked to any ordinary pattern of meat consumption. It is possible that additional cultic horse heads are represented in the Dereivka horse tooth assemblage. Bibikova observed that many of the horse metapodials (hind- and forefoot bones) from Dereivka were found in groups of two or three near large skull or mandible fragments, and speculated that many of these might have been votive deposits. If stallion heads were systematically selected for ritual use, the tooth sample derived from those heads might not tell us anything about ordinary meat consumption practices. One explanation for the age and sex patterns revealed in the Dereivka horse teeth could be that prime stallions were preferred for ritual use.

Finally, it should be noted that the Dereivka horse bones have not been curated or described in a consistent manner. Telegin's final excavation season was in 1967. Bibikova's 1967 and 1969 reports in Ukrainian journals listed 2,255 horse bones from Dereivka, representing at least forty-four individuals. Telegin's book on the Sredni Stog culture in 1973 listed 2,412 horse bones from Dereivka and a minimum of fifty-two individuals. He did not comment on the source of the additional 157 bones. Bibikova noted that fifteen of seventeen sexually identifiable tooth rows were male, and that nearly 23 percent of the forty-four or more individuals represented in the horse bone assemblage were immature.

In 1988, when Levine conducted her study, about half of the bones had been discarded. Levine found only ten sexually identifiable tooth rows (nine of which were male), and the minimum number of individuals had fallen to sixteen. She observed that only 7 percent of the postcranial bones were immature (unfused or fusing). Bibikova's count of immature individuals cannot be compared directly with Levine's count of immature bones, but the discrepancy between 23 percent and 7 percent does raise the strong possibility that many of the bones of immature animals were discarded before 1988. In that case the age-at-death statistics from Dereivka cannot be relied upon.

It is in this context that Anthony and Brown's recent studies of bit wear (see below) on the horse teeth at Dereivka are important. Bit wear identifies a specific human-horse interaction that cannot occur in the wild. The cult stallion at Dereivka was bitted. The presence of a single horse that was regularly and repeatedly bitted is sufficient to document the beginnings of riding.

The Ural Mountains and Kazakstan

G. Matyushin has suggested that horses were domesticated as early as 6500 B.C. in the northern Russian forests. On the Kama River drainage, in the southwestern piedmont of the Ural Mountains, numerous horse bones have been found in combination with numerous elk and beaver at Neolithic sites like Mullino II and Davlekanovo. This evidence suggests a forest-steppe environment. Domesticated sheep and cattle have also been reported from the same levels. The stratigraphic sequences and dates for these sites have been questioned, however, throwing doubts on the chronology. The only basis for a claim of domestication is the fact that horses appear here in surprisingly high percentages. Until the stratigraphic sequence in these sites is better understood, it is best to reserve judgment. In any case Dereivka has more compelling evidence for domestication.

Yet another candidate for early horse domestication is located far to the east in northern Kazakstan. The site of Botai, south of the city of Petropavlovsk, has yielded over 300,000 animal bones, 99 percent of which are from horses. The site, a settlement with the remains of at least 153 semisubterranean dwellings, was occupied repeatedly or continuously between about 3500 and 2500 B.C. There are no other known domesticated animals except the dog. No copper artifacts have been recovered. Other Botai-culture sites have been found in the steppe region around the Ishim River, and of all the recovered bones over 90 percent are from horses. The Botai culture appears to represent a specialized exploitation of horses by indigenous hunting societies in the steppes of Inner Asia that probably included some domestication.

During the same period in the eastern European steppes, from Ukraine to the Ural River, the Yamna (Pit-Grave) culture regularly used domestic horses in an economy based on horse and ox cart transport, the herding of sheep and cattle, and the manufacture and exchange of copper ornaments and weapons. The

7. Diagram of a properly adjusted bit positioned on the tongue in the gap between the anterior and cheekteeth.

Yamna culture developed out of several earlier regional cultures, one of which was the Sredni Stog culture. While Yamna tribal groups used wheeled vehicles, worked copper, and herded sheep and cattle in the steppes west of the Ural River, the Botai culture did none of these things in the steppes east of the Ural River. The single aspect of the Yamna economy that may have diffused eastward was the practice of horseback riding, although it is also possible that horse domestication developed independently in the Botai region.

Brown and Anthony have recently examined a small collection of the Botai horse teeth. They found that 25 percent of the sample of lower second premolars exhibit bit wear. Some of the Botai horses, therefore, were ridden or driven. The excavators, V. Zaibert, A. Kislenko, and S. Olsen, believe that the Botai people rode domesticated horses to hunt wild horses in much the same manner that American Indians rode horses to hunt buffalo, while keeping no other domesticated animals except dogs. Brown and Anthony's results support this view.

Bit Wear and the Origins of Riding

Some particularly skeptical archaeologists have concluded that there is little convincing evidence for horseback riding or even for horse domestication in Europe before about 2500 B.C. At this point the reader might be tempted to agree. Despite many years of work by numerous gifted scholars, the evidence for early horse domestication remains elusive. The current tendency among zooarchaeologists, exemplified by Levine and Uerpmann, is to approach the Dereivka claims with cautious doubt. Given the analytical difficulties just reviewed, bit wear might be the best method for identifying the skeletal remains of domesticated horses.

When and where did horseback riding begin? The oldest firmly dated picture of a horseback rider was carved on a cylinder seal in Mesopotamia about 2150 B.C. during the Ur III Period (figure 2). In the steppes the oldest pictures of riders probably are petroglyphs carved on a stone outcrop at Kamennaya Mogila, near Melitopol in Ukraine, but they are difficult to date with any certainty. Before 1989 there was no direct evidence for riding in the steppes that could be assigned confidently to a period earlier than 2000 B.C. Those who argued that riding began earlier had to rely on frustratingly indirect evidence. Indirect clues included perforated antler tines found at Dereivka and other sites of the Sredni Stog culture (4500-3500 B.C.), argued to have been cheekpieces for bits; zoomorphic stone mace heads, carved in the shape of horse heads with incised lines that might represent halters or bridles, found in sites scattered from the Balkans to the Caspian and dated broadly to about 3500-3000 B.C.; and the simple assertion that horse herding was impossible without horseback riding. If the Dereivka horses were domesticated, as this argument hypothesized, riding must have existed. None of these artifacts or arguments were conclusive, however.

The search for direct, conclusive archaeological evidence for the use of horses as transport animals has now focused on identifying bit wear on ancient horse teeth. Bit wear is the damage that occurs on the anterior occlusal surfaces—the chewing surfaces—of the second premolar teeth (P_2's) when a horse chews the bit. Horses can be controlled without bits, so the absence of bit wear does not indicate that horses were not ridden or driven. However, the presence of bit wear clearly indicates bitting.

As early as the 1970s, archaeozoologists such as Juliet Clutton-Brock mentioned the possibility that bit wear might explain certain features seen on ancient horse teeth. In articles published in 1989 and 1991 David Anthony and Dorcas Brown formally defined bit wear. Their definition was based on a comparison of the wear features seen on the teeth of feral and domesticated horses. Natural occlusal and dietary wear was observed on the teeth of twenty modern feral horses (never bitted) from Nevada and the Atlantic barrier islands; this natural wear was compared with wear from metal bits observed on the teeth of ten modern domestic horses. Recently these researchers have examined the teeth of forty-two additional modern domestic horses and have conducted riding experiments on previously unbitted horses with bits made of rope, leather, and bone. They have recognized bit wear on many archaeological horse teeth, but two cases are particularly important: Malyan in Iran, dated to 2000-1900 B.C., and Dereivka in Ukraine, dated to 4200-3750 B.C. The bit wear at Malyan is the earliest unambiguous evidence for the use of the bit in the Near East, although copper stains on donkey teeth from Akkadian Tell Brak in Syria might suggest earlier bitting. The bit wear at Dereivka is the earliest evidence for the use of horses as transport animals anywhere in the world.

What is bit wear, and how is it produced? A bit normally rests on a horse's tongue and gums in the space between the cheekteeth, or premolars, and the front teeth, or incisors (figure 7). When the reins are pulled, the bit presses into sensitive soft tissue, causing the horse to turn its head if the rein is pulled on one side or to tuck its chin down if both reins are pulled. Horses can use their tongues to elevate and retract the bit, lifting it off the sensitive gums and into the grip of their upper and lower second premolars, where it can no longer cause discomfort.[6] The position of the bit between the teeth was documented by Hilary Clayton and R. Lee in fluoroscopic X-ray photographs that showed the action of a bit in living horses' mouths (figure 8).

It is difficult for a horse to keep a bit between its teeth. Because the corners of the lips are positioned forward of the premolars, the horse must push the bit back with its tongue and grasp it between its teeth to prevent the cheek corners from pushing it forward onto the gums. Bit wear is caused by two factors: (1) the horse must firmly grip the bit between its premolars in order to hold it in place, and (2) the bit nevertheless slips back and forth over the chewing surfaces of the premolars. Slippage affects the lower premolars more than the uppers, so bit wear is more pronounced on the lower teeth. Usually it is confined to the chewing surface on the anterior third of the lower premolar (P_2), because it is difficult or impossible for the horse to push the bit back into its cheeks far enough to affect the posterior part of the tooth.

When a horse chews the bit, two things happen to the anterior part of the premolars. First, on a microscopic level the front third of the chewing surface becomes covered with abrasions and pits where spalls (chips) have been removed (figure 9B). It is the location and intensity of this wear that is diagnostic: a bit causes intense wear that is confined to the front third of the chewing surface of the anterior portion of the premolar. Wild horses often have microscopic scratches on their teeth, but natural abrasions are never concentrated exclusively on one

6. The first premolar is very small or more commonly absent in modern horses.

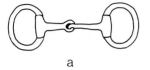

a

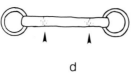

d

b

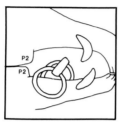

e

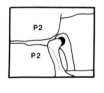

c

f

8. *Diagrams of a jointed snaffle bit (a–c) and a Mullen mouth loose-ring snaffle bit (d–f). Diagrams b and e show the bits correctly adjusted in the horse's mouth; c and f show the bits raised by the horse's tongue so they rest clinched between the upper and lower premolars, leading to bit wear on the lower premolar. The arrows on diagram d point to tooth wear on it. (Drawings after flouroscopic X-ray photographs by H. Clayton and R. Lee)*

cusp of the anterior premolar.

Second, on a macroscopic level (visible without magnification), the slippage of the bit back and forth across the front corner of the premolar produces a wear facet or bevel that can be measured. A pronounced bevel can be diagnostic by itself among horses more than three years old. (Younger horses often have irregular teeth that may exhibit natural "dips" resembling beveling.) The mean bevel measurement for the feral horses studied by Anthony and Brown was only 0.78 millimeters (0.03 in.), and the majority measured 0.5 millimeters (0.02 in.) or less (figure 9A). Among frequently ridden domesticated horses the mean bevel measurement was 3.6 millimeters (0.14 in.), and the majority measured 4 millimeters (0.16 in.) or more. A bevel measurement of 3 millimeters (0.12 in.) or more on the premolars of a mature horse is considered a reliable indicator of bit wear.

In 1989 Anthony and Brown studied the horse premolars in the collections of the Ukrainian Institute of Zoology in Kiev. High-resolution casts were made of lower second premolars from a wide variety of sites ranging from 25,000 years to just 1,000 years old. Those older than 4000 B.C. showed no beveling or microscopic evidence of bit wear.

The Dereivka cult stallion, however, exhibited bevel measurements of 3 and 4 millimeters (.2 and .25 inches), well within the range considered diagnostic of bit wear. The beveling affected only the anterior portion of the chewing surface of its lower second premolars. Microscopic spall pits and abrasions covered the same part of the tooth and did not occur on the posterior chewing surface or on other surfaces (figure 10). Moreover, because the Dereivka cult stallion was deposited in a head-and-hoof ritual, the matching upper jaw was preserved and can be fitted against the lower. There is no malocclusion that could account for the wear. The Dereivka cult stallion was bitted.

Recent riding experiments by Anthony and Brown with bits made of bone, leather, and rope suggest that the Dereivka cult stallion was bitted with a hard bit (perhaps bone) repeatedly over a long period of time (at least 300 hours of riding time) and had been regularly bitted in the months before its death. Bitting implies that the stallion was either ridden or used to pull a vehicle. Derievka was occupied about 4000 B.C., 500 years before the earliest evidence for the invention of the wheel, so the Dereivka cult stallion was most likely a mount. It is the earliest horse thought to have been ridden anywhere in the world.

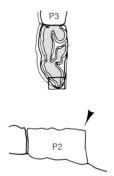

The P$_2$'s from just four of the fifty-two or more horses represented at Dereivka were available for Anthony and Brown's 1989 investigation. One individual was less than 2.5 years old and still retained its deciduous teeth, two displayed no evidence of bit wear, and one (the cult stallion) was bitted. It is impossible to determine whether horseback riding was widespread at Dereivka on the basis of

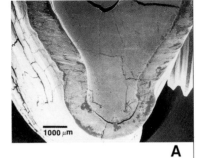

such a small sample. However, in a settlement where one horse was ridden regularly, it is very probable that riding was a familiar and important activity.

Some specialists who feel uneasy with such an early date for riding think that the cult stallion deposit at Dereivka might date later than the rest of the site in which it was found: perhaps people living at a later time dug into the Copper Age levels at Dereivka and placed the horse-and-dog deposit there. No evidence of such a disturbance was detected when the cult stallion deposit was first found, and the excavator has emphasized that it was covered by a Copper Age midden. However, a radiocarbon date of 2915 B.C. (4330±120 B.P.) was recently obtained from a fragment of bone from the skull of the cult stallion, suggesting that the skull is about 1,000 years younger than the Copper Age level in which it was found. This was the only anomalous radiocarbon date from Dereivka. Radiocarbon-age ranges for the seven other bone and shell samples from the site overlap between 3750 and 4200 B.C. An obvious explanation for the inconsistency is that the cult stallion skull was covered with thick layers of glue and lacquer for twenty-five years while it was on display at the Institute of Zoology in Kiev, before the bone fragment was removed for dating.

Glue and lacquer percolate easily and extensively through bone, contaminating the old carbon of the bone with small amounts of modern glue carbon. Bone contaminated in this way would yield an anomalously recent radiocarbon date. The Kiev laboratory that produced the date did not isolate the horse bone carbon from that of the modern glues and lacquers, a procedure that can be performed in only a few radiocarbon laboratories in the world, so the carbon was almost certainly contaminated. Nevertheless, the new date does cloud the current chronology of horse domestication.[7]

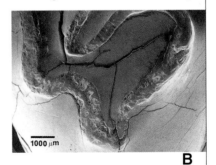

Brown and Anthony also detected bit wear on at least five P$_2$'s from Botai (26 percent of the measurable P$_2$'s) and on three P$_2$'s from Sergeivka, an early Bronze Age site near Botai. Both sites are located in northern Kazakstan. Botai is dated by radiocarbon to about 3600 to 2500 B.C.; Sergeivka is later. Horseback riding appears to have become a widespread practice in the western Eurasian steppes by perhaps 3000 B.C.

---

7. A fragment of bone from the cult stallion was being analyzed by the Oxford University Radiocarbon Laboratory as this volume went to press. The results may clear up the question of the date of the cult stallion.

9. Comparison of unbitted and bitted horse premolars:
A. Lower second premolar of an eight-year-old island pony from Assateague, Maryland: scanning electron micrograph of natural wear from chewing. Diagrams above show the chewing surface depicted in the photo and a side view illustrating the lack of a bevel. The fine parallel striations in the photograph represent normal wear caused by grinding food.
B. Lower premolar of a five-year-old racehorse: scanning electron micrograph of the bit wear. Diagrams below show the chewing surface and a side view with bevel. Note the spalling and pitting of the enamel surface in the photograph.

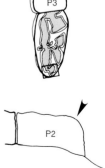

The First Riders

The customs that define the Sredni Stog culture (including Dereivka) were learned and maintained by people living between about 4500 and 3500 B.C. in the forested river valleys that wound through the dry grasslands north of the Black Sea. The people lived in small valley-bottom homesteads (two to four light-

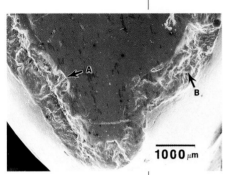

ly built structures), their material culture was relatively simple, and they kept herds of cattle, sheep, and pigs. There is no direct evidence for Sredni Stog agriculture, but grinding stones and flint blades with cereal "sickle polish" on the cutting edges are common artifacts, so they probably did raise grain. They ate horses in larger numbers than any earlier or contemporary culture of the same region. At Dereivka 61.2 percent of the identified animal bones were from horses, representing a minimum of fifty-two animals (probably many more) and at least 6,800 kilograms (15,000 lbs.) of meat. They also rode horses, and included horses in their rituals.

1000 μm

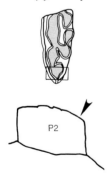

10. Lower premolar of the Dereivka cult stallion: scanning electron micrograph of the bit wear (top), diagram of the chewing surface showing the area in the photo (center), and a side view showing the presence of a bevel. Note the center-origin spall (A) and the abraded step fracture (B) in the photo.

P2

1 cm

What impact did riding have on the lives of the Sredni Stog people and other ancient Europeans? One way to answer this question is to look at the example of those American Indians who also lived in grassland environments, used a similar bone-and-stone tool technology, and acquired horses from Europeans under circumstances that permit a close examination of the implications of riding. For them riding was a revolutionary innovation that completely reoriented many fundamental aspects of their lives. In both North and South America the former dominance of farming tribes over hunting tribes was reversed within two generations after the hunters acquired horses. Religion, status, personal identity, warfare, economic productivity, commerce, and the boundaries of tribal territories all were redefined once riding began.

Horseback riders could move two to three times farther and faster per day than people on foot. Resources, enemies, allies, and markets that had previously been beyond effective reach suddenly became obtainable. Subsistence and economic survival in the dry grasslands, an uncertain and risky proposition for pedestrian hunters, became predictable and productive for mounted hunters. Sedentary horticultural villagers whose river-valley settlements had been the centers of population and economic productivity in the region became vulnerable to lightning-quick raids by enemies who could not be pursued or punished. Many of these villages were abandoned, and their occupants became mounted hunters in self-defense.

This, for example, was the case with the Plains Indians, including the Cheyenne, many of the Sioux, and the Arapaho. Warfare increased in intensity and social importance, both because horses became an easily stolen standard of wealth and because mounted societies redrew ethnic boundaries that had been based on pedestrian travel distances. Trade and exchange systems extended farther, became socially more complex, and carried a higher volume of goods (including horses) than had been possible before. It is difficult to identify an aspect of Plains Indian culture that was not affected by horseback riding. In North America this flurry of innovation went on for a century (from 1650 to 1750) without direct European interference, permitting a new type of native culture to evolve largely on its own terms.

One would expect a newly mounted Sredni Stog population to have entered into radically altered relations with its regional neighbors, as happened with the American Indians. In fact, important changes did occur. To the west, in the forested uplands between the Dnieper River and the Carpathians, the large agricultural towns and numerous small villages of the Cucuteni-Tripolye culture were the centers of population and economic productivity in the region from about 4500 B.C. to about 3500 B.C. Copper metallurgy, two-story buildings, rituals associating female figurines and grain, and the manufacture of technically sophisticated polychrome ceramic vessels distinguished Cucuteni-Tripolye settlements from those of the Sredni Stog culture.

However, during the late Sredni Stog Period (the period represented at Dereivka), Cucuteni-Tripolye copper ornaments appeared in Sredni Stog graves in both numbers and varieties that had never before appeared east of the Dnieper River. In addition, copper ornaments of Cucuteni-Tripolye type and spectrographic composition appeared in cemeteries 900 kilometers (559 mi.) to the east, at, for example, Khvalynsk on the middle Volga, presumably acquired through Sredni Stog middlemen. At the same time the largest Cucuteni-Tripolye settlements ballooned in size to over 300 hectares (741 acres) and 1,000 structures, representing unprecedented population concentrations that can best be explained as defensive in nature. Finally, cemeteries resembling those of the Sredni Stog culture appeared about 3800 B.C., 600 kilometers (372 mi.) to the west of the Dnieper in what is now eastern Hungary and western Romania.

Horseback riding would have led to just such changes—the enrichment of the Sredni Stog culture, the extension of long-distance trade and communication across the grasslands, the defensive concentration of neighboring sedentary farming populations, and the actual movement of Sredni Stog groups into resource-rich areas that they had never before been able to exploit.

These social and economic changes are important enough by themselves. However, Ukraine at 4000 B.C. is also a candidate for the time and place in which Proto-Indo-European, the mother tongue that spawned all Indo-European languages, was last spoken in a unified speech community. After this date the speakers of Proto-Indo-European dispersed, and their varied dialects were adopted in different geographic areas, ultimately evolving into languages as diverse as modern English, Russian, and Persian. Recent scholarly opinion, however, is divided on the question of the location of the Proto-Indo-European homeland, partially because the mechanism that might have propelled Indo-European speakers outward from Ukraine has not been clearly identified. Horseback riding and its accompanying social changes might have provided such a mechanism.

Horseback riding alone did not open the steppe environment to efficient exploitation by human societies. Sredni Stog settlements and cemeteries remained largely within the forested river valleys rather than out in the steppes. After about 3500 B.C., however, the steppes north of the Black and Caspian Seas witnessed the evolution of the Yamna (Pit-Grave) culture, which appears to have been derived partially from a Sredni Stog background and partially from the Repin and Khvalynsk cultures of the middle Don-Volga. The evolution of the Yamna culture marked a watershed in the cultural ecology of the Eurasian steppes.

Yamna settlements and cemeteries are occasionally found far out in the steppes, reflecting the first appearance of societies that made regular use of deep-steppe pastures and resources. Wheeled vehicles also appeared for the first time in Eurasia about 3300 B.C., during the era of the Yamna culture. Although heavy and clumsy, these solid-wheeled ox carts and wagons could transport enough tents and supplies so that herders did not have to depend on the river valleys. For the first time groups of herders could spend long periods, perhaps the spring and summer months, moving their sheep and cattle from pasture to pasture deep in the steppes.

Carts and wagons were so important that they were buried in high-status Yamna graves, perhaps as a symbol of the spiritual journey to distant pastures in the afterlife. It was the combination of rapid, long-distance transport represented by the horse and the slow bulk transport represented by the ox cart that finally transformed the Eurasian steppes from a hostile barrier to a corridor of intercultural communication.

Reading List

Anthony, David W. "The 'Kurgan Culture,' Indo-European Origins, and the Domestication of the Horse: A Reconsideration." *Current Anthropology* 27 (1986), 291-313.

_____ . "The Domestication of the Horse," in *Equids in the Ancient World*, vol. II, ed. by R. H. Meadow and H-P. Uerpmann. Wiesbaden: Ludwig Reichert Verlag, 1991. Pp. 250-77.

_____ . "A Continent for a Horse." *Pacific Discovery* (Columbian quincentennial issue) 45 (1992), 16-22.

Anthony, David W , and Dorcas Brown. "The Origins of Horseback Riding." *Antiquity* 65 (1991), 22-38.

Anthony, David W., Dimitri Telegin, and Dorcas Brown. "The Origin of Horseback Riding." *Scientific American* 265 (1991), 94-100.

Bökönyi, Sandor. *History of Domestic Animals in Central and Eastern Europe*. Budapest: Akademiai Kiado, 1974.

Clutton-Brock, Juliet. *Horse Power: A History of the Horse and the Donkey in Human Societies*. Cambridge, MA: Harvard University Press, 1992.

Davis, Simon J. M. *The Archaeology of Animals*. New Haven: Yale University Press, 1987.

Ewers, John C. *The Horse in Blackfoot Indian Culture*. Washington, DC: Smithsonian Institution Press, 1955.

George, M., Jr., and O. A. Ryder. "Mitochondrial DNA evolution in the genus Equus." *Molecular Biology and Evolution* 3 (1986), 535-46.

Hyland, Ann. *Equus: The Horse in the Roman World*. New Haven: Yale University Press, 1990.

Levine, Marsha. "Dereivka and the Problem of Horse Domestication." *Antiquity* 64 (1990), pp. 727-40.

Littauer, Mary A., and J. H. Crouwel. *Wheeled Vehicles and Ridden Animals in the Ancient Near East*. Leiden: Brill, 1979.

Mallory, James. *In Search of the Indo-Europeans*. London: Thames & Hudson, 1989.

Murray, Jaqueline. *The First European Agriculture: A Study of the Osteological and Botanical Evidence Until 2000 B.C.* Edinburgh: Edinburgh University Press, 1970.

HORSES IN HISTORY

JULIET CLUTTON-BROCK

*I*t is hard for us today to comprehend the
enormous importance of the horse in the development of nearly all the great civilizations of the world. Before the invention of mechanical power, draft animals were
the only source of transport and haulage, other than people themselves. Because of
its great speed and resilience, the horse became the invaluable partner of the traveler, soldier, and invader. Without the horse Alexander the Great and Genghis Khan
could not have made their Asian conquests. There could have been no European
Crusades to the Holy Land, and the Spanish followers of Columbus could not have
destroyed the civilizations of the Aztecs and the Incas in the Americas.

The Horse in the Ancient World
Ancient Mesopotamia

There were two civilizations in ancient Mesopotamia (Iraq) that had
great influence on the early history of the horse and donkey. In the south, in
Babylonia, the Sumerian empire lasted throughout the third millennium B.C. In
the north the Assyrian empire lasted from 2,000 B.C. until it fell in 612 B.C.

The Sumerians, like the ancient Egyptians, were great believers in hierarchy and order. As such, they made lists on clay tablets of everything that concerned
them in their daily lives, using a type of writing known as cuneiform. Many thousands of these tablets have been retrieved from sites throughout Mesopotamia. It
seems clear from recent decipherment of the cuneiform texts that the domestic
donkey was the common agricultural draft animal of the Sumerians, while small
numbers of captive wild onagers were kept for cross-breeding with donkeys. The
hybrid offspring were large powerful animals that were yoked in teams and used to
draw primitive vehicles with disk wheels. These animals would have been about as
large as the early domestic horses, which are mentioned only occasionally in the
cuneiform texts from around 2050 B.C. One three-year accounting tablet records
37 horses, 360 onagers, 727 hybrids, and 2,204 donkeys.

From the eighteenth century B.C. on, throughout western Asia and
Egypt, the elite members of society traveled in light, fast, horse-drawn chariots with
spoked wheels. That the horse replaced the donkey as a mount is indicated by the
earliest depictions of men on horseback. In these the rider is seated well back on
the loins of the horse, in the "donkey position," rather than behind the withers as
is usual for horse riding. It is not until the eighth century B.C. that Assyrian riders
are shown seated like modern riders, at their ease, bareback behind the withers.

The Assyrian Kings

The ancient palaces of Assyria were decorated with elaborately carved
bas-reliefs that give us an incredibly detailed picture of Assyrian life in the first
millennium B.C. The most numerous and grandest of the stone reliefs come from

Facing page, see figure 1.

palace walls at Nimrud and Nineveh. Many, like those from the palace of Assurbanipal (668-627 B.C.) at Nineveh (figure 1), portray scenes of hunting and war. They depict hunting from horseback or chariots in marvelous detail, showing the pageantry of the nobility and the suffering of the conquered. Recently it has been demonstrated that an Assyrian archer could shoot an arrow from a galloping horse without a proper saddle or stirrups because of the clever style of the their bridle. Instead of being held in the hands, their reins were attached to a neck collar that was kept in position by a weighted tassel in front. To direct the horse, the rider needed only to pull the collar to the right or the left and apply pressure with his legs.

Ancient Egypt

There are no fossil records of wild horses from North Africa after the end of the Pleistocene period (about 12,000 years ago), so it is certain that the horse was not domesticated in Africa. It was apparently brought into Egypt by the Hyksos rulers, who first seized power in the region of the Nile Delta in about 1720 B.C. and then moved south into Nubia. The Hyksos (meaning "princes of foreign countries") had a wide network of contacts throughout western Asia, and would have had access to all the most recent technologies of their day, including horses and chariots for use in royal processions and hunts. The Hyksos rulers were ousted in about 1639 B.C. by a new family of kings (Dynasty XVII), who inherited the royal chariots.

Just as the Paleolithic cave paintings from France and Spain show what the wild ponies of Europe looked like toward the end of the last ice age, 12,000 years ago, so the paintings from ancient Egypt are a vivid memorial to the earliest chariot horses. Remarkably, all these horses look like the modern Arab with their small heads, slender bodies, and fine limbs. The famous gold base of the ostrich-feather fan (figure 2) found in the tomb of Tutankhamen (Dynasty XVIII) is engraved with a chariot and horses that have ostrich plumes on their bridles, bronze cheekpieces, tassels on the harness, and groomed manes and tails. These horses of 1300 B.C. exemplify the pageantry and splendor that has accompanied royal parades throughout history.

The Horse in the Old Testament

The first mention of the horse in the Old Testament is in the story of Joseph saving the people of Egypt from the great famine described in Genesis 47:17 (King James Version): "and Joseph gave them bread in exchange for horses, and for the flocks, and for the cattle of the herds, and for the asses." From this time on (from ca. 2,000 B.C.), the chariot horse played an integral part in the endless wars fought between the peoples of western Asia. The Israelites came to depend on a supply of horses and chariots from Egypt to defend themselves against Syria and the Assyrians. This policy was clearly denounced by the prophets: "Woe to them that go down to Egypt for help; and stay on horses, and trust in chariots, because they are many; and in horsemen, because they are very strong" (Isaiah 31:1), and "Now the Egyptians are men, and not God; and their horses flesh, and not spirit" (Isaiah 31:3). One of the most evocative of all descriptions of the war horse is given in the Book of Job:

He paweth in the valley, and rejoiceth in his strength: he goeth on to meet the armed men. He mocketh at fear, and is not affrighted; neither turneth he back from the sword. The quiver rattleth against him, the glittering spear and the shield. He swalloweth the ground with fierceness and rage: neither believeth he that it is the sound of the trumpet. He saith among the trumpets, Ha, ha; and he smelleth the battle afar off, the thunder of the captains, and the shouting.

Job 39:21-25

The Greek Empire

Throughout the Bronze Age empires of Egypt, Crete, and the Near East, battles were fought by lines of chariots that crashed together in combat. However, from the beginning of the historical period in Greece, around 700 B.C., until the end of the Roman empire, chariots were used only for transport to the scene of a battle. Once the fighting began, the chariot was left with a driver, while the warriors attacked on foot with a lance or javelin.

After 550 B.C. wars became more serious events and were fought by heavily armed foot soldiers and mounted archers. The Greek horse was, however, still only the size of a modern pony (less than fourteen hands[1]) and, therefore, could not carry armor heavy enough to repel spears hurled in large numbers by foot soldiers. Also, archers could not fight in heavy armor and stay on horseback without a saddle and stirrups, which were still unknown at this time in the classical world.

Xenophon and the Art of Horsemanship. The most famous writer on the subject of horses from the classical period was Xenophon, a rich Athenian (427-354 B.C.). Xenophon is most famous for his treatises on horsemanship and hunting, which, like those of the later Roman writers on husbandry, are remarkable for their obvious concern for the welfare of animals.

1. A hunting scene from the new palace of the Assyrian king, Assurbanipal (668-627 B.C.), at Nineveh (northern Iraq), showing the king hunting onagers from horseback with the aid of mastiffs. (Copyright British Museum)

2. The gold base of an ostrich-feather fly whisk belonging to Tutankhamen (reign ca. 1336-1327 B.C.), showing the king's triumphal return with his kill after the hunt. (Photo courtesy of the Robert Harding Picture Library)

---

1. A hand is a unit of measure equal to ten centimeters (4 in.).

Xenophon told the horseman everything he needed to know about how to choose, mount, train, exercise, and feed a horse. He also gave advice on the proper type and size of armor for both horse and rider and how to hurl a javelin. All of this, it must be remembered, was accomplished without stirrups and with only a cloth for a saddle. Since stallions were not castrated, Xenophon recommended that a horse should always be muzzled when led out of its stable to avoid injury from conflict between stallions. Because there were no horseshoes to keep the hooves evenly worn, Xenophon advised that the horse should stand for some time each day on a floor of small rough stones. Every person who owns a horse today should read Xenophon for his timeless advice, good sense, and compassion.

Alexander the Great. Bucephalus, owned by Alexander the Great for seventeen years, is the most famous horse of the ancient world. It was a black stallion, bred in Thessaly and given to Philip of Macedonia in 343 B.C. The horse bucked and reared in front of Philip and was ordered to be taken away, but Alexander, Philip's twelve-year old son, had seen that Bucephalus was shying away from his own shadow. Alexander turned the stallion's head so it was facing into the sun and leapt onto his back. Bucephalus was given to the boy, and the king accurately predicted that Macedonia would never hold his son. Alexander the Great, although he died at the age of only thirty-two, conquered the lands from Greece to Afghanistan and founded the largest empire the world had yet known.

The Ancient Greek Chariot in Sport and Pageantry. Although the chariot became obsolete as a weapon of war in the classical period, it remained in use for sport and processions. The chariot was always constructed as a two-wheeled car, harnessed to a pair of horses by a central pole. Often, however, another pair of horses was harnessed to the outside of the central pair, to make the chariot a *quadriga* (figure 3). In later times even more horses, up to ten in number, were added to the chariot.

The earliest-known description of a chariot race is recounted in the *Iliad,* a Homeric poem believed to have been composed around 750 B.C. The *Iliad* is about the Trojan War, supposedly fought 500 years earlier by the Greeks to recover their queen, Helen, who had been kidnapped by the King of Troy.

Homer recounts that the race was a central event in the funeral games organized by Achilles for his close friend Patroklos, who was killed during the war. The chariot race was run by five contestants across the open plain outside the city of Troy. The participants raced to a goal and back again to where Achilles would judge the winners. The goal was a standing wooden post with two white stones on either side of it. One of the drivers, Antilochus, received this advice from his father:

> *Approach the goal very closely, drive your chariot and horses near; but bend a little towards the left side of the horses from your well-joined chariot; and cheering on the right hand horse, whip him and give him the rein with your hands. Let your left hand horse move close to the goal, so that the nave of the well-made wheel may seem to touch the goal post, but avoid touching the stone, lest you wound your horses and break your chariot in pieces, which would be a joy to others and a disgrace to yourself.*

Iliad 23. 331-60, translated by M. Hammond, 1987

The Olympic Games. According to legend, games were first held at Olympia in honor of Zeus in 1222 B.C. The first Olympiad was in 776 B.C., when the prize was won by Coroebus, and from then on the games were held every four years at the time of the first full moon after the summer solstice. Four-horse chariot races were introduced to the games at the twenty-third Olympiad (684 B.C.), and mounted horsemen competed in races at the thirty-third (648 B.C.).

The Great Panathenaea. In the fifth century B.C., the zenith of classical Greece, the chariot was featured in spectacles in the hippodromes, or race courses, as well as all processions. The most important of these events was the Great Panathenaea, which is represented in the frieze of stone reliefs around the top of the Parthenon in Athens, built between 447 and 432 B.C. The Great Panathenaea, originally a religious celebration, was the oldest and most important festival in Athens. It was held around the middle of August in the third year of each Olympiad with a smaller festival being held in all other years. One of the many contests that took place was a race by the charioteers' companions, who demonstrated their skills by leaping out of their chariots while the horses were going at full speed, a scene that is dramatically depicted on the stone reliefs of the Parthenon.

3. *A Greek four-horse chariot, depicted on a black-figured Panathenaic amphora from the Kuban group, fifth or early fourth century B.C. (Copyright British Museum)*

The Roman Empire

The Romans were not great equestrians. Although they used horses for riding, warfare, and racing, the horse was not as much a part of Roman life as it appears to have been in classical Greece. The ox was the most common beast of burden and plow animal, while mules and asses, used for traction, were the next most popular animals.

Despite the fact that horses were not used in warfare to any great extent, the Romans did have a saddle with horns in both the back and the front, although it lacked a girth strap and stirrups. The pommels performed practically the same function as stirrups in allowing the rider to brace himself and regain his position in the saddle if he slipped. The Romans are credited with inventing the first horseshoes, known as *hipposandals.* They had a metal sole and a piece that cupped over the top of the hoof for attachment with leather thongs (figure 4). Because they were not nailed onto the hoof, the shoes were removable. The modern style of horseshoe that uses nails came much

4. *Roman* hipposandal, *one of the earliest-known horseshoes. (Photo of reproduction courtesy of the International Museum of the Horse, Lexington, Kentucky)*

later, having been first recorded at the end of the ninth century in Siberia and much of Europe.

Columella, the Roman writer on agriculture, divided horses into three classes of breeding stock. The first, or noble, stock supplied horses for the circus and the Sacred Games. The second class of stock was used for breeding mules, and, according to Columella, the offspring fetched a price as high as any of the noble stock. The third class was the common breeding stock that produced ordinary mares and horses. The sporting horses and the mule-breeders were attended to with great care and fed well. These horses were allowed to mate only in alternate years at the time of the spring equinox, so that the foals would be born a year later, when the pasture was most lush. Common horses, however, were pastured all together, with no fixed breeding season.

Much can be learned about the horse in Roman times from the works of Julius Caesar (100-44 B.C.), who wrote his own account of his army campaigns. During the Gallic Wars, from 58-52 B.C., Caesar had between six and eleven legions in Gaul and at least 4,000 cavalry men, all of whom were mercenaries or were recruited from foreign countries. Horsemen were not usually employed in the battle lines but provided support for the foot soldiers and were used as messengers. While in Gaul, Caesar was in awe of the local people and their horses, although these people too, did not fight on horseback. Instead, they dismounted, leaving their well-trained horses to stand perfectly still in readiness for a quick retreat.

Perhaps the most graphic of Caesar's written accounts is that of his invasions of Britain in 55 and 54 B.C. Crossing the English Channel with a large number of ships carrying soldiers and horses, he was met by the Britons, who still fought from horse-drawn chariots. The British tactics were to drive wildly about, hurling their javelins, which, when combined with the galloping horses and the noise of the heavy wheels, threw the enemy into disorder. Although this unfamiliar method of warfare could not dislodge Caesar's invading army, it was nearly a hundred years before England was forced to become a part of the Roman empire. By this time (A.D. 43), the Romans ruled all of western Europe, North Africa, and the Near East. The empire lasted for another three hundred years before Rome's power declined.

Despite its complicated political and social structure, the huge Roman empire depended entirely on oxen, horses, mules, and donkeys for all its land transport and postal services. That there were shortages of wood as well as horses is reflected by laws preventing the excessive loading of wooden carts. The postal carriages were allowed to carry a load of only 1,000 pounds (one Roman pound equaled 0.34 kilogram or 0.75 English pound), and a cart could not carry more than 600 pounds. The saddle and bridle of a postal horse were not to exceed 60 Roman pounds, and the maximum weight for the saddlebags was just 35 pounds. If found to be heavier than these weights, the saddle was to be cut in pieces and the saddlebags confiscated. The weights appear to be rather low, but the Roman horse was only pony-sized and unshod. Additionally, the weight that the wooden axle of the cart could bear was strictly limited, and the roads often must have been extremely muddy.

Outside the Roman cities there were increasing threats from invading barbarians. For this reason shepherds were forbidden to own horses for fear they would be captured and used by the brigands. To prevent infiltration of Rome by foreigners, all citizens were to be dressed in togas while in the capital city and were not allowed to wear boots or trousers, the clothing of barbarian horsemen.

The Roman Chariot Race. Horse racing was as popular in the Roman period as it is today. The four-horse chariot, or *quadriga*, was most commonly used, but there were also races between two-horse chariots and between mounted jockeys. There was a specially built racecourse, or circus, in every main city. For a description of Roman horse racing, see "Roman Chariot Racing" in chapter 6.

Compassion for animals is evident all through the writings of both the ancient Greeks and Romans. It is not surprising because, not only did the wealth of the people rest in their livestock, but animals and people lived closely together. In the Roman empire's waning years efforts to control shortages of food, fuel, and many other resources led to the passage of ever more stringent laws. Many of these laws were compiled in A.D. 438 during the reign of Theodosius II, forming the Theodosian Code. One law of the Theodosian Code decreed that the state should pay for food for horses that had been weakened by age or by chariot racing.

Horses of the East
The Scythians

From the first millennium B.C. until the great empire of Genghis Khan in the Middle Ages, the nomadic peoples of the steppes of eastern Europe and Asia had no rivals as horsemen. The land of the Scythians covered a vast area from directly north of the Black Sea eastward and north to Mongolia and southern Siberia. The Scythians are better known to us than any society without written language in the classical period because they were described by Greek writers like Herodotus and Strabo and by inference by Homer in the *Iliad*. These writers were in awe of the Scythians' strange way of life. In the fifth century B.C. Herodotus wrote about the Scythians and other mysterious tribes who inhabited the land; "To the northward of the furthest dwellers in Scythia, [where] the country is said to be concealed from sight and made impassable by reason of the feathers [snow] which are shed abroad abundantly" (IV. 7).

More dramatic than any written descriptions are some of the archaeological discoveries from the Scythian culture. The great Scythian graves on the steppes north of the Black Sea have yielded a vast array of splendid objects of gold and other materials, many of which depict horses (figure 5). The inclusion of horse sacrifices in the burial chambers confirms much of what Herodotus wrote about the Scythians. While the ancient Egyptians and the Assyrians were building massive temples and palaces and perfecting the horse chariot for warfare and hunting, the Scythians were developing into an elite society of

5. *Scythian horse carved on antler. (Drawing by Sandra Olsen; original in the Hermitage Museum, St. Petersburg, Russia)*

nomads who had no settled places except for the tombs where they buried their dead. They were peaceful people for long periods except when their sacred tombs were vandalized. However, where their territories impinged on those of other cultures, they were prepared to fight. Indeed, they contributed to the fall of the Assyrian empire in the late seventh century B.C.

The Scythians lived in movable felt tents (yurts) and owned many elegant, yet portable, belongings. They had trading links throughout the Near East, as well as with China. Their beautifully made horse cloths, harnesses, carpets, and clothes were ornamented with gold. Horses were their most highly valued possessions and were, therefore, sacrificed for the final burial of a king. Herodotus described a Scythian burial in this way:

> *Fifty of the best of the late king's attendants are taken, . . . and strangled, with fifty of the most beautiful horses. When they are dead, their bowels are taken out, and the cavity cleaned, filled full of chaff, and straightway sewn up again. This done, a number of posts are driven into the ground, in sets of two pairs each, and on every pair half the felly [rim] of a wheel is placed archwise; then strong stakes are run lengthwise through the bodies of the horses from tail to neck, and they are mounted up upon the fellies, so that the felly in front supports the shoulders of the horse, while that behind sustains the belly and quarters, the legs dangling in mid-air; each horse is furnished with a bit and bridle, which latter is stretched out in front of the horse, and fastened to a peg. The fifty strangled youths are then mounted severally on the fifty horses.*

Herodotus, IV. 72, translated by G. Rawlinson, 1964

Archaeological excavations of a group of frozen tombs at Pazyryk, near the Ob River in Siberia, conducted between 1929 and 1949, revealed some amazing discoveries. Dating to the last half of the fourth and the early part of the third centuries B.C., these tombs are younger and farther east than the Scythians, but there is obviously a strong cultural connection. Much of what Herodotus wrote about the Scythians has been corroborated from the excavations of these tombs. Because water from melted snow seeped into the tombs and froze, preservation of perishable material like cloth and leather is remarkable. Five large tombs and a number of small ones were excavated. Each of the large tombs contained the remains of between seven and fourteen horses, totaling at least fifty-four skeletons. Nearly all had been riding horses and were buried with saddle cloths, bridles, bronze or iron bits, and whips. Some had very elaborate felt masks and headdresses still in place on their skulls. The horses' ears had been notched to show their ownership, their manes were clipped and covered with leather, and their tails were plaited or knotted. One tomb contained a four-wheeled carriage with a draft pole and four harnessed horses. Two of the horses wore yoke saddles and reins, while the other two wore traces.

The excavation of these remarkable tombs provides a detailed picture not only of the Pazyryk horse gear, but also of the kinds of horses and of how they were fed and stabled in the fourth century B.C. There were four sizes of horses in the tombs. The mummified coats of those wearing masks were still obviously shiny. These were the tallest, with withers heights of around fourteen hands. The smaller, stockier horses, measuring around thirteen hands at the withers, were obviously less valued.

The frozen tombs of Pazyryk may seem to record the exotic way of life of an ancient and extinct society, but nomads of the Eurasian mountain steppes have a remarkable history of at least three thousand years of continuity that includes horses. In the isolated mountain province of Tuva, southeast of Pazyryk, fermented mare's milk *(koumiss)* has always been an important part of the nomads' diet. Mare milking for the purpose of making *koumiss* continues to be performed from the Don River in western Russia across Mongolia (chapter 7), and up to the nineteenth century in Tuva, when a man died, his horse was killed and buried with him.

Horses in China

There is some archaeological evidence to suggest that there may have been domestic horses in China as early as the Lungshan Period (3000-2300 B.C.). As in Europe and the rest of Asia, however, it was not until the Bronze Age, around 1500 B.C., that the horse became of crucial importance for transport and warfare. Remains of the first chariots in China have been found in sacrificial pits belonging to the Shang Dynasty (from 1400 B.C.), together with the bones of nearly a hundred horses. The horses stood about 13.3-14.3 hands at the withers and had heavy heads and stocky bones, showing a resemblance to the modern Przewalski horse.

Chinese horses gradually increased in size, but remained heavy in build until after the Qin Dynasty (221-206 B.C.). When Qin Shi Huang (the first emperor of the Qin Dynasty) died in 210 B.C., he

6. One of the terra-cotta horses from the mausoleum of Qin Shi Huang (259-210 B.C.), the first emperor of the Qin Dynasty, Shansi Province, China. (Photo courtesy of the Robert Harding Picture Library)

was buried in what was probably the most astonishing mausoleum ever constructed. The central tomb has never been excavated, but in three vast underground chambers located 1.5 kilometers (1 mi.) east of the mausoleum, approximately 7,000 life-sized figures of soldiers, over 500 chariot horses, and 116 cavalry horses, all made of terra-cotta, and 130 actual battle chariots were buried. The terra-cotta army represents Qin Shi Huang's own army, which repulsed invaders from the north and unified China. The largest pits contain a combination of foot soldiers, cavalrymen, and chariots with large quantities of actual bronze weapons. The smallest pit contains only a cart, four pottery horses, sixty-eight warriors, and thirty-four bronze weapons. It may have been the command post for the battle formations found in the other two pits.

The terra-cotta horses stand an impressive seventeen hands in height, about the stature of a modern Thoroughbred (figure 6). Their chests and backs are broad and they have a round conformation. Manes are clipped to stand erect, and the tails are tied up on the chariot horses and braided on the cavalrymen's mounts. The horses' forelocks are prominent and parted in the middle, sweeping up on both ends like a mustache. The chariot horses were outfitted with real harnesses and the soldiers' horses bore leather saddles, but only remnants of these artifacts are now preserved. Each wooden chariot was pulled by four terra-cotta horses.

In addition to the terra-cotta army, two remarkable bronze carriages were excavated from the outer walls of the burial mound. Each is harnessed to four bronze horses, which are of the same stocky build as the clay models. One carriage is larger than the other and is approximately half life-size. Measuring 3.17 meters (10.4 ft.) in length, 1.06 meters (3.5 ft.) in height, and weighing 1,241 kilograms (2,736 lbs), it is covered with a very thin canopy of cast bronze and was originally lined with silk. The four terra-cotta horses are harnessed as in a *quadriga*, that is, the inner two are yoked to a pole and the outer pair are held with traces. The carriage is divided into two compartments, a forward one for the driver, who is seated with reigns in hand, and one in the rear for the passenger. A canopy covers the body and there are just two spoked wheels, complete with brakes.

A century after the death of Qin Shi Huang, news of the first "heavenly horses of Ferghana" was brought to the Western Han emperor by the great traveler Chang Chi'en. Ferghana is located in a mountain range of the same name, southeast of Tashkent in the easternmost part of modern Uzbekistan. It served as the eastern outpost of the classical (European) world. The Ferghana horses were larger and more fine-limbed than any in China. They were said to "sweat blood," probably the result of a parasite that causes slight bleeding of the skin and so colors the foamy sweat of a galloping horse.

In 104 B.C. and again in 102-101 B.C., the Chinese Emperor Han Wu-ti sent two large expeditionary forces 3,000 kilometers (1,864 mi.) west to Ferghana to obtain these horses by force. Over 3,000 horses were collected, but only 50 "blood-sweating" and 1,000 inferior horses survived the long desert journey back to China. Because the Ferghana horses were believed to be "heavenly," they were to be used at the emperor's funeral. They became a legend and were a focus for many beautiful paintings and sculptures in Chinese art.

The Tang Dynasty (A.D. 618-907). Like several of the Chinese dynasties, the Tang was founded by a leader with Turkic ancestors who excelled in the art of warfare from horseback. The Tang armies, like their predecessors, received their horses from the nomadic herdsmen of the grasslands. The second emperor of the Tang Dynasty directed his armies to expand in all directions. Their military success was paired with considerable cultural achievements. The capital of Changan was a match for any European city of its day, and the Silk Road was opening trade routes with the West. As new pottery glazes of green, blue, brown, and gold were developed, ceramic technology was used to create the well-known Tang horses (figure 7), which are so commonly reproduced today. The fact that horses were regularly depicted in clay figures is a tribute to their importance among the Tang aristocracy and military.

The Empire of Genghis Khan (A.D. 1162-1227)

Genghis Khan was the greatest nomadic horseman of all time. He was born in 1162 in a tent on the banks of the Onon River in Mongolia and was named Temujin. His father was a minor Mongol chieftain of noble descent, who died when the boy was thirteen years old. His mother retained power, but they were surrounded by warfare between rival nomads until 1206. Temujin then proclaimed himself first emperor of the Mongol empire and adopted the name of Genghis Khan, which in Chinese means "ruler of all." He conquered northern China in 1215 and then, always on horseback, advanced westward.

The world of Genghis Khan became a nomad empire that extended from the Mediterranean to the Pacific. It was based on the tribal loyalties of pastoralists and nomadic horsemen. These men were reared in the saddle and had little experience with urban civilizations, but were unified and manipulated by the remarkable organizing ability of their single leader, the Khan.

Marco Polo (A.D. 1254-1324) and His Journeys

From the age of seventeen Marco Polo spent twenty years traveling around the empire of Genghis Khan's grandson, the great Kublai Khan (1260-1294). The remarkable account of Marco Polo's journeys tells much about the way of life of the nomadic horsemen. These people had apparently inherited many customs from the ancient Scythians, including the burial of the later Khans in the Altai Mountains, accompanied by the ritual killing of people and horses.

While in Persia, Marco Polo saw fine horses that were to be exported to India, where apparently they could not be bred because of the heat. In China, Marco Polo described how the Great Khan left his palace every year on August 28 to inspect his stud of snow-white stallions and more than 10,000 snow-white mares.

The method of travel of the nomadic armies was highly organized. The horsemen could travel for ten days, subsisting only on horses' blood, which they drank from a pierced vein. Perhaps the most remarkable of all Marco Polo's anecdotes are his descriptions of the messenger services that were set up to keep the Great Khan in touch with the whole of his vast empire. There were said to be 10,000 posts stationed forty to forty-eight kilometers (20-30 mi.) apart along all the main highways. Each post was equipped with a luxurious rest house and a complement of 400 horses, which were provided by the inhabitants as part of the system of taxation. Two hundred of the horses were put out to graze on the pastures, while the other 200 were held ready to be taken on to the next post by the messengers. Marco Polo's comment was that the whole organization was so stupendous and so costly that it baffled speech and writing.

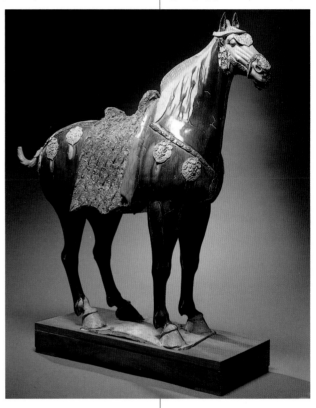

7. *Glazed earthenware horse from the Tang Dynasty (ca. A.D. 618-907), height eighty-one centimeters (32 in.). (Courtesy of Carnegie Museum of Art; photography/Peter Harholdt)*

Horses of the West
The Middle Ages

Feudal Europe. After the fall of Rome to the Vandals in A.D. 410, there was a period of turmoil throughout Europe followed by the Dark Ages and then the establishment of feudalism in the early medieval period. The elite class of feudal knights had total power over their tenants, or vassals, and their single role was to be armed horsemen always ready for battle. For entertainment the knights took part in jousts and practiced the art of venery, or hunting.

Their way of life was extremely expensive. Armor was becoming increasingly complicated as the art of war became more and more elaborate. In the eighth century military equipment for one man cost as much as twenty oxen. The armor grew so heavy that stronger, stouter horses began to be bred or imported to carry the weight of the knight and his weapons. Even so, it seems that most of the horses were still only pony-sized. Their small stature did not prevent them from carrying heavy loads, however, especially as the tactics of fighting were by shock combat at close range. Once at the line of battle, the cavalry did not have to travel over great distances.

The Farm Horse. In western Europe during the Middle Ages, there were no grazing lands where vast numbers of horses could be reared, so only small numbers of farm horses were kept to provide breeding stock for transport animals. On the land oxen were used for plowing and haulage.

The Welsh Laws of Hywel Dda, written around A.D. 940, provide insight into the status of the horse and other animals at the beginning of the Middle Ages:

The value of a young foal of a mare is four pence until fourteen days after its birth. . . . If it attain the age of one year and a day it is worth forty eight pence. If it attain three years of age, it is worth sixty pence; and then it will be time to tame it with a bridle and to teach it its duty, whether as a stallion, a palfrey, or a serving horse. . . . the value of a palfrey [riding horse] is one hundred and twenty pence. The value of a pack horse, is one hundred and twenty pence. The value of a serving horse is sixty pence. The value of a stallion is the price of his two stones [testes], with two mares, and he himself forming the third; that is, one hundred and eighty pence. . . .The value of a filly is four pence for the first fourteen days after her birth; sixteen pence when a year old; thirty two pence when two years old; and then she must be set to work. . . . her qualities are to draw a car up steep ground and down it, and to breed colts, and if she do not possess these qualities, one third of her price must be returned. . . . Neither horses, mares, nor cows ought to be yoked to the plough; and if they should be so, and the mares and cattle suffer an abortion from it, there can be no redress. . . . Four horse shoes and their complement of nails are worth two pence. The price of a saddle is eight pence.

Owen, 1841

The Battle of Hastings and the Bayeux Tapestry. The loss of England to the Normans at the Battle of Hastings in 1066 is one of the landmarks of European history. Almost every incident that occurred during the battle is well known from written accounts and from the embroidered portrayals on the Bayeux tapestry (figure 8). The Norman invader brought 7,000 troops across the English Channel in boats, and half of these men were mounted. The tapestry shows that ten horses were carried in each ship so there must have been 350 ships for the horses alone. The invading army was much better organized than the English, but its main strength lay in its mounted archers who rode with the new invention of stirrups. The English, too, rode with stirrups, but when it came to the fighting, they dismounted to form a wall of shields in the old-fashioned way. This outmoded fighting technique cost King Harold his life and the English their country.

The Crusades. By the end of the eleventh century, the supremacy of the armed horseman was firmly established throughout Europe and knights began to look farther afield for extension of their power. As early as the first Crusade, 1096-1099, the motive was the conquest of territory. The mounted knights wanted to take possession of lands in the East, while the pious pilgrims, marching on foot, wished to see the walled city of Jerusalem returned to Christian rule. None of their innumerable battles and skirmishes with the Turks, Arabs, and Egyptians could have been fought without thousands of horses on all sides. It must have required great organization to provision men and animals both on the long journeys and at the scenes of battles, especially in the arid land of Palestine.

8. A scene from the Bayeux tapestry (ca. 1070-1080), showing Norman cavalrymen advancing on the English at the Battle of Hastings. Notice that they are wearing suits of chain mail, are armed with lances, and are preceded by archers. (Photo courtesy of the Robert Harding Picture Library)

Increasing Demands on the Medieval Horse. Before the fifteenth century, British horses were pony-sized and were very limited in the sizes of loads they could pull or weight they could carry. Henry VIII (1491-1547) made a concerted effort to increase the size of British horses through a series of decrees. In 1535 he insisted that all large landowners had to keep at least two mares with heights of thirteen hands or over. In 1541 he prohibited stallions under fifteen hands from grazing on common land in the Midlands and the southern counties of England. Large horses from Hungary, Spain, France, Poland, Denmark, and Sweden were imported into Britain in the fifteenth and sixteenth centuries. It is true that stronger horses of greater size were being bred at this time in Europe, both for draft and cavalry needs. After all, the weight of a soldier, his armor, and his horse could exceed 200 kilograms (450 lbs) (figure 9), enough to push the limits of any pony. There is a misconception, however, about the size of medieval cavalry horses. Size is relative, and although these animals were taller and more robustly built than their predecessors, were not the enormous draft horses we see today. Mary Littauer has studied the question extensively by examining the size of medieval horse armor and other evidence, and has shown that most cavalry horses of the time would not have exceeded fifteen hands in height and would have more normally been around fourteen hands or a little more.

The Arab Horse in Britain and the First Thoroughbreds

There are two breeds of horse that had their early history in the hot deserts of Arabia and North Africa: the Arab (chapter 8, figure 8) from western Asia and the Barbary or Barb from the coastal belt of Morocco, Algeria, and

Tunisia. Physical characteristics that distinguish the pure Barb from the Arab are its slight Roman or "ram-like" facial profile, sloping croup (rump), and low-set tail.

The first written account of an Arabian horse in Britain was in A.D. 1121, when Alexander I, King of Scotland, presented to the Church of St. Andrew's an Arabian horse with costly furniture, Turkish armor, many valuable trinkets, and a considerable estate. From that time on, Turkish and Barbary horses were occasionally imported in efforts to improve the speed of the British ponies. In 1616 James I paid 500 pounds to a Mr. Markham for a celebrated Arabian horse, but it received little acclaim in Britain. After this purchase Arabs were not imported until Charles II sent his master of the horse to the Levant to purchase brood mares and stallions.

A Thoroughbred (chapter 8, figure 12) is any horse whose pedigree is recorded in the *Stud Book*, which was first printed in 1791 and has been published periodically up to the present day. All modern racehorses and Thoroughbreds cited in the *Stud Book* are descended from three stallions: the Byerley Turk, the Darley Arabian, and the Godolphin Arabian. Little is known of the Byerley Turk, which may have been either an Arabian or a Turkoman. In the words of the *Stud Book*, "He was Captain Byerley's charger in Ireland in King William's wars," which would have been in about 1689. It seems the captain took the horse from a Turkish officer at the siege of Budapest. The Byerley Turk did not sire many well-known horses except Jig (in about 1705), the sire of Partner, a chestnut colt that became the best racehorse of his day. Partner was put to stud in 1728.

At the beginning of the reign of Queen Anne, the Darley Arabian from Aleppo heralded a new era in horsebreeding. According to the *Stud Book*, "Darley's Arabian was brought over by a brother of Mr. Darley of Yorkshire, who, being an agent in merchandise abroad, became member of a hunting club, by which means he acquired interest to procure this horse." The Darley Arabian was the most influential of the founders. His direct descendants were the Devonshire Flying Childers and the Bleeding or Bartlett's Childers, the great grandsire of Eclipse, probably the best-known racehorse of all time.

The Godolphin Arabian was a Barb. A brown bay about fifteen hands in stature, he had been seen drawing a cart in Paris by a Mr. Coke, who brought the horse to England and gave him to a Mr. Williams who, in turn, presented the horse to the Earl of Godolphin. The horse's value was unknown until 1731, when he was being used as a teaser on the mare Roxana, who was to be mated with a stallion named Hobgoblin. However, because Hobgoblin refused to have anything to do with Roxana, the Godolphin Arabian was allowed to mate with her. The resulting foal was Lath, which became the most-celebrated racehorse of his day after Flying Childers.

Eclipse, sired by Marsk with his dam Spiletta, was born on April 1, 1764 during an eclipse of the sun. He was a chestnut with a white blaze down his face, and his lower right hindleg was white. On his rump were black spots, which were said to be inherited by generations of his male offspring. Eclipse was said to be a thick-winded horse that puffed and roared so as to be heard at a considerable distance. He was bred by the Duke of Cumberland and sold on the Duke's death to Mr. Wildman, a sheep salesman, for 75 guineas. Colonel O'Kelly at first bought a half share in the horse from Wildman for 650 guineas, but later bought him out for an additional 1,100 guineas. Eclipse ran for only two seasons, beginning in 1769 when he was five years old. He finished twenty-one races, the last being for the King's Plate at Newmarket, and he was never defeated. Then he was put out to stud and sired 334 offspring that were all winners, making an incredible £25,000 for his owner in service fees. Eclipse died on February 25, 1789, at the age of twenty-five years.

The English Jockey Club was founded in 1750 and purchased the racing ground at Newmarket in 1753. For more on English racing, see chapter 6.

The Domestic Horse in North and South America

During the late Pleistocene, it will be recalled from chapters 2 and 3, there were several species of wild equids living throughout North and South America. These all became extinct, along with many other herbivores and their predators, about 10,000 years ago. The causes of the extinctions are not fully understood, but they probably resulted from climatic change and perhaps overhunting by humans. Native Americans were, therefore, without the benefit of horses until European explorers appeared on the scene.

When the Spanish followers of Christopher Columbus arrived in the Americas after 1492, their most effective weapon against the native civilizations was their ability to move rapidly on horseback. The ships of all the voyages were loaded with horses, but so many died during the sea crossing that the part of the ocean between Spain and the Canary Islands was called the Gulfo de Yeguas (Gulf of Mares) in later times. The part of the Atlantic just east of Mexico that is infamous for its ceaseless calms became known as the Horse Latitudes, possibly because so many horses died while the ships waited for the breeze to stir. Despite the hazards at sea, by 1503 there were sixty to seventy horses on the island of Hispaniola.

The first region of North America to be colonized by the Spanish was the area around Mexico City, where there was good grazing for livestock. Although at first horses were slow to breed, within a few years of 1550 there were said to be 10,000 horses in the area of Querétaro. These all

9. German armor for man and horse, late fifteenth century. (Photo courtesy of The Board of Trustees of the Royal Armouries, H M Tower of London)

were descended from a few domestic horses that had been released on the grasslands, but because they had no predators, their numbers rapidly increased. In South America as well, introduced horses soon began to breed in the wild. The city of Buenos Aires was first founded by Pedro de Mendoza in 1535, but he was forced to abandon the settlement because of a food shortage. He and his compatriots fled across water into Paraguay, leaving behind five mares and seven horses. From these, and presumably from additional horses lost by travelers, there was a great population explosion.

Three vast regions of the Americas provided grasslands suitable for expansion of the feral horse populations: the prairies that stretch north all the way from Mexico to Canada, the llanos (plains) of Venezuela and Colombia, and the pampas of Argentina and Uruguay.

Native Americans of both continents slowly began to recognize the value of the horse. They learned its management partly by trial and error and partly from the Spanish from whom they received horses through barter and raiding. By the beginning of the seventeenth century, members of many of the Plains people of North America had become highly skilled horsemen and their way of life had been transformed.

Before they obtained horses, the only forms of transport the peoples of North America had were the canoe, dugout, and dog sleigh or travois. The Plains people hunted bison by driving them on foot. Once they became horsemen, however, their hunting techniques and warfare assumed new patterns and rituals. The Blackfoot hunted bison either by a surround or in open chase. In the surround a large number of horsemen encircled a herd and milled around it, shooting down animals as they rode among them. The chase involved a straight rush by mounted men, each of whom singled out an animal to shoot and then rode alongside it for the kill. A skilled hunter mounted on a trained horse could kill enough animals in a single morning to feed a family group of twenty as well as their dogs, with enough meat left over for drying. A successful equestrian hunter, therefore, had plenty of leisure time for caring for his horses, making weapons, and raiding enemy camps (figure 10). Bison hunts were controlled by strict social rules. There were severe penalties for anyone who hunted bison before the appointed time. Among the Cheyenne there were only three recognized crimes: homicide, disobeying the rules of the bison hunt, and repeated horse theft. For committing any of these the culprit was severely beaten.

As in North America, the Pampas and Patagonian people of the southern continent had perhaps fewer than 200 years during which their culture was dependent on the horse. In Paraguay feral horses became so numerous that people who took the trouble to catch them could have as many as they wanted. The horsemen lived a nomadic existence and were renowned for their bravery. They rode bareback, sometimes by merely clinging on, sometimes almost under the horse's belly, and often with only a bitless bridle. The native people rapidly succumbed, however, to European diseases like smallpox and measles. The resulting feral horses that escaped or wandered away from dying villages were all but exterminated by European firearms, because they interfered with domestic stock by luring away the mares and competing with cattle for grazing land. Today, however, feral populations of mustangs descended from Spanish and other European horses are sizeable in areas like Wyoming and Nevada.

Summary

In the mythology of ancient Greece, the centaurs were a race of beings from Thessaly with the heads and trunks of men joined to the bodies and legs of horses. Perhaps the myth arose from the first sightings of horsemen by southern Greeks about 3,000 years ago. Since then the worldwide partnership of man and horse has been so close that the two might just as well have been true centaurs.

It is hard to imagine what history would have been like without the horse. Without raiding armies of nomads on horseback, many of the great ancient civilizations would probably still be flourishing (unless they would have destroyed all their local resources by now). The grasslands of the world might still be teaming with herds of wild animals, and human populations would be isolated as physical and cultural entities adapted to their local environments. Without the horse the diffusion of people, culture, and technologies all would have been much slower.

Xenophon, who died in 359 B.C., wrote this advice to a cavalry officer: "Those who are taught and accustomed to leap across ditches, to vault over walls, to spring up on eminences, to descend from them with safety, and to ride at full speed down steep grounds, will have as much advantage over those who are unpracticed in such exercises as winged animals have over those that can only walk." Today humans are, indeed, winged animals, but this miracle of technology could never have been achieved without the development of technology that originally depended on the horse.

10. Mounted Kiowa men in traditional warriors' clothing (1898). (Photo by F. A. Rinehart of Omaha provided by the Carnegie Museum of Natural History)

Reading List

Clutton-Brock, J. *Horse Power: A History of the Horse and the Donkey in Human Societies.* London: Natural History Museum, 1992.

Contamine, P. *War in the Middle Ages.* Oxford: Basil Blackwell, 1986.

Crosby, A. W. *The Columbian Exchange: Biological and Cultural Consequences of 1492.* Connecticut: Greenwood Press, 1972.

Dent, A. *The Horse Through Fifty Centuries of Civilization.* London: Phaidon Press, 1974.

Ewers, J. C. *The Horse in Blackfoot Indian Culture with Comparative Material from Other Western Tribes.* Smithsonian Institution Bureau of American Ethnology Bulletin 159. Washington, D.C: Smithsonian Institution, 1955.

Greenhalgh, P. A. L. *Early Greek Warfare: Horsemen and Chariots in the Homeric and Archaic Ages.* Cambridge: Cambridge University Press, 1973.

Hammond, M., translator. *Homer: the Iliad.* London: Penguin Books, 1987.

Hyland, A. *Equus: The Horse in the Roman World.* London: Batsford, 1990.

Littauer, M. "How Great Was the Great Horse?" *Light Horse,* December 1963, 350-52.

_____. "V. O. Vitt and the horses of Pazyryk." *Antiquity* 45 (1971), 293-94.

Owen, A. *Ancient Laws and Institutes of Wales.* London: Commissioners of the Public Records, 1841.

Pharr, C., translator. *The Theodosian Code and Novels and the Sirmondian Constitutions.* Princeton: Princeton University Press, 1952.

Rawlinson, G., translator. *The Histories of Herodotus.* 2 vols. Everyman's Library, no. 405. London: Dent, 1964.

Rudenko, S. I. *Frozen Tombs of Siberia: The Pazyryk Burials of Iron-Age Horsemen.* London: J. M. Dent and Berkeley: University of California Press, 1970.

Trow-Smith, R. *A History of British Livestock Husbandry to 1700.* London: Routledge & Kegan Paul, 1957.

_____. *A History of British Livestock Husbandry 1700-1900.* London: Routledge & Kegan Paul, 1959.

White, L., Jr. *Medieval Technology and Social Change.* Oxford: Oxford University Press, 1962.

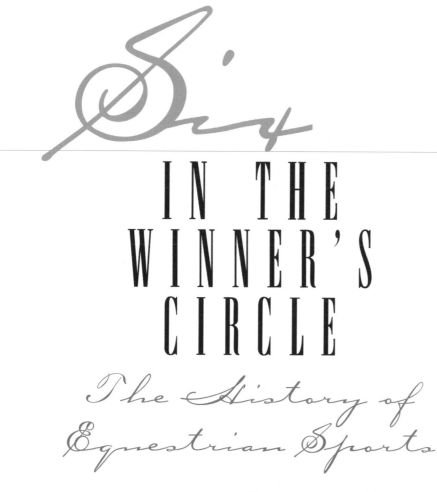

Six
IN THE
WINNER'S
CIRCLE

The History of
Equestrian Sports

SANDRA L. OLSEN

Since the Iron Age (1500-1000 B.C.) equestrian skills have been honed through games, races, and other competitions. The role of equestrian sports has far exceeded simple entertainment for the masses; it stimulated excellence in horsemanship that paid great rewards on the battlefield. Before mechanized vehicles and advanced weapons, those cultures that could mount massive cavalries generally had an enormous advantage over less-prepared societies. Competitions helped maintain soldiers' skills through peaceful times and generated countless improvements in equipment and breeding that in many cases altered the outcome of history.

Not all sports have their origin in military training, however. The rodeo was developed as a means of demonstrating the many skills necessary on the farm or ranch. Hunting for sport and outgrowths like competitive jumping evolved from hunting out of necessity. Harness racing emerged from informal, spontaneous competitions among drivers on the road, not unlike teenagers drag racing in the 1950s and 1960s in the United States. Through the ages most leisure sports have been regulated, performed, and largely attended by the wealthier side of society.

Because of the powerful motivation to gain a competitive edge and win the prize, equestrian sports can count a number of improvements as their most positive achievements. These include the systematic development of breeds that are stronger, healthier, swifter, more intelligent, or more attractive. Horse tackle has become more effective, more streamlined, and better suited to specific tasks. Advances in lighter-weight vehicles can be attributed to chariot racing early on and harness racing later, though this development is less important to us today than it once was. The communication between rider and mount has progressed to astounding levels through the sophistication of training seen not only in the haute école ("high school"),[1] but in any form of equestrian competition. No doubt, the investment of time, talent, and resources in training a horse for competition has also led to better care for the health and well-being of the animals. Lastly, the continuing popularity of equestrian sports has contributed to the maintenance of skills that would otherwise rapidly decline or disappear.

These sports must be seen as an important link with our past, which in some cases stretches back two to three thousand years or more. Human culture relied heavily on horses from the time of their domestication at least 6,000 years ago until the turn of the twentieth century. Motorized vehicles may have replaced four-legged transportation in most practical aspects of our lives, but in these sports there can be no substitute for the grace, beauty, speed, strength, endurance, maneuverability, and animation of the horse.

Facing page, see figure 5.

---

1. The haute école is advanced equitation, or the art of riding on horseback.

Scythian Equestrian Sports

Some of the earliest records of equestrian acrobatic events were reported for the nomadic Iron Age culture known as the Scythians (700-200 B.C.) that started in Central Asia. These great warriors, who spoke an Iranian language, eventually charged across the Eurasian steppes from Hungary to Siberia on horseback. There are descriptions recorded by their Greek neighbors to the south of a variety of Scythian equestrian games and events. Skills that were performed at trials included standing on the horse's back while it galloped, changing riders at full speed, lassoing, and hunting rabbits with a lance at full gallop. This last event may have been the forerunner of the modern Central Asian game known as *buzkashi* (see below), which involves a dead goat or calf and up to a thousand riders.

The Scythians used a simple pillow that was strapped onto the horse for a saddle. They had no true stirrups, but depictions of leather loops hanging down from the saddle are interpreted by some as functional stirrups. Artistic representations of Scythian riders on horseback never actually show the rider's feet in the loops, however. The absence of stirrups is highly significant, because without stirrups a rider cannot stand up and have a firm position on the horse, making it difficult for him to thrust with a lance or dagger or to use his upper body in a physical confrontation with another rider. This would impact the Scythians' abilities in peacetime competitions, as well as in battle.

Greek Competition and Horse Training

Although the Greeks knew the marauding Scythians quite well, they could never match their abilities in horsemanship. Greek horses were said to be inferior to those of the Scythians. Despite the fact that horses played a minimal role in the Greek military, they were important characters in religion and were featured heavily in Greek sports. The Olympiad, which started in 776 B.C., featured harness races with two or four mules. The first large-scale, organized horse races were initiated by the Greeks in specially constructed hippodromes, or arenas. The chariot, which was introduced in Greece about 1500 B.C., was used more in sports than in battle because of the country's mountainous terrain. Homer's *Iliad* (ca. 750 B.C.) refers to chariot races that were supposed to have taken place at athletic games during the Trojan War, around 1200 B.C. Two-horse chariot races preceded those with four horses, which began to be depicted on vases in 680 B.C. *Quadrigas* (chapter 5, figure 3), two-wheeled carts drawn by four horses, appeared in the Olympic races during the twenty-fifth Olympiad. The first races involving bareback riders were held at the thirty-third Olympic competition, in 648 B.C.

If the Greeks were not feared for their large cavalries, they were at least prolific writers on the subject of horses. In about 400 B.C. Simon, the Athenian knight, wrote the first known book on the professional training of horses and riders, but unfortunately only a small scrap of it exists. Slightly later Xenophon (430-354 B.C.), an advisor to Philip of Macedonia, wrote two treatises on horses: *Hipparchikos* (the riding master) and *Perihippikes* (the art of horsemanship), which covered such topics as how to train, groom, mount, ride, and stable a horse. As a cavalry general Xenophon focused on achieving the highest level of cooperation between a soldier and his mount in the throes of battle.

In his writings Xenophon copes with the great difficulty of achieving a graceful mount onto a standing horse without the aid of stirrups. The Greeks usually rode bareback, but they failed to teach their horses to kneel for mounting like the Scythians did. According to Xenophon, the rider should hold the reins in his left hand loosely, grab the mane in his right hand, and leap onto the horse's back with his leg bent, using his spear if necessary to assist his vault. He warns against presenting an "uncomely spectacle from behind" since short tunics, rather than trousers, were the normal attire for Greek soldiers.

In addition to step-by-step instructions on how to break a horse and train it for normal riding, Xenophon covers advanced equitation. He discusses several topics including the "religious processional," the "brilliant horse," and the "airs of passage." The religious processionals were elaborate spectacles involving the cavalry, like those depicted in the frieze around the Parthenon. The "brilliant horse," which was recorded in a text about the Thesean games of the first part of the second century B.C., was a hard-earned title achieved only by the finest beasts that had received best training in dressage and aerial skills. Unfortunately, the exact technical abilities required to receive this accolade have been lost to us.

The earliest documentation of training horses to flex their haunches tightly and raise their forelimbs into the air is in Xenophon's writings. Among the airs of passage that Xenophon describes are those that were later adopted in the European high schools of the Renaissance and are still performed by Lipizzaners at the Spanish Riding School of Vienna. These probably include the levade, mézair, and courbette (see below). There is disagreement on whether such advanced skills in equitation were developed by the Greeks primarily for battle or for exhibition at processions. Horses naturally attack one another or predators in combat by rearing up and lurching forward, so this trait could have been applied in war to attack the enemy who was on horseback. In 496 B.C. Herodotus described a Persian governor in Cyprus who attacked foot soldiers in just this manner. On the other hand, Mary Littauer has argued that rearing would have been very impractical because it exposed the unprotected belly of the horse to attack by lance or other weapons. Xenophon himself does not recommend rearing as a useful military tactic, but does suggest that it created an impressive spectacle at public processions.

Xenophon advises soldiers to maintain a level of military preparedness during peacetime by regularly riding across country at full gallop, taking obstacles as they are encountered. This Greek practice preceded the earliest cross-country English steeplechase and similarly inspired low-level jumping skills. There are no accounts of the Greeks using artificial structures for jumping or holding official jumping competitions or races with jumps. Since they usually rode bareback and had no proper saddle and no stirrups, the Greeks were necessarily limited in their equestrian feats. Greek horses were also small and cobby, so they were not strong jumpers.

The most important aspect of Xenophon's writings was his emphasis on humane treatment in training horses. It was his philosophy that a rider could achieve far more from a horse by rewarding it periodically and by encouraging it to do what it naturally wanted to do. By forcing a horse to do something through the use of a painful curb bit or by striking it on the head, the rider would never achieve the best results and the horse would appear tense and awkward rather than graceful and proud. He discusses at length how to get a horse to hold its neck and head high in a manner that comes naturally to the horse without inflicting discomfort.

Xenophon has come to be known to many as the Father of Dressage. His writings are often attributed with having influenced teachings in equestrian high schools during the Renaissance, but Littauer has shown that there is virtually no reference to his work by any of the masters who revived and further developed dressage during the sixteenth and seventeenth centuries.

The fine vases made by the Greeks are an important source of detailed information regarding their use of horses. Black-figured vases from the sixth century B.C. depict, for example, aristocratic horsemen hunting wild boar, armed with javelins and followed by hounds. This sport was nearly abandoned by the fifth century, however, and Xenophon barely mentions it. The decline in hunting is probably related to the fact that by that time most of the wild animals had been driven into the more rugged terrain, accessible only on foot. While he was on his Asiatic campaigns, in 401 B.C. and later, however, Xenophon reports that Persian nobles had large game parks for hunting and Persians hunted foxes from horseback with tridents. The Macedonian leader Alexander the Great (356-323 B.C.) went fowling and fox-hunting on his horse Bucephalus.

Roman Chariot Racing

Although the Roman army depended heavily on its cavalry, horses were perhaps appreciated even more for their roles in festivals and sports. The Romans borrowed the idea of the hippodrome from the Greeks but called it a "circus." These large arenas were built primarily for chariot racing, but were later the scene for ridden horse races, competitions in which the rider dismounted and completed the race on foot, the Troy Game (a sport for noble children involving stunts on horseback), boxing, wrestling, gladiator competitions, and other events. Equestrian acrobatics at circuses included such events of skill as a man standing on the back of one of a team of two horses and leaping from its back to the other.

Chariot races started out fairly simply, but evolved into more and more elaborate affairs as time went by. Originally they were nothing more than races around two posts at opposite ends of a field. Then tracks were built with a long barricade down the middle and bleachers on the sidelines for spectators. Eventually, the circus became an enormous permanent structure to be found in every Roman city of significant size.

In its final form the circus was a U-shaped arena with tiered seating all around the U, but not at the open end. The floor was usually sand and there was a barrier running down the middle for most of the length of the course. At either end were turning posts, around which the chariots had to swing. The *Circus Maximus* (figure 1) in Rome was the largest of the Roman racecourses and seated two hundred thousand spectators. Its dimensions inside the arena were 580 by 79 meters (1,900 ft. x 260 ft.), with an area twelve times that of the colosseum. Construction of the *Circus Maximus* was first recorded by the Elder Tarquin (616-578 B.C.). Some emperors had dust of red lead oxide (minium) or green malachite sprinkled over the arena for a dramatic effect.

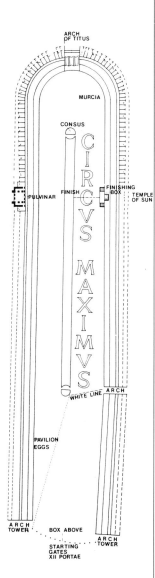

1. Architectural plan of Circus Maximus. *(Drawing courtesy of John Humphrey)*

Whereas there were traditionally no more than twelve races per day, Caligula (A.D. 37-41) held a festival in which there were twenty on one day and twenty-four the next. The winning Greek charioteer received olive garlands or palm branches, but during Roman times these were replaced with monetary payments. Juvenal (A.D. 60-140), a Roman poet, collected winnings that were said to be the equivalent of the wealth of 100 lawyers. Another charioteer during the reign of Domitian (A.D. 81-96) won fifteen pieces of gold in just one hour. Initially, the chariot drivers were either slaves or working class fellows who dreamed of obtaining wealth and accolades, but after a time the bulk of the prizes went to the faction or individual who owned the chariot.

As the popularity of chariot racing grew, the noble classes and eventually the emperors became involved in the races themselves. Caligula, Nero (A.D. 54-68), Vitellius (A.D. 69), Commodus (A.D. 180-192), and Caracalla (A.D. 211-217) all participated by actually driving the chariots or by having their own teams of charioteers. So serious were these competitions that the emperor often had rival charioteers poisoned or opposing spectators slain. Like modern-day hooligans the fans sometimes got carried away in the enthusiasm of the sport. As a result many insurrections began at the races. Perhaps the bloodiest was when the Byzantine army had to kill thirty thousand people to stop the revolution started at the events held to commemorate the fifth year of Emperor Justinian's reign (A.D. 527-565).

Roman chariots pulled by teams of different sizes were called by different names: *biga* (two horse), *triga* (three horse), and *quadriga* (four horse) (figure 2). Emperor Nero, who was a champion in his own right, introduced races with chariots pulled by ten horses into the Olympics. The *hippodromus* type of chariot, used by the Romans, was a lightweight two-wheeled vehicle that was open in the back.

The Roman circus spread rapidly throughout the empire. In the west chariot racing was patterned after that performed in the *Circus Maximus*. The races were financially supported by the wealthy nobility and the emperor. In Rome there were four circus factions, independent organizations that were given the finances so that their charioteers, horses, and other staff could conduct the races. Each faction was associated with a particular color, which was worn by its charioteers. The spectators' allegiance was to the color representing the faction they supported.

In the eastern part of the empire, however, the competitions more closely resembled those of the Greek Olympic games, although most of the arenas were modeled after the Roman circus rather than the hippodrome. Here, chariot racing with two or four horses was just one of many events featured with riding and non-equestrian athletics. The chariots and horses were paid for by wealthy individuals who hired the driver or even entered the race themselves on occasion. In place of large factions with their associated colors were individual sponsors who received the prizes and honors when their chariots won.

Horse and chariot races were already somewhat important to Near Eastern people, so it is not surprising that under Roman rule (64 B.C.-A.D. 395),

2. Roman bronze pitcher from Pompeii showing a man in a quadriga *(four-horse chariot). (Reproduction by De Angelis Sabatino and Sons, ca. A.D. 1900; courtesy of Carnegie Museum of Art; photography/Peter Harboldt)*

circuses appeared in Beirut, Antioch, Jericho, and Alexandria. One such circus was built probably by at least A.D. 190 in Tyre, the old Phoenician capital on the southern Lebanese coast. Its popularity was supposed to have thrived into the fifth century A.D. This large arena had exterior measurements of 480 by 92 meters (1,575 x 301 ft.) and reportedly could handle as many as twelve chariots at a time. The circus at Tyre was only discovered in 1967 and, because it had been covered by six meters (19.6 ft.) of sand, at the time of its excavation it was one of the best preserved of all those that are known.

Through the time span in which the Roman empire flourished, riding skills degenerated. Eventually the army had to relearn military equitation from the Teutons, but these Germanic people then lacked any of the fine techniques of Xenophon or the later haute école.

Medieval Jousting and Tournaments

The Age of Chivalry (A.D. 1000-1600) was a colorful time in history that conjures up images of noble knights competing in jousting events in full armor. It is difficult to imagine just what it would have been like to be seated on top of a horse in full armor. At first the horses were small and fast, but as chain mail and leather shirts covered with metal discs were replaced by whole metal armor, the horses had to be more sturdily built. Armor was heavy and uncomfortable, as well as restrictive of movement and visibility, but it did afford protection from the lance or spear. The horse had to be able to carry the man, his armor, his weapons, the saddle, and the horse's armor, which could total as much as 200 kilograms (450 lbs.). This meant that the massive draft horses used to pull plows and wagons had to be engaged for battle and tournament.

The knight's riding techniques became simpler and less refined as time went by. Because of his cumbersome armor, he could no longer guide the horse with his thighs but had to direct it instead by shifting his weight. Spurs and the extremely painful curb bit were also used to control the horses. Use of the curb bit had to have approached torture for these poor mounts, especially since its design in the Middle Ages was less humane than modern ones. Today, curb bits are generally used only by very experienced riders with a gentle hand and only with skilled horses.

The knights' horses were not required to be well trained either, since both the horse and the rider were limited in their movement by the armor. Basically, a horse needed to gallop in a straight line so that its rider's lance could hit the opposing rider with as much force as possible to unseat him.

Jousting and tournaments provided tests by which a humble squire could work up to becoming a knight of some repute. It is unclear whether the French or the Germans invented the tournament, but the earliest documented death during a contest was that of Geoffri de Preuilly, a French knight who wrote the first tournament rules in 1066. There were a number of games of skill performed at such tournaments. One of the safer games, played early in the tournaments to demonstrate the rider's skill, was tilting at the ring. Ring jousting, as it is often called today, involved a player riding at full gallop with the goal of threading a small ring suspended from a gallows onto the point of his lance. Progressively smaller and smaller rings might be used until all ties were broken and only one winner remained. Another form of competition was the *quintain* (figure 3), in which the participant attempted to stab or decapitate an effigy while at full gallop. The dummy could be designed so that if the rider failed to strike it in the correct place, it automatically struck the rider. The most popular competition, jousting, involved the confrontation of two horsemen who would ride toward each other in parallel lanes, separated by a waist-high barrier. Riding "at full tilt," each would attempt to knock the other out of his saddle. Even when blunt lances were used, serious injury or death could occur, especially given the risk of falling from the horse in a heavy, rigid suit of armor. Dangers included choking on the dust and being trampled by the horse.

The knight used a special jousting saddle with stirrups set so that he could ride "long," legs straight and feet forward, while his lance was tucked tightly under his arm for maximum strength and power. If his horse was struck or came to an abrupt stop, the knight was at risk of being thrown over the horse's head. If, on the other hand, the rider received a harsh blow, he was pushed backward. A high cantle on the back of the jousting saddle was meant to prevent the rider from falling off the back of the horse. Through time, the armor worn by man and beast alike became things of beauty, with virtually every piece being ornately decorated for exhibition.

In cities like Venice, Florence, Milan, Lisbon, Madrid, Paris, and Brussels, tournaments were held in central plazas. They were also often held out in the countryside, where there was plenty of space for the competitors, spectators, and gamblers. Because tournaments were displays of military prowess at large gatherings, those in power feared that these events could get out of control and lead to civil unrest. In time English kings began requiring that a license be obtained in advance to alert local sheriffs of the upcoming event. The popular tournaments continued as a spectacle long after armor ceased to be worn in battle, however, and the competitions were eventually even associated with important church events or weddings.

Dressage: The Art of Riding

The term *dressage* is derived from the French verb *dresser*, which means "to train." Its purpose is to train the horse to respond to the rider's commands so that the rider can guide it through certain tasks. Basic training in dressage is necessary for any horse that is ridden and begins between the ages of three to five years. At age five the horse can be evaluated as to its suitability to go on to a higher level of training.

As we have seen, the origin of training horses to be ridden properly is credited to two famous Greeks, Simon the Athenian and Xenophon. After their writings, however, there was a nearly 2,000-year gap in the literature on horse training. In 1550 Federico Grisone, an Italian nobleman and famous instructor at the riding academy in Naples, revived interest

3. Modern jousting demonstration showing a modified quintain *in which a watermelon substitutes for an effigy of a human head. (Photo by S. Olsen)*

through his publication *Gli ordini di cavalcare* ("the orders of riding"). In contrast to Xenophon's emphasis on humane tactics to train horses, however, Grisone used the painful curb bit and advocated striking the horse between the ears. For the next fifty years, the Italian masters led in training horsemen in precision riding.

Prominence in equestrian skills then shifted to France with the development of the haute école. Around the beginning of the seventeenth century four French equestrians played significant roles in this: Solomon de la Broue, Antoine de Pluvinel, Gaspart de Saunier, and F. Robicon de la Guérinière. De la Broue, trained in the Neapolitan school by the famous Italian equestrian Giovanni Pignatelli, wrote the first French publication on equitation in 1594, entitled *Le Cavalerice François* ("The French Cavalry"). De Pluvinel, Louis XIII's riding master, published an important volume in 1623 entitled *Le Maneige Royal* ("The Royal Riding School"). De Saunier eliminated the use of the painful bridlebits and the curb rein. In the early eighteenth century de la Guérinière revived the Greeks' humane training techniques, fitting his horses with soft bits. He also introduced the dressage position in which the rider's thighs are positioned securely against the horse and are used for guidance. His volume was published in 1733. It is to de la Guérinière's philosophy that the birth of modern dressage is attributed.

To the British hunts and races were always more popular than the "high school" equitation of the continent. The only exception was the English Duke of Newcastle, William Cavendish, who, having been influenced by French manège, wrote a treatise on training horses in 1657. He is associated with inventing the curb rein and advised the foreshortening of the movements performed in the haute école. His doctrine of harsh treatment and abbreviated executions led to very unnatural, uncomfortable actions by the horse.

Through the centuries an elite faction of the European military handed down dressage techniques through cavalry schools. Noblemen and courtiers at the royal courts were also required to be well versed in dressage. The picture in the twentieth century is very different, however. The last of the cavalry schools closed after World War II and royal courts rapidly dwindled. Interest in dressage shifted away from the military and aristocrats, becoming an athletic event practiced by a broader cross-section of the social classes.

At the 1912 Olympics in Stockholm, dressage was introduced as one of the official sporting events. Prior to this century dressage was primarily a man's sport, but in the 1952 and 1956 Olympics, Liz Hartel of Denmark won a silver medal. In the 1968 Olympics Liselott Linsenhoff of Germany was the first woman to win a gold medal.

The Spanish Riding School and the Haute École

The supreme expression of equitation has been reached in horses trained in the haute école. The Spanish Riding School in Vienna, Austria, and the Cavalry School at Saumur, France, are the only two institutions that meet haute école standards today. The philosophy behind haute école is that the movements shall all be ones that horses perform under natural conditions when defending themselves from predators or in struggles for dominance with other horses. These natural movements are then cultivated by the trainers to their highest level of competency. Artificially developed movements like the marching step are not permitted.

Although the training for both horse and rider involves maximum concentration and discipline, it is never harsh or cruel. The goal is to perform perfectly and gracefully by means of subtle instructions conveyed through the reins and the rider's body.

De la Guérinière's methods formed the foundation for the Spanish Riding School in Vienna, which is still considered the pinnacle of dressage exhibition. It is the home of the majestic white Lipizzaner horses, so famous around the world for their remarkable dressage feats, including the "airs above ground." In 1562 the first exercise ground for horses was laid out in the Josephsplatz in central Vienna, but the cold winters proved difficult for trainers. Ten years later a wooden building was constructed and the Spanish Riding Hall was opened. The school's name refers to the geographic origin of the Lipizzaner horses, which were derived from a blend of Iberian, Arabian, and Berber stock. The Lipizzaners themselves are named after Lipizza, Italy, where the breed was developed in 1580. The present baroque building that houses the stately Riding School Hall was completed in 1735.

The means by which the highest standards of dressage are met at the Spanish Riding School are interesting. The horses and riders are trained by the riding master (Bereiter), and the head riding master (Oberbereiter). The young rider is placed on an older, experienced horse, which lets the rider know every time he makes even a minor error. The rider thus learns to control his own gestures tightly and to sit in the proper manner to guide the horse. The transfer of skill and knowledge from experienced rider to young horse and then through mature horse to young rider ensures the continuance of a high level of excellence in perpetuity at the school.

The training program consists of three stages. The first deals with the forward gaits: the walk, trot, and canter. The second level is the lower (or campaign) school, where the horse is taught to flex its hindlimbs under its body and to bring its hooves close together. This training prepares the horse for all of the gaits, turns, and figures. When the campaign school training is completed, the horse is able to perform all the simple and complex gaits and responds quickly to the rider's actions. By the fourth year, if the horse shows promise, it is promoted to the haute école. It is then that the horse learns the exercises on the ground and above the ground.

The stallion is first exposed to the lunging rein between the ages of six to twelve weeks of life. Riding begins in its first year, although this is done with great care and moderation since Lipizzaners are slow to mature. Members of this breed do not reach their full size until a remarkably late seven years of age, but they can continue to perform through their mid-twenties, when most horses have reached their maximum life expectancy.

In order to develop the proper seat, the riders practice extensively on the lunging rein and without stirrups. This discipline eventually allows the rider to move with the horse as though they were one and the same creature. All the above-ground movements are performed without the use of stirrups. To perfect concentration and control, a movement devised by de Pluvinel may be performed "between the pillars," which are two closely spaced posts, located near the center of the exhibition hall. The horse must perform the movement perfectly between

4. The levade in the hand performed by a Lipizzaner horse at the Spanish Riding School, Vienna, Austria. (Photo courtesy of the Spanish Riding School)

5. The courbette performed by a Lipizzaner horse at the Spanish Riding School, Vienna, Austria. (Photo courtesy of the Spanish Riding School)

the pillars without touching them. The final test of training involves performing the movements on a long rein, with the instructor standing on the ground near the hindquarters of the horse. The horse is then guided only by the gentle motions of the reins.

The rigorous training results in the perfect execution of the following:

Exercises on the Ground
Gallop change: The horse is trained to change its step when the rider commands.
Pirouette: The horse turns 360 degrees on its haunches with the head facing out. This is a collected canter pivoting around one hindleg. Only six to eight strides are permitted.
Piaffe: The horse does a cadenced trot in place.
Passage: This is a slow deliberate trot in which each diagonal pair of legs is raised alternately with a period of total suspension in midair with each stride.

Airs Above Ground
Pesade: The forelegs are lifted and flexed so they are at a forty-five degree angle to the ground.
Levade: The hindlegs are flexed until the hock is nearly resting on the ground, while the forelimbs are bent at the knee joint (less than in the pesade). The whole weight of the body is on the hindlimbs and the rump is almost parallel with the ground (figure 4).
Mézair: The horse performs a series of levades. It first raises its forelegs in a levade, then lowers them to the ground and brings the hindlegs forward, and repeats the levades in succession.
Courbette: The horse first performs a piaffe, rises to a pesade, and then leaps forward on its hindlegs two to six times without lowering its forelimbs to the ground between jumps (figure 5). This is one of the most difficult movements, and only a few horses are ever able to perform it.
Croupade: From a stationary piaffe position, the horse leaps in the air with its forelimbs bent and its hindlegs tucked under its belly.
Ballotade: This is like the croupade, except that the hindlegs are extended.
Capriole: This is like the ballotade except that the horse kicks its hindlegs forcefully as it extends them. It looks like a leap combined with a backward kick. It is the most difficult movement of all.

Performances by the famous Lipizzaners are still held in the Riding School Hall to the delight of thousands of spectators. The finale is the grand quadrille (figure 6) performed by eight horses and riders.

Polo

The fast-pace sport of polo is a game played by two teams on horseback using mallets with long, flexible handles to drive a wooden ball (figure 7). The aim is to hit the ball into the opponent's goal. Like other sports designed to sharpen the responses of cavalrymen, polo requires considerable skill and well-trained horses.

Polo was reputed to have been invented during the reign of the third king of Persia, Darius I (522-486 B.C.), whose empire stretched from the Indus River in southern Asia to the Balkans and from

Armenia to Egypt. The Persian horses of his time were extremely well-bred, highly prized specimens, although the Persians' riding skills failed to advance to the level of their enemies, the Scythians. Originally polo was called *chaugan*, a name that persists for the polo mallet in America today. The Tibetan term *pulo*, from which the modern name for the sport is derived, is the word for the plant root out of which the wooden ball was carved.

Polo was brought into India by Muslims from the northwest and Chinese from the east. The game became very popular in India, but by the time the English arrived, it was found only in the northwestern and northeastern frontiers. English tea plantation owners in Assam adopted the sport and, in 1859, founded the Silchar Club, which has the distinction of being the oldest polo club in the world. With the start of the Silchar Club, members devised the first set of rules for the modern version of polo. They played on Manipuri ponies, which stood only twelve hands[2] in stature. At first there were nine riders per team, but the number was reduced through time to seven and eventually four, as it is today. Throughout the 1800s the wither height limits were continually raised until they were eventually eliminated completely in 1919. Today, the average height of a polo "pony" is slightly more than fifteen hands.

Buzkashi

One of the most difficult and fastest equestrian sports ever developed is *buzkashi*, which in Turkish means "to steal a goat." Its ancestry goes back probably at least to the Scythians, and slight variations on its theme are played by Mongols, Kazaks (see chapter 7, figure 8), and Turkic people throughout Central Asia. The center for *buzkashi* today is Afghanistan. In *buzkashi*, a headless goat or calf skin is filled with sand and soaked in water overnight. The aim of the sport is for one rider to seize the skin from the *hallal*, or "circle of justice," ride out around a post, and return the bag to the *hallal* before any of his competitors can take it from him. The number of players ranges from ten to over one thousand, and at times it becomes a free-for-all. *Buzkashi* horses are highly valued and the wealthy *beys* (noblemen) are among the few people who can afford to own them. Because the riders attack one another vigorously with whips to retrieve the goat skin for themselves, many injuries are sustained during the competition. It can be so dangerous that only the very finest riders are generally allowed to compete.

2. A hand is a unit of measure equal to ten centimeters (4 in.).

6. *The grand quadrille performed by the Lipizzaner horses at the Spanish Riding School, Vienna, Austria. (Photo courtesy of the Spanish Riding School)*

7. *Polo game at the Middleburg Polo Club, Virginia. (Photo by Crowell Hadden, Jr.)*

The Equestrian Games of the Mongols

Horse racing has a long history in Mongolia, where it undoubtedly served to keep the horses and their riders competitive and skilled in preparation for military campaigns. Today racing is done more for entertainment and out of a sense of tradition. The exhilaration of the race is just one expression of the passion for life that Mongols enjoy.

Horse races are at the center of most social gatherings in Mongolia. Mongol racing differs from its European and American counterparts in that it does not take place on prepared racetracks, but rather is cross-country. The races are generally at least fifteen to twenty-five kilometers (10-15 mi.) long, across the open, fenceless grasslands of the steppes. The short-legged, sturdy Mongol ponies outrun all other horses under these conditions, but do poorly in short sprints on prepared tracks where a larger Chinese horse with a longer stride can quickly overtake them. The jockeys are usually boys of fifteen years or younger who wear short, colorful riding coats and no boots. Instead of a saddle, a small felt triangle is tied to the horse's back.

One traditional race is a big annual event. It begins at dawn, with each rider mounting his horse at his own home. He must ride to each of his neighbors' houses, dismount, engage in polite conversation, drink the traditional beverage known as *koumiss* (fermented mare's milk), and get back on his horse to continue his visitations. By the end of the day, the riders are so intoxicated from the *koumiss* that they can barely stay on their horses. Despite their worsening condition, they ride at high speed from one house to the next, tilting and righting themselves as they go. The rider who manages to visit all of his neighbors and stay on his horse until sunset is the winner.

The Mongols have other forms of entertainment involving the horse. One is the "bride chase," or *Khis-Kouhou*, in which the young men chase the young women and try to kiss them, while the young women fend them off with whips. Another tradition is the *papach-oinu*, in which players have ten minutes to try to steal as many of their competitors' hats off their heads as possible within the confines of the playing field.

The American Rodeo

Unlike many of the sports discussed here, the rodeo is a recent invention. Its origin can be traced through two lines of descent, Buffalo Bill Cody's Wild West Exhibition (figure 8) and the more authentic expression of the cowboy's work-related skills.

Colonel William F. Cody, otherwise known as Buffalo Bill, founded the Wild West Exhibition in 1882 to educate the masses in what the taming of the western frontiers was supposed to have been like. Cody himself had led a colorful life in the West before it was settled, working as a freight messenger, a Pony Express rider, a soldier in the Union Army, a stagecoach driver, and a buffalo hunter for the Kansas Pacific Railroad. Later in life, he became a melodrama actor, a member of the Nebraska legislature, and the owner of an irrigation company, a gold mine, and a western film company.

Although Cody had experienced the West more fully than most people and his motto was Everything Genuine, his exhibition was not a realistic depiction of actual events or people. He seemed to understand that flamboyance was needed to entertain and had no scruples about providing what the people wanted. What is important in the context of the history of the rodeo is the acts that Cody featured. The Wild West opened with the Grand March, followed by a bareback pony race, a 100-yard race between an American Indian on horseback and one on foot, a shooting exhibition, riding of wild Texas steers, and roping and riding of wild bison. It concluded with the Grand Hunt. It is clear that modern rodeo, which portrays cowboy skills far more realistically, received its impetus from Cody's show.

There were over eighty other companies that performed similar shows, but Buffalo Bill's Wild West was the first, the most successful, and the longest-lived exhibition of its type. In 1913, however, despite its great success, it lost so much money that creditors took possession and Cody had to declare bankruptcy.

The peak years for the professional cowboy in America were from 1867 to 1892, after much of the West had been conquered and the Civil War was over, but before the railroad had really taken hold in the West, most of the land was settled, and automobiles were invented. Cowboys were and are generally the employees of large ranch owners. Average cowboys are in their twenties because they must have incredible physical endurance. Their skills in handling the horses they ride and the livestock they manage are the essential part of their job, so developing their talents is important to the business. Although it is not necessary to participate in a rodeo to hone riding and roping abilities, this competition provides cowboys with the opportunity to receive recognition for these skills. The ranch owners may reap the financial benefits of having a trained and effective staff, but at the rodeo, the cowboy hopes to become a star in his own right. This situation is not unlike that of the Roman charioteer who competed with a team and a vehicle financed by the nobility or the jockey who races a horse of a wealthy owner, except that in the rodeo the prize and the glory go straight to the cowboy himself.

8. Buffalo Bill Cody with the performers of the Wild West Exhibition, ca. 1915. (Photo courtesy of the Buffalo Bill Historical Center, Cody, WY)

At the end of the nineteenth century, life for the cowboy, his horse, and the livestock could be harsh and cruel. Cowboys were nomads who worked eighteen hours a day and seven days a week when they were on a drive. The horses were ridden most of that time, and both rider and mount often went for days with little food or water. They encountered every form of hazard that the elements could bestow, including floods, droughts, blizzards, tornadoes, and prairie fires. The attraction of living out under the sky and owning nothing but a bedroll was the adventure of it all.

The cowboys' methods of training and working with horses differ radically from those put forth by the dressage masters in the riding schools. Traditional bronco-busting consists of destroying the horse's spirit by harsh treatment designed to establish human supremacy as quickly as possible. The goal is to capture an adult wild horse and then rope, saddle, bridle, and beat it into submission on the first riding. The bits used are uncomfortable and the spurs extreme: in fact, the whole manner with which the horse and the livestock are handled can be cruel. Cowboys are equally hard on their coworkers, especially the "tenderfoot" or "pilgrim." They test the inexperienced by a variety of hazing techniques guaranteed to winnow out all but the bravest.

Ranching and the rodeo are inseparable. In the Great Plains virtually every rancher and cowboy takes some interest in rodeo, whether as a present or past competitor, an official, an organizer, or just a spectator. Like their predecessors on a long drive, modern cowboys in the rodeo circuit are nomadic.

The modern rodeo is divided into two primary categories: the rough stock and the timed events. The first includes saddle bronc riding, bareback bronc riding, and bull riding. Timed events consist of calf roping, steer wrestling, and steer roping. A third category, barrel racing, is the only competition in which women are normally allowed to compete, although this is changing with the addition of all-female bareback bronc and bull riding. Other events include a wide range of children's competitions like goat tying, relay races, and flag races, but female and children events are secondary to the adult male competitions.

Fox Hunting in Great Britain

Hunting on horseback has always taken precedence over dressage in Great Britain. It originally was done out of necessity with the game likely to have been red deer, fallow deer, or wild boars. For centuries hounds, horses, and humans sped through forests hunting for food. Because of intensive clearing for pastures, the shrinkage of forests eventually led to a decline in the number of deer and wild boar in Britain. At the same time, foxes were being hunted proportionately more because of their threat to expanding sheep herds.

With a series of British enclosure acts, beginning in the twelfth century and peaking between 1450-1640 and 1750-1860, the common public pastures were gradually replaced by private fields enclosed by hedges and fences. As a result hunting became increasingly difficult. The construction of fences, hedges, and ditches around small plots of private land meant that horses had to be trained to leap over obstacles with ease during hunts.

Fox hunting gradually evolved into a popular sport. Viscount Lowther, in 1660, was the first to be accredited with keeping a pack of hounds strictly for fox hunting. In 1726 Squire William Draper of Yorkshire was said to have spent a large part of his leisure time hunting foxes to spare his lambs. The modern form of fox hunting is attributed to Hugo Meynell in the eighteenth century. It was at this time that the hunt livery, or uniform, became standardized, although it has changed somewhat over the years according to fashion.

The hunt is led and directed by the master. His huntsman uses a copper horn and his voice to control the hounds. Two or three "whippers-in" assist the huntsman in keeping the hounds in a pack. Other members of the master's entourage may include earth stoppers, grooms, second horsemen, and terrier men. Earth stoppers are supposed to close any dens, burrows, or drains temporarily on the day of the hunt to prevent the fox from hiding from the hounds. Grooms and second horsemen are expensive options that are provided only at the more affluent hunts or by some of the members themselves. The second horsemen, if present, provide fresh horses for the master and huntsman when needed. Terrier men carry terriers on horseback, in dog carts, or on foot to rout the fox out of its den or a drain pipe.

Before the race begins, those participating formally acknowledge the master and his team of assistants at the meet, where wine is sometimes served to the mounted hunters. At the signal the hounds take off to draw out the fox from the cover where it is hiding and the chase begins. If the fox is killed, the master awards the brush (tail), mask (head), and footpads to those hunters present at the death, while the hounds are fed the fox's body.

9. The huntsman and the hounds at a meeting of the Orange County Hunt, Middleburg, Virinia. (Photo by Janet Hitchen)

The sport reached its peak of popularity just prior to World War I, when fox hunting began to be regulated by the Master of Foxhounds Association. Both world wars led to shortages of men and feed for the hounds, leading to a severe reduction in the sport. After World War II, many anti-fox-hunting groups tried to have the sport abolished, but the bill was defeated in 1949 in the House of Commons. By the 1960s, fox hunting was as strong as it was around the turn of the century, with 230 official packs of foxhounds in Great Britain and Ireland. Fox hunting in Britain today is again extremely controversial and legislation may soon ban it entirely.

In the United States there are about 100 packs of hounds officially registered with the American Masters of Foxhounds Association (figure 9). The native gray fox and imported red fox are hunted. No particular breed of horse is required, but the ideal breed is a Thoroughbred, although ponies are also used. In the 1920s and 1930s, the "Irish Hunter," a cross between a large Irish Draught Horse and a Thoroughbred, was preferred.

10. A typical "Timber Race" steeplechase over fences at the Glenwood Race Course, Middleburg, Virginia. (Photo by Janet Hitchen)

Steeplechasing

A natural outgrowth of fox hunts is the steeplechase (figures 10 and 11), a race across country and over a number of obstacles. Its name comes from the tradition of racing from one obvious landmark on the British landscape to another, usually church steeples. As jumping over obstacles became a necessity during hunts because of the British enclosure acts, it started to develop a competitive aspect. One of the most famous and earliest recorded steeplechases was held in 1752 in County Cork, Ireland, between Cornelius O'Callaghan and Edmund Blake. The race was four miles long and ran from Buttevant Church to St. Leger Steeple. The prize, which went to Blake, consisted of generous portions of port, claret, and Jamaican rum.

11. Steeple race known as the "hunts course" at Great Meadows Course, The Plains, Virginia. (Photo by Janet Hitchen)

By about 1850 steeplechasing split in two directions, one for amateurs that retained aspects of its origins in hunting and another that evolved into professional competitions. Tom Colman organized the first St. Albans' steeplechase in 1830 for a sweepstakes of twenty-five sovereigns. Sixteen competitors performed that day. In 1839 the most famous steeplechase of all, the Grand National at Aintree, began outside Liverpool. The four-mile course over plowed ground had twenty-nine obstacles, including small banks, stout walls, and two streams. A bay horse named Lottery won it that year in fourteen minutes fifty-three seconds, five minutes longer than it takes to run the course today.

The Aintree course today is four and a half miles long and has thirty fences, some of which have developed worldwide reputations for the tolls they extract from horse and rider alike. The Grand National remained the only steeplechase competition that offered a substantial prize until the 1960s, when several others began to approach it in winnings.

For the steeplechase the stirrup leathers are longer than usual, and the rider sits with his or her legs well forward and braced against the stirrup irons. There is no specialized breeding industry for steeplechase horses, although some Anglo-Irish lineages are known for their jumping abilities. Chasers are usually older than horses that run in flat races, because the stiff jumps and the long steeplechase courses necessitate great power and stamina.

Show Jumping

Both the British and the French can take credit for initiating the skill of jumping horses over obstacles in competition (figure 12). Two lines of competitive jumping—one military and one purely for sport—developed from its beginnings in the eighteenth century.

The first civilian show jumping competition was held in 1865 at the Royal Dublin Society's annual show, where competitions for wide and high leaps were conducted, and by the twentieth century the sport was firmly established. Audiences can appreciate jumping events because, unlike dressage with its elaborate grading system, it is easy and quick to see whether the rider has been successful in his or her delivery.

12. Show jumping at the Upperville (Virginia) Horse Show, the oldest horse show in America. (Photo by Janet Hitchen)

At the turn of the twentieth century, Federico Caprilli, an Italian cavalry officer, developed the "forward seat," which is now the standard position for all equestrian activities involving jumping, including steeplechasing, show jumping, and fox hunting. In it the rider shifts his or her weight forward to just behind the withers and, at great speeds or over jumps, places it entirely in the stirrups.

International open jumping has grown rapidly in Europe since World War II. The increasingly difficult courses have honed the abilities of horse and rider alike. As a result show jumping has become incredibly specialized and now shares little in common with cross-country steeplechases or other equestrian sports.

The 1912 Olympic Games in Stockholm were the first in modern times to allow equestrian events. At that time the maximum height of show jumping obstacles was 1.4 meters (4.5 ft.) Many of the obstacles were only 1.1 meters (3 ft. 7 in.). By 1960 the highest was 1.6 meters (5 ft. 3 in.) and the lowest was 1.3 meters (4 ft. 3 in.), just below the highest of 1912. In addition to the height increases, the obstacles have become closer together and the breadth of some has increased. Through time, then, competitions have become much more difficult with more horses being eliminated or disqualified and more injuries occurring to both horses and riders. The risks and required skill have driven many amateurs out of the competition and greatly reduced the number of talented competitors.

Horse Racing (Flat Racing)

Horse races date back at least to the time of the Iron Age Scythians and are undoubtedly the equestrian events with the longest continuity. On the European continent races were recorded by the Greeks. The Romans preferred chariot races to ones with mounted riders, but they occasionally held some on horseback. The Palio di Siena, which is still run every year, is the only existing example of a once-common Italian tradition. The winners, according to tradition, receive a *palio*, an expensive piece of brocade cloth.

The earliest-known racetrack in England was one commissioned by the Roman Emperor Lucius Septimius Serverus between A.D. 208 and 211 in Yorkshire. Horse racing continued on after the Romans forfeited control of England. In 1074 William Fitzstephen described informal horse races at Smithfield, in London, where horses were tested before being sold. In 1174 one of the earliest records of an official English horse race was made. Between that time and the sixteenth century, horse racing was primarily "the sport of kings" and wealthy nobility. Under the last Tudors and early Stuarts, royal studs were found at Hampton Court and Tutbury.

Newmarket, in Suffolk, England, was a small town where King James I (who reigned from 1603 to 1625) chose to build a hunting lodge. His son, Charles I, sponsored the first spring and autumn races at Newmarket and, in 1634, financed the first Gold Cup race there. Horse racing suffered a brief setback during Oliver Cromwell's reign (1649-1658) when he declared racing illegal. However, Charles II (1660-1685) picked up the torch and expanded the races at Newmarket to numerous contestants running a series of four-mile heats. He increased the prizes and set up official guidelines and arbiters. Newmarket was then to become famous as the home of Thoroughbred breeding, which began in the eighteenth century (see chapter 8). During the reign of Charles II, the course at Epsom opened near London. For the past two hundred years it has been the home of the famous Derby.

Horse racing spread rapidly in the eighteenth century throughout Britain and Ireland. Small tracks sprang up everywhere, but only at Newmarket were the rules strictly enforced. Professional jockeys began to replace royalty and nobility on the tracks and professional trainers became common. Queen Anne continued the tradition set by Charles II and founded Ascot in Berkshire in 1711. Today it is the venue for the Royal Ascot, the world-famous four-day event held annually in June. Since 1807 racehorse owners have enthusiastically competed for the Ascot Gold Cup. Today the six classic races in England are the One Thousand and Two Thousand Guineas races at Newmarket, the Derby and the Oaks at Epsom, the St. Leger at Doncaster, and the Ascot Gold Cup.

The Jockey Club, founded in 1752, began in Newmarket and eventually spread throughout England. This organization was responsible for establishing a set of strict rules regulating tracks, races, breeding, and licensing that still help to keep the sport as honest and fair as possible. At the time of its formation and long after, its power was in the hands of a few influential people.

Until 1744 most of the horses that ran in races were over five years of age, but in that year a race for four year olds was introduced. Twelve years later races for three year olds were initiated. In 1786 the longest running race for two year olds was established at Newmarket, the 1,000-meter July Stakes.

Horse racing was one of the first sports to be taken up by the English colonists of Virginia. By 1620 short contests between two horses were being held on village streets and on paths through the forest. Horse racing was legalized in 1630 by the colonial governor. Because of the thick forests, however, proper racecourses were not established in Virginia until the end of the seventeenth century, when exhausted tobacco fields were converted.

In New York tracks were set up much earlier. The first formal racetrack in America was built in 1665, just one year after the Dutch surrendered New Amsterdam to the British, near today's Aqueduct track on Long Island. Known then as New Market, after the famous English racing center, it held the first races in America in which a trophy was awarded. The Governor's Cup, presented by the first governor of New York, Sir Richard Nicolls, started a tradition of giving utilitarian items like tankards, punch bowls, plates, spoons, teapots, and candlesticks as trophies. Maryland, too, was important in the history of racing, with more than twenty racing centers in existence prior to the Revolutionary War.

George Washington, as an active member of the landed gentry of Virginia, bred and raced horses inside the colony and elsewhere. The only account of his winning, however, was a race in which he hotly disputed the outcome until the judges reversed their decision and awarded him the cash prize.

The Triple Crown is the most famous group of American races today. The trophy for the Triple Crown is awarded to the racehorse that wins all three of the big American races: the Kentucky Derby, the Preakness Stakes, and the Belmont Stakes. As of 1996, only eleven horses had won the American Triple Crown. The first winner was Sir Barton, in 1919. Between 1948 and 1973, fifteen

13. Thunder Gulch, the 1995 Kentucky Derby winner, just before crossing the finish line at Churchill Downs. (© Churchill Downs, Inc. and Kinetic Corporation)

racehorses won two of the three races, but none could win all three. Finally, in 1973, Secretariat broke the jinx and won the Triple Crown. These races are run by three year olds, primarily Thoroughbreds.

Since 1875 the Kentucky Derby has been held at Churchill Downs in Louisville, Kentucky, in early May (see figure 13). The first winner was Aristides, whose net winnings for the race were $2,850. Over 10,000 fans attended the first Kentucky Derby. The Preakness Stakes, the second of the classic races, is run two weeks later at Pimlico in Baltimore, Maryland. It is slightly older than the Derby, having been in existence since 1871. The Belmont Stakes, the final race, is run at Belmont Park, New York, three weeks after the Preakness. The Belmont Stakes, the oldest of the three, was first run in 1867 at Jerome Park. In 1920 the famous horse Man O' War (figure 14) won it.

The first record of a horse race in Australia was in 1821, in Sydney. By 1840 the rage had spread to every state and virtually every village and town. The importance of the horse, the love of Thoroughbreds, and the desire to gamble ensured racing's popularity before the turn of the century. Today horse racing is well established and on the first Tuesday of November everyone takes off work for the Melbourne Cup, the most important competition since it began in 1861. Today the Cup offers the largest stake of any race in the world.

Horse racing actually served as an inspiration for the invention of motion pictures, and, in turn, photography has become an integral part of racing.

In 1872 Eadweard Muybridge, a well-established photographer of his day, was commissioned by Leland Stanford, previous governor of California, to settle a bet. Stanford bet a friend that all four of a trotter's feet leave the ground at one point in its stride. His friend claimed that at least one foot is on the ground at all times. Muybridge took a series of photographs that eventually proved Stanford right.

Inspired by this wager, Muybridge continued to capture motion on film. In 1880 he developed the zoopraxiscope, the precursor of the movie projector. In 1883 Muybridge set up a studio in a wooden shed at the University of Pennsylvania. One of his series was of the first dean of the Department of Veterinary Medicine, Dr. Rush Shippen Huidekoper, jumping his mare Pandora.

14. Man O'War with his groom in 1920. (© Churchill Downs, Inc. and Kinetic Corporation)

Today photography is used to record entire races. Until recently the chief means by which a winner of a close race was determined was through photographing the finish line as the horses crossed. Hence, the term *photo finish* is used to indicate a tight competition in which the results are not known until the last moment.

Trotting and Harness Racing

The earliest record of trotting was made around 1300 B.C. in Asia Minor, where it was used in pulling war chariots. Much later the Norfolk Trotter, a breed whose sire was born in the twelfth century in Norfolk, England, drew attention to the advantage of developing horses that had a natural talent for trotting. However, the three countries that have produced the best lines of trotters are Russia, France, and the United States. Count Alexei Gregorevitch Orlov started a line of horses on his breeding farm in 1773 that eventually produced Bars I, the founding sire for the Orlov Trotter breed. This is a large breed, standing at about seventeen hands. The Orlov Trotter was the supreme trotting breed for about 100 years, until the arrival of the French Trotter on the scene. The fastest breed today is the American Standardbred (chapter 8, figure 15), founded by the famous trotter Hambletonian. Its genetic background includes the Norfolk Trotter, the now extinct Narragansett Pacer, and, most significantly, the English Thoroughbred (chapter 8, figure 12). That Thoroughbred was Messenger, a stallion that arrived on the American shores in 1788. It is claimed to be ancestral to over 90 percent of all American Standardbred horses today. The Standardbred has a very gentle temperament and is an extremely consistent performer. In 1879 the National Association of Trotting Horse Breeders set the standard qualifying time for a horse to trot a mile at 2:30. The name *Standardbred* originally referred to any horse that could perform at the official time limit during a trial. Later, however, this designation was transferred to the specific breed, and a stallion's genealogy, instead of his performance, became the test of whether he was a Standardbred.

The first trotting races in America were performed with a rider and became very popular in colonial New England. The sport can attribute part of its popularity to 1802 legislation that banned horse racing throughout the whole Northeast because it "led to immorality." Trotting was permitted by a technicality, however, because the horses did not run as fast as possible. One of the earliest speed records was won in 1806 by Yankee, who trotted a mile in 2:59 at Harlem, New York. Between 1818 and 1830 trotting races began to be held on public tracks in New York, Philadelphia, Boston, Baltimore, and Trenton.

In the United States harness racing with a vehicle began only around 1830. Its tardy appearance resulted from the fact that prior to that time horse-drawn vehicles were heavy and clumsy and roads and tracks were rough. The sport owes its beginning to improvised races with all sorts of vehicles on regular roads in rural areas and villages across the country. From 1830 on, vehicles, roads, and the horses themselves were gradually improved. Traffic on the road-ways increased as well, however, making it prudent to limit such competitions to racing tracks that sprang up chiefly on both coasts. Lightweight sulkies replaced ordinary road vehicles around 1850, and harness racing simultaneously edged out trotting under saddle. The early sulkies had high wheels (up to 2.1 meters, or 7 feet, in diameter) with iron tires and high seats. An important date in harness racing was 1892, when regular sulkies were replaced by the "bike," a very light vehicle with pneumatic tires on low, ball-bearing wheels. The bike sulky immediately knocked more than four seconds off the world's trotting record for a mile, dropping it from 2:08 3/4 to 2:04. The seats on the bike sulkies were lowered after a while, when drivers realized they did not need to see over the horse. The old sulkies weighed between fifty and sixty pounds, whereas the bikes are less than twenty-eight pounds.

During the last half of the nineteenth century, unscrupulous gambling and fixed races led to a decline in the character of the spectators, and harness racing became greatly stigmatized. The sport lacked any formal regulations until 1870, when the National Trotting Association was founded. Not only did the organization clean up the sport, but it also helped to unify it across the country under the same set of guidelines. Following this massive housecleaning, harness racing became one of the most honest sports in the United States.

The long-held two-minute speed barrier finally fell when the pacer Star Pointer covered a mile in 1:59 1/4 in 1897. Perhaps the most-celebrated harness

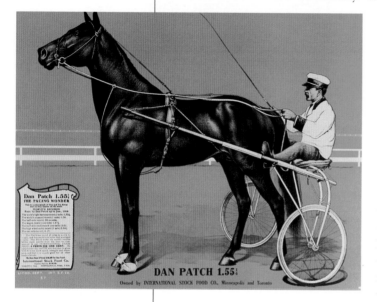

15. A 1906 color lithograph advertising the famous harness racehorse Dan Patch, known for his record pacing time of 1 minute, 55 3/4 seconds for one mile. (Photo courtesy of the Harness Racing Museum and Hall of Fame, Goshen, NY)

racer of all time, however, was a pacer called Dan Patch (figure 15). In 1905 the stallion paced a mile in 1:55 3/4, but the record was questioned because of the equipment he was wearing to maintain his gait. Nevertheless, a fantastic public relations pitch had fans turning out everywhere just to see him.

In 1940 pari-mutuel betting was legalized at Roosevelt Raceway in New York, but during this time drivers were able to jump over the starting line prematurely. This either altered the outcome of the race or caused innumerable false starts that delayed races and irritated fans. In 1946 a mobile starting gate was designed to be carried on a car so that the horses could run behind it in unison to the starting line. As the car crossed the line, the driver sped up and left the horses far behind. This ensured that all the horses had the opportunity to cross the line at the same time. The next important invention was the wheel disk, which prevented the horses' hooves from getting caught in the spokes. In 1976 the driver's position was moved back from over the axle to behind it, lifting much of the weight off the horse (figure 16).

Summary

Equestrian sports are clearly as diverse as the cultures and time periods that gave rise to them. An examination of the history of these sports makes it possible to understand better the varied and complex relationships that have developed between horses and humans through the millennia. Equestrian athletes have had to work within the limitations of their mounts, but it is obvious from the examples in this chapter that the creativity of the human performer, coupled with the speed and agility of the horse, allows spectacular feats to be accomplished.

16. Cam's Card Shark, the 1994 Harness Horse of the Year, being driven by John Campbell. During his last year of racing, Cam's Card Shark won fifteen of eighteen races and came in second in two others. (Photo courtesy of the Harness Racing Museum and Hall of Fame, Goshen, NY)

Reading List

Anderson, J. K. *Ancient Greek Horsemanship.* Berkeley: University of California Press, 1961.

Blackstone, S. J. *Buckskins, Bullets, and Business: A History of Buffalo Bill's Wild West.* New York: Greenwood Press, 1986.

Boutros, L. *Phoenician Sport: Its Influence on the Origin of the Olympic Games.* Amsterdam: J. C. Gieben, 1981.

Dossenbach, M., and H. D. Dossenbach. *The Noble Horse.* New York: Portland House, 1987.

Edwards, E. H. *Encyclopedia of the Horse.* New York: Crescent Books, 1990.

Humphrey, J. H. *Roman Circuses: Arenas for Chariot Racing.* London: B. T. Batsford, Ltd., 1986.

Lawrence E. A. *Rodeo: An Anthropologist Looks at the Wild and the Tame.* Knoxville: University of Tennessee Press, 1982.

Littauer, M. A. "After Seeing the Spanish Riding School, Part I." *The Chronicle of the Horse,* February 5, 1965, 26-27.

———. "After Seeing the Spanish Riding School, Part II." *The Chronicle of the Horse,* February 12, 1965, 22-25.

Littauer, V. S. *The Development of Modern Riding: The Story of Formal Riding from Renaissance Times to the Present.* New York: Howell Book House, 1991.

Reuter, W. *The Lipizzaners and the Spanish Riding School.* Innsbruck, Austria: Pinguin-Verlag, 1982.

Wrensch, F. A. *Harness Horse Racing in the United States and Canada.* New York: D. Van Nostrand Co., Inc., 1948.

Seven
HOOVES ACROSS
THE STEPPES

The Kazak Life-Style

VICTOR A. SHNIRELMAN
SANDRA L. OLSEN
PATRICIA RICE

*H*orse cultures have developed all around the world, including North Africa, Arabia, the North American Plains, and the Argentinean pampas, but nowhere are equestrian traditions as deeply established as in the Eurasian steppes. Much has been written and discussed about the highly respected and feared Mongol armies of the eleventh through sixteenth centuries, but more recent horse cultures have not been as vividly described. Many groups, such as the Mongols of Mongolia and China and the Bashkirs of Russia, could be highlighted here, but the Kazaks set a fine example of the pervasiveness of equine-related traditions in certain societies.

About the Kazak People

Today approximately seven million Kazak people live in the very heart of Eurasia, inhabiting a large territory from the northern Caspian area in the west to the Altay Mountains in the east and from the southern Ural Mountains in the north to the Kyzyl-Kum Desert and the Tian Shan Mountains in the south (figure I). Their territory sprawls some 3,200 kilometers (2,000 mi.) from east to west and 2,400 kilometers (1,500 mi.) from north to south. They largely occupy newly independent Kazakstan, but other groups of Kazaks live in the Xinjiang Uygur Autonomous Region of northwest China and in western Mongolia.

The Kazaks speak a Turkic language that is closely related to other languages of the steppes, such as Kyrgyz, Turkmen, and Tatar. In appearance they are generally an Asian people with short stature and straight black hair, but with facial features that reveal a varied ancestry including Mongols from the east, Turkic people from the south, and Europeans from the west. Nominally, they have been Sunni Muslims since the eighteenth century, but continue to practice many older traditions, including shamanism.

This chapter discusses traditional beliefs that are still practiced by Kazaks in Mongolia, China, and some areas in southern Kazakstan, but change is occurring rapidly in all regions. The most "westernized" Kazaks are those whom the Soviet government settled on collective farms in Kazakstan. For them many traditions have been abandoned or are practiced only on very special occasions. After the Russian revolution the Soviet government strongly encouraged the abandonment of nomadism in Kazakstan. The greatest shift occurred between 1929 and 1933, when the percentage of Kazaks settled on collective farms rose from 7.4 to 95 percent. The current government of Kazakstan is trying to find a balance between ethnic identity and economic progress.

The Kazaks' origin is somewhat clouded because of the shifting tides of steppe nomads through time and the paucity of written records. After the disintegration of the Golden Horde (the medieval Tatar-Mongol nomadic empire) in

Facing page, see figure 2.

the fifteenth century, the people split into separate tribal groups, one of which probably formed the core of the Kazaks.

During the mid-sixteenth century the one million or so Kazaks became a recognized entity led by one khan (ruler) and divided into three political units: the Elder, Middle, and Young Hordes (figure 1). The Elder Horde's territory was the area south of Lake Balqash to Lake Ysyk and from the northwest edge of the Tian Shan Mountains west to Tashkent, Uzbekistan. The Middle Horde occupied most of central Kazakstan, with concentrations along the Irtysh, Ishim, Tobol, and Chu Rivers. The Young Horde claimed the western steppe between the Aral and the Caspian Seas and along the lower valley of the Syr Darya River.

The origin of the Kazak name is more obscure than the history of the Kazaks' formation as a group. It is most likely a derivative from the Turkish word *qaz*, meaning "to wander." Some believe the name came from uniting two tribal names, *Kaspy* and *Saki*. Still others say that it is derived from the Mongol word *khasaq*, which refers to a wheeled cart used to transport felt tents. Many Kazaks claim that their name comes from the Turkish words for white, *ak*, and goose, *kaz*, because of their legend that they descended from one of these birds.

Traditional Kazak Economy

Until recently the economy of the Kazaks was almost completely based upon pastoralism. The entire Kazak culture was devoted to the herding of horses, sheep, cattle, and camels. They practiced very little agriculture and existed almost entirely on the products of their herds.

Today many changes have taken place and nomadic life is retained only in remote areas, like the Tian Shan Mountains of northwestern China and in western Mongolia. Outside of this area, most Kazaks live on collective farms and care for herds or raise grain, or are industrial workers in cities. In Kazakstan, which was partitioned into state-controlled collective farms by the Soviet government, much of the land has now been privatized and more of the traditions are being reintroduced.

1. Map of the Kazak region.

It might be thought that the traditional Kazaks who spend their lives wandering across the landscape with very few material possessions would be completely egalitarian and classless. Such is not the case, however, and, in fact, they have often been referred to as having a patriarchal-feudalistic society. Wealth is measured according to the size of one's herds and the control one has over winter grazing territory in areas where the climate is relatively mild. The richest Kazak leaders are the most nomadic, because their large herds allow them to take greater risks and lose a few animals along the way. Because they are able to spread their herds out in small groups across the landscape to minimize the effects of localized climatic or environmental disasters, there is a tendency for the rich to get even richer. In addition, they can afford to have their poorer relatives care for each of these smaller herds. Because the wealthy are more mobile, they can get to fresh pastures more quickly and stake a claim. Once someone has camped in an area, he is rarely pushed out by later arrivals, unless the latter are the powerful, who maintain privilege over the best winter feeding grounds year after year. The herds of the wealthy thus tend to grow larger through time, while the middle class or poor are lucky to maintain their herd size. Although one large-scale bout with ice or deep snowfall can transform a rich man into a poor one overnight, it can completely wipe out the herds of average pastoralists. The lower-class Kazaks are semisedentary and often own a few cows. The poorest work for the wealthy as hired hands; in the past they were sold as slaves to farmers.

Hunting and fishing were more important in the past than in the present, but both are still practiced. In the northern steppes, furbearing animals like the marmot, wolf, and muskrat (introduced from North America) are important for the warm clothing they provide. Deer, moose, saiga antelope, and waterfowl are among the more commonly hunted species. Fishing for pike, perch, trout, carp, and other species provides a minor supplement to the diet for people living along permanent rivers.

A minimal amount of farming is carried out by the Kazaks. Agriculture is always very marginal because of the low precipitation, poor soil, and short growing season. The range of crops includes wheat, millet, rye, peas, and even rice in the south. Among the nomads only families that can spare a few members to stay and mind the fields can participate in planting. This is done on the high side of a river rather than the shoal, which is subject to flooding. Irrigation is usually required in the south, because rainfall is so low. Farming equipment consists of a plow drawn by a pair of horses, oxen, or camels and a sickle or harvesting knife. A few branches may be tied to a horse's tail so that clods of soil are broken up as the animal is led over the freshly plowed field. Those Kazaks who do not farm rely on exchange of some of their livestock products for grain supplied by more sedentary cultures, like the Uygur people in China and the Russian communities in Kazakstan. In previous centuries one means of obtaining grain was by raiding farming villages and stealing their grain supplies.

Adaptations to the Environment

The region where the Kazak people live is a mosaic of various natural features encompassing large rivers, harsh deserts, high mountains, and featureless lowlands. In general, however, Kazakstan is a vast plain that incorporates four major ecozones forming bands running from east to west. Starting in the north, the forest-steppe zone occupies just 7 percent of modern Kazakstan, the steppe (grass-covered plain) about 20 percent, the semiarid steppe another 20 percent, and the desert more than 40 percent. Across central Kazakstan the climate becomes more severe from west to east, with the vegetational growth period shrinking and annual rainfall and temperatures dropping as one moves eastward.

Both the forest-steppe and steppe zones are characterized by a harsh continental climate with a short vegetational growth period. Winter is very severe here, since the mean snow depth is about thirty to fifty centimeters (12-20 in.) and the ground is snow-covered for 140 to 160 days of the year. High winds are characteristic of winter in the steppes.

It is possible to practice farming in both the forest-steppe and steppe zones, but low annual rainfall, especially in the south, makes it too risky to rely heavily on agriculture. Early fall and late spring frosts are hazardous to farming in north and central Kazakstan. Much of the soil is very saline or alkaline and not conducive to plowing because it is thick clay that dries out and hardens when turned up. Because of all the problems with the climate and soil, agriculture is not so successful as animal husbandry in this region.

Great temperature fluctuations occur from time to time in the winter, causing disastrous conditions for pastoralists. When a thaw is followed closely by a severe frost, the result is a thick ice covering known to the Kazaks as *djut*. Livestock cannot break through it with their noses or hooves, so that much of the herds may starve if the herdsmen are not able to drive them to better pasture in time or if vast regions are affected. Usually *djut* occurs once every six to twelve years, and in the past up to 25 percent of the herd could die in a few days. Rich Kazaks are known to turn into beggars overnight as a result of a heavy ice storm. An old proverb states, "One *djut* is as much to a rich man as one arrow is to a great warrior."

Unusually deep snowfall can also lead to serious disasters and the loss of thousands of animals within a few days. Sheep and goats are sometimes buried in snowdrifts, and cattle may lose their way or be unable to feed on the concealed grass.

Another dangerous situation occurs when spring precipitation is insufficient to produce good pasture. In the past fodder was rarely stored through the winter, and only small numbers of the very young or weak animals could be kept in the shelter of Kazak homes.

South of 50° latitude in Kazakstan, the region is semiarid steppe to desert. Because dry farming is difficult in such an arid climate, prior to current irrigation practices nomadic pastoralism was the only option for inhabitants of this region. The aridity necessitated migration in order to provide sufficient food for the herds and to avoid permanent destruction of the land. In this century collective farms have reduced, but not totally eliminated the mobility of the herds. Meadows are sparsely dispersed along the large river valleys and there is suitable water for the herds only during the winter. Although there are sufficient water and forage in some permanent sand basins, these must be utilized sparingly. Overexploitation causes the ground surface to become broken by the livestock, resulting in rapid erosion that turns the area into a sea of shifting, grassless sand.

For this reason herds visit such places only in the winter, moving on to the semi-arid steppe in springtime. Winter pastures are situated where areas of dense, tall grass can be found. Shrubs like wormwood and glasswort are the most characteristic plants in the semiarid steppe and desert zones. These species can only be used for forage in the winter, when frosts diminish their strong odor and bitter taste. Pastures are usually chosen near lakes and rivers and in basins well protected from the searing wind and harsh snowstorms.

The richest pastures are located in the north to northcentral forest-steppe and steppe. Today large areas are used for agriculture and are lost to the pastoralists. In former times Kazaks used to set prairie fires there to rejuvenate the vegetation and increase productivity of the pastures.

Livestock Requirements

Vast areas are necessary to maintain the livestock. A horse requires at least twenty hectares (49 acres) of pasture annually in the steppes, and a sheep needs from five to seven hectares (12-17 acres). Both have to have two to five times that area in the desert and semiarid steppe. The various domestic animals have diverse requirements for pasture and are differentially adapted to nomadic migration, water shortages, and winter conditions. These factors thus affect herd composition. For example, cattle and camels cannot cope with deep snow without human assistance. Sheep and goats can graze for themselves if the snow depth is less than ten to twelve centimeters (4-5 in.). On the other hand, horses can easily get forage from beneath twenty-five centimeters (10 in.) of snow or more. Thus, it is clear that horses and small livestock are the most appropriate species for the northern steppe and forest-steppe regions. This pattern of livestock preference is characteristic of groups all over the Eurasian steppe belt, from the Kalmyks and northern Kazaks in the west to the northern Mongols in the east. Camels are more reliable than horses in the southern semiarid steppe and deserts. For this reason camels and sheep predominate in the herds of the Turkmens, southern Kazaks, and southern Mongols. Cattle are poorly adapted to long migrations, but are more appropriate for seminomadic to sedentary conditions where provisions for supplemental feeding are available. Thus, there are far more cattle in the herds of seminomads and those settled on farms than in those of true nomads. The Kazaks borrowed cattle from the Kalmyks in the eighteenth century, and cattle continued to be of minor importance to them until very recently when the size of their herds increased along with greater sedentism.

As a result of these factors, the composition of Kazak herds varies from one region to the next depending on local conditions. Despite variations in species proportions within herds, however, one value system prevails throughout the Kazak territories: camels are the most highly valued animals, horses are second, sheep third, and cattle fourth. In the past wealthy stock owners had the largest herds of camels, horses, and sheep and were more completely nomadic. Cattle were the main livestock of the poor, sedentary commoners. Large herds and their demands for vast pastures led to the dispersed patterns of Kazak settlement and the low population density of just one to one-and-a-half persons per square kilometer (0.39 sq. mi.).

Seasonal Migrations of the Herds

There is much variation in the distances covered in yearly migrations by different groups of Kazaks, ranging from 30 to 650 kilometers (19-404 mi.) depending on the geographic conditions and cultural traditions. In some extreme cases in the nineteenth century, the length of seasonal migration routes was over 1,000 kilometers (621 mi.) in one direction. The longest migrations are referred to as meridional since they are made chiefly in a north to south direction. Smaller movements of the herds are more typical today. Seasonal pastures are much closer to one another in the north, where the lengths of individual routes are only between 5 and 100 kilometers (3-62 mi.). In the north migrations can be radial, like the spokes of a wheel, as well as meridional. In addition, there are many more choices of winter campsites in the north because of the richer supply of natural water resources. In the south, winter camps are more rigidly associated with particular geographic features like lakes and river valleys.

In the north winter pasture sites are chosen with respect to the grazing demands of sheep. During the critical winter period horse herds are driven up to 250 kilometers (155 mi.) away from the sheep herds to avoid competition. To emphasize the danger of competition between different species, the Kazaks say, "A hundred sheep will be satisfied with what one horse requires." Wintering horses in northern pastures allows more intensive exploitation of local forage, providing horses with the superior grasses of the forest-steppe and the steppe and protecting them from the *djut* that is more characteristic of the south.

Herding horses away from the other livestock and the camp is possible because of their great mobility. Horses are supposed to be able to cover up to fifty kilometers (31 mi.) a day through snow. The average horse herd, whether communally or individually owned, consists of 400 to 600 horses that are driven and controlled by two or three highly skilled horse-herders. Thus, while the other domestic animals stay close to the settlements and are controlled by many residents, horse herding is much more nomadic and involves a smaller number of people. Those horses that are excluded from herd migrations and are left to graze in protected areas during the winter are emaciated horses, workhorses needed in the village, milk mares, mares foaling in winter, and prized racehorses.

In the event of an unusually deep snow, the Kazaks bring the various animal herds together for grazing. The horses go into an area first to break the snow crust with their hooves and eat the tips of the grass. They are followed by camels and cattle that eat the middle parts of the grass stems. Finally, sheep and goats finish the feast by eating close to the roots. Under extreme conditions, then, horses become rescuers of the herds and sustain the wealth of the pastoralists. In other cases people shovel the deep snow with implements and even their hands to open wide trenches so that their sheep can forage. To minimize losses, wealthy stock owners divide their horse herds into smaller units that are dispersed over different areas and tended by their poorer relatives. Under this practice, both parties have specific rights and obligations toward each other. In short, it is not easy to herd horses in winter, and the Kazaks say, "A poet-singer can herd horses in summer, but only the bravest of the brave can do it in the winter."

In mid-March the herd owners divide their herds into small breeding groups, much like the family bands observed among wild horses. Each new group contains eight to nine two-year-old mares and one stallion of four years. The group is segregated in a stable or by hobbling the females and tying all of them to a rope that is tied around the neck of the stallion.

In the early spring pregnant mares that were taken out to graze are driven back home to foal so that the newborns can be housed temporarily indoors. At the moment of foaling, a person is supposed to strike the mare three times, saying "Be a pacer," "Be a runner," or "Be milky." The Adai, one of the Kazak tribes, deliver the foals of well-bred stallions on luxurious carpets. According to their belief, if one cannot manage this, the colt might lose its parents' fine qualities.

The nomadic Kazaks try to leave the winter grounds as quickly as possible in the spring to allow regeneration of the winter pastures and to drive poorly fed livestock to fresh meadows in the north or up into the mountains. The initial migration to the summer grounds resembles a parade. After all material property is loaded onto the backs of camels, the first camel is led by an elegantly dressed young woman on horseback. Colorfully adorned girls on nicely decorated horses follow alongside the caravan. Large horse herds and sheep flocks bring up the rear. Once armed warriors, seated on the fastest steeds, galloped in front of the procession.

The starting day of the trek to the summer feeding grounds is marked by a festival in which each family prepares an elaborate feast for visitors. The most respected elder selects the starting day, usually sometime in mid-May. Because newly born animals of the various species differ in their abilities to migrate, the different kinds of livestock are kept and driven separately. Since the colts begin to follow the mares very early, horse herds can be kept several kilometers away from the temporary spring camps.

At this time of year, the pastoralists busy themselves with animal grooming, breeding, gelding, branding, and milking. The Kazaks usually begin to break in the yearlings in the spring, riding on the colts' backs until they are tired. If they are training an adult horse, they keep it hungry for two days before mounting it.

Whereas snow cover is the critical factor for herding during the winter, heat and aridity are the major concerns in the summer. In China summer pastures are situated primarily in the mountains. The Kazaks try to keep livestock close to natural water resources. If none can be found, they dig wells. Common folk move only two to three times per summer. The rich herd owners have to be more mobile, because they need more pastureland to enable their vast herds to reach maximum weight. Fresh pastures allow animals to achieve a good weight during the summertime. The old Kazak proverb, "A rich man's campsite is inviolable," reflects the rule that once was honored within each clan. In general the pastures were divided among various clans, and a stranger avoided staying too long in alien territory because of possible punishment.

As in the winter, the different types of herds are kept apart while grazing. Horses are pastured radially from eight to fifteen kilometers (5-9 mi.) around a central spring or well and sheep three to five kilometers (2-3 mi.) from it, unless a river or stream is available nearby. Most of the livestock are kept at the camp at night, except for the horses, which are pastured at night. Nocturnal grazing avoids the daytime heat and the irritating biting insects that distract the horses while feeding. The milk mares are kept in the camp during the day, but they and the colts join the herd at night. The horse herd may be driven into the camp twice a day for drinking, if necessary.

The Kazaks work hard during the summer, producing and storing dairy products and manufacturing needed materials, like hides, cordage, felt, and wool cloth. From September on through autumn, they begin to wean the colts from the mares. Special wooden devices are put around the colts' jaws to keep them from reaching the udder.

In the late summer the nomads return to their winter camps. On their way they visit autumn pastures, migrating in groups of up to several hundred households. Thus, in the autumn the herds are much larger and have to move faster than in other seasons. Upon reaching the winter grounds, the nomads again disperse into small groups that occupy separate pastures not far from one another. The main slaughter for meat takes place in the late fall, and the meat is frozen or prepared for use throughout the long winter.

The Household and Personal Possessions

Nomadic Kazaks must have dwellings that are portable. One form of housing used by Kazaks is the yurt, a felt house that can be quickly assembled or dismantled (figure 2). Yurts were and in some cases still are the house of choice for many nomadic Asian groups, including those in Afghanistan, Tibet, Kyrgyzstan, Mongolia, and northern China. The complete house can be set up in about two hours and disassembled in a little over an hour, using the labor of only three people. The yurt is supremely well designed for mobility. Usually three or four horses or camels can carry the disassembled house units, and an equal number of pack animals are needed to carry the contents. Women traditionally set up and take down the yurts, although at times men may be called in to assist with the heaviest poles.

The walls of yurts are made of a wooden latticework frame consisting of eight to twelve trellis sections that fold up like an accordion when not in use. When it is time to set up the household, the one-and-a-half-meter-high (5-ft.-high) sections are opened out and lashed together to form a circular enclosure. Made of red willow saplings, they are bound by leather thongs and wool or horsehair ropes that run through holes drilled at each of the intersections of two perpendicular poles. A gap is left on one side of the circular structure to accommodate a sturdy door frame to which a brightly painted wooden door is attached. The floor of the yurt provides between twenty and thirty square meters (215-323 sq. ft.) of floor space and is generally about five to six meters (16-20 ft.) in diameter, although a sumptuous one can reach twenty-five meters (82 ft.) across. The roof frame consists of willow sapling rods that open out in a radial pattern, much like an enormous umbrella, with a large hole in the center for the smoke to exit. Horsehair rope is used to lash the roof spokes to the trellis wall frame and thick felt sheets are then wrapped over the top and around the outside of the yurt to provide the roof and wall coverings. These too are lashed securely to the lattice wall frame with rope.

2. Kazak camp, showing a yurt, clay oven, and small ramada, in Tian Shan Mountains, Xinjiang Uygur Autonomous Region of northwest China. (Photo by Sandra Olsen)

For the most part a yurt is designed to hold an older couple, perhaps one of their married sons, his wife, and their small children. The larger ones, however, can accommodate as many as twenty people. In different seasons or according to their needs, the family can expand or contract the dimensions of the yurt. A tall yurt is built during the summer to improve ventilation, while a lower one is constructed in the fall to keep the warmth close to the floor. If the people are migrating from one camp site to another over a long route, they can just spread the roof supports open, cover them with felt, and crawl under them to sleep rather than set up the whole house. The thick woolen felt protects the people from the hot sun during the summer months and from the cold and damp in the winter. During the winter the central hearth warms the yurt quite efficiently. A yurt was once the only dwelling for the southern Kazaks year round. In the north, however, traditional people spent their winters in subterranean dwellings made of turf or in log structures with six to eight walls, resembling Navajo hogans. Modern villages on collective or privatized farms in the north consist of rectangular Russian-style log or frame houses. In China and Mongolia the people may live in brick houses in the winter.

3. Inside a typical yurt with a Kazak family at Tian Chi (Heavenly Lake), Xinjiang Uygur Autonomous Region of northwest China. The two small children danced for their guests while the mother served tea containing sheep fat and a variety of cheeses and breads. Note the lattice framework of the walls, the radial roof supports, and the colorful wall hangings. (Photo by Sandra Olsen)

4. Young Kazak girls embroidering velvet bags and saddle blankets at a camp at Tian Chi (Heavenly Lake), Xinjiang Uygur Autonomous Region of northwest China. (Photo by Sandra Olsen)

The interior of a yurt is not only warm and comfortable, but also extremely beautiful (figure 3). Intensely colored woolen rugs are laid face down over the roof poles so that they show through between the framework, forming an ornate ceiling. Similarly, the interior walls are covered with vibrant, finely stitched cotton quilts. The floor may be bare ground, sheets of plywood, or a low wooden platform. Felt rugs decorated with appliqué are spread over the floor. Bedding and pillows are then placed on the floor on either side and in the rear, opposite the front door. Silk curtains provide privacy for married couples. The area near the entrance is reserved for kitchen equipment, while the rear serves as the reception area and sleeping quarters. The head of the household and his wife sleep on the right, while the son and daughter-in-law sleep on the left beside the clothing, trunks, and horse tackle.

The nomadic Kazaks minimize their possessions because of their need to keep their loads light on the journey. The contents of their homes consist of a cauldron, a teakettle, a few dishes, the necessary bedding, wooden chests to carry their belongings, and colorfully stitched cloth or leather bags hung from the trellis to hold food and odds and ends. Spare saddles and bridles are hung inside out of the weather.

To a large extent, even the clothing of Kazak people is adapted to their nomadic life-style and inclement climate. A horseman generally wears a white cotton shirt trimmed with embroidered patterns under a darkly colored velvet jacket. The trousers are loose-fitting to provide freedom of movement while riding. Leather riding boots are also a necessity. Intricately embroidered hats are still worn by both men and women. The women, who ride astride like the men, may wear trousers for riding, but normally prefer long dresses.

Clothing, like the houses, is elaborately decorated with embroidery and appliqué work, all done by the women of the household (figure 4). The women also make felt from sheep wool to be used for the yurt coverings, rugs, saddle blankets (figure 5), and so forth. They weave woolen rugs for the floors and walls of the yurt. To protect the family from the extreme cold, women stitch fur hats, coats, and gloves. The most-prized possessions of the household are the embroidered wall hangings (figure 3), each of which can take a woman two years to complete.

Horses in Kazak Culture
Horse Breeds, Types, and Colors

Each Kazak tribe once had its own breed that was, accordingly, named after the tribe. The three most ancient breeds mentioned in Kazak myths were the Argymak, Karabaiyr, and Kazanat, all of which were ridden by warriors. All three vanished during the nineteenth century.

Cutting across breed lines, the Kazaks categorize horses into three major types and several minor types, primarily for their suitability to perform certain tasks. The three major types are the Berik (workhorse), the Zhurdak (intermediate type), and the Zhuirik (racehorse). The Berik is a strong, sturdy horse possessing qualities that make it useful for herding sheep, driving cattle, and transporting people and products. Generally, Beriks are small in stature with robust legs and short, thick manes and tail hair. These are primitive traits, resembling those of the wild Przewalski horses (see chapter 3). Their strongest attribute is their remarkable endurance, regardless of harsh climatic conditions, food and water shortages, or heavy work conditions.

The Zhurdak is an intermediate type between a workhorse and a racehorse. Most are taller, thinner, and faster than the Beriks. Their best quality is their ability to maintain their stamina over lengthy distances. Because of this attribute, they are preferred for long migrations, short migrations under arduous conditions, and tracking horse thieves. With sufficient training, they can become excellent trotters.

The Zhuirik is a racehorse that is used primarily in short races of two to ten kilometers (1.25-6 mi.). The best Zhuiriks, however, can maintain a high average speed over distances of forty to one hundred kilometers (25-62 mi.). Racehorses vary in size, but the tall, strongly built ones are favored. Desirable traits are intelligence, agility, maneuverability, and, of course, speed. Zhuiriks are ridden to herd horses and are ideal for rounding up stragglers that have wandered off. Of all the horses, Kazaks value Zhuiriks most of all. People believe the ability to run fast is inherited through the female line and hence try to preserve the purity of a line of good runners through controlled breeding. The colts are trained by special experts. Other types recognized in the Kazak classification scheme include trotters, amblers, pacers, traveling horses, and even horses specifically chosen to be ridden by clan or tribal ambassadors.

In the same way that Arctic people have a large vocabulary for snow and Peruvian Indians for potatoes, the

5. Kazak man with his horse at Tian Chi (Heavenly Lake), Xinjiang Uygur Autonomous Region of northwest China. Note the ornately embroidered saddle blanket. (Photo by Sandra Olsen)

6. Herd of the Kazak breed of horses in north-central Kazakstan, showing typical bay coloring. (Photo by Sandra Olsen)

Kazaks have over 300 words for horse colors. The most frequent color among the herds is what Westerners would call bay (figure 6), but Kazaks further distinguish sixty-two subtypes of that shade. Their favorite colors for horses are dark gray and speckled. A gray horse is associated with the "cult of a cloudless sky." If a man comes from good family origins, he is said to be descended from a dark gray horse because it represents wealth and fortune. White represents purity, justice, and honesty in the Kazak culture, so white mares are chosen occasionally to be sacrificed at important occasions such as the sudden appearance of a relative after a long absence, the finding of a relative that was missing in battle, the ending of a livestock plague, honoring a newly elected khan, or the strengthening of a truce. In order to indicate ownership of a particular horse, the horse-herder brands the colt's thigh and notches its ear in a characteristic manner. When horses are rounded up in a herd, each horse-herder checks off his horses based on their coat colors and types, rather than by merely counting them.

Equine Veterinary Practices

Kazak pastoralists use a combination of both folk veterinary medicine and techniques familiar to the West. For instance, the Kazaks cut into a tumor and pack it with grain and roots of a medicinal herb. In the case of stomach pains, they give the horse a powder made from dry snake skin dissolved in water. Blood-letting, cauterizing of open wounds, stitching of lacerations, and bone-fixing are practiced on horses. The Kazaks' knowledge of parturition techniques is quite impressive. Treatments are also known for about thirty kinds of equine diseases. Epidemics are a serious threat, however, because the shortage of antibiotics means that disease can sweep through the land and kill thousands of animals within a few months.

The Many Utilitarian Roles of Horses

Hunting once played an important role in Kazak subsistence. To hunt prey, horses were used, along with whips, spears, bows and arrows, lassos, and later the gun. Wild onagers (Asian asses) were hunted from horseback for their delicious meat and the useful leather they provided.

More important than their use in hunting was the role horses played in Kazak military life in the past. A warrior had to be a superb rider, first and foremost. Excellence in riding allowed him to approach his enemy swiftly, effect a surprise attack, and vanish suddenly before retaliation could occur. The Kazaks' chief weapons were originally designed primarily for mounted battles. Among a warrior's arms were a composite bow, iron-tipped arrows, a saber, a lance, and a thick whip.

In the nineteenth century and even in modern times, horses have been used to make hay, to harrow, to thresh grain, and to pull carts and sleighs. Throughout history and continuing on into the present, horses have served as an important source of food, in both the milk and the meat they provide.

Horse-related Equipment and Tackle

Wheeled vehicles are sometimes utilized for seasonal migrations in the north, while pack animals (horses and camels) provide the primary means of transport in the south. Carts pulled by oxen are used primarily by the seminomadic Kazaks. The great majority of Kazaks ride only horses; it is considered shameful to ride a camel or an ox, especially since the latter is a symbol of poverty.

Horse tackle is highly ornate among the Kazaks. There are several local styles of saddle. The popular *kazak eri* saddle consists of a birch frame that can be elaborately decorated with gilding, silver, and semiprecious stones on the most valuable ones. Pack saddles are worn by packhorses. Women's saddles are the most beautiful. The seats are covered with leather, and a felt sweat cloth is placed underneath. Kazak bridles consist of leather headstalls and reins with iron bits. Specialized craftsmen occupy themselves with the production of horse harnesses. Stirrups are either wooden or steel. Horse blankets and saddle bags are usually quite colorful and may be made of felt, woven cotton, or embroidered velvet. For special occasions bright tassels may be added to the bridle. Riding crops and whips consist of a sapling handle with either a short or a long rope of braided leather (figure 7). Horses are not normally fitted with shoes except in icy conditions, and then only those that are being ridden are shod.

The Kazaks have only a few types of pastoral implements. A *kuruk* is a long birch pole with a hair loop at the tip that is used to catch horses. Horse hair lassos serve the same function. Leather or horsehair hobbles, iron hobbles, and special three-legged hobbles are employed to keep horses from escaping or wandering very far. Wooden or stone basins are used to water the livestock.

Some pastoral implements, like a tether for a colt, a colt's halter, a bridle, and a pole snare (*kuruk*), have magic qualities. These are rarely given away by their owner, and it is forbidden, especially for women, to step over a tether or a snare. Violations of these rules can result in grave misfortune.

7. Seven-year-old Kazak boy on horseback, Tian Chi (Heavenly Lake), Xinjiang Uygur Autonomous Region of northwest China. (Photo by Sandra Olsen)

Products from Horses and Other Livestock

Meat and dairy products are the main foods in the nomads' diet. They milk practically all of their domestic animals—camels, horses, cattle, sheep, and goats. Milk products are their chief staples from early spring until late fall. Kazaks have a wide variety of recipes for processing their dairy products and preparing their meals, but they rarely use fresh milk. Several kinds of hard and soft cheeses, as well as yoghurt, butter, and other products are made.

Koumiss, a fermented drink made from the curd of mare's milk, is their favorite beverage. Today it is still regarded as an extremely healthy drink, said to contain everything required by humans, including protein, fat, carbohydrates, salt, and five times the amount of vitamin C found in cow's milk. The Kazaks believe that *koumiss* can cure forty diseases, and the fate of a sick person is questionable if he or she does not consume *koumiss* or horse meat. This mildly alcoholic beverage (ranging from about 1 to 2.5 percent alcohol) is prepared in skin bags or wooden barrels. A ferment is added, and the milk is whipped for a long time—the longer the better—to aerate the milk and stimulate fermentation. Grains of the previous year's dried *koumiss* are the preferred fermenting agent, but lacking these a horse's thigh, horse meat sausage, fresh horse skin, a horse tendon, or even a copper coin encrusted with verdigris may be added to initiate fermentation. *Koumiss* can be made in a day, after which it is poured out into various vessels or a deep wooden bowl. Its flavor is affected by the fermentation process and the container in which it is prepared. Kazak people value *koumiss* prepared in a skin bag most of all and distinguish several kinds of *koumiss* based on taste and quality.

Various wooden vessels are utilized in the *koumiss* economy, as well. These include large wooden bowls with lids for storage, carved scoops for dipping out the *koumiss*, and cups with handles for drinking it. In general *koumiss* requires a whole set of specialized vessels. On the other hand the same wooden vessels can serve to whip either *koumiss* or butter.

Like other Inner Asian nomads of Turkic origins, the Kazaks traditionally arrange a solemn ceremony of communal *koumiss* drinking after the first annual mare milking. Members of the community and other guests, especially those who look after the mares, are invited. The ceremony begins with a prayer to the horse protector *Kambar-ata*. He is asked to be gracious, to reward the herd with fertility, to protect the people from enemies and evil in general, to provide a mild winter, and to maintain peace. Women begin the ritual *koumiss* drinking, after the drink is offered to other guests in an order based on their social status, from the most respected *aksakals* (leaders) to the poorest commoners. Even youngsters, seated near the yurt entrance, are served *koumiss*. This is the only event during which women's wrestling takes place.

In the autumn a purification ceremony is held to signify the end of the milking season. During the festival women drink the remaining *koumiss* because it symbolizes fertility. Generally, any celebration, especially weddings and funerals, provides justification for *koumiss* drinking.

There are more than forty terms for *koumiss* in the Kazak language. Its importance in Kazak life and their world view is reflected in their proverb, "Marry a girl if she has a good mother," that is, if her mother is good at preparing *koumiss*. It is thought a sin to pour out leftover *koumiss* from a cup or to spill milk on the ground in general. This is considered an irritation to ghosts that might provoke misfortune for the person responsible. Several highly nutritious drinks are produced by mixing *koumiss* with the milk of other animals. Children are fed these beverages for their health, and herders take the drinks with them to the pastures for refreshment.

Both wild and domestic animals provide meat as a staple for the nomads, especially in winter when there is a scarcity of dairy products. Each family owns a large cast-iron cauldron in which meat is boiled. Animal slaughters take place mainly in November and December, and chiefly young male horses and sheep that are not suitable for breeding are fattened beforehand in preparation. Up to ten horses, two camels, and thirty rams are slaughtered in late fall by the wealthier households. Poor people, on the other hand, kill only one goat or one sheep. The slaughter is performed according to tradition, whereby the animal's legs are tied and it is tumbled onto its side. Its legs are oriented toward the west and its head to the south. Usually the owner carries out the slaughter, although he may ask a relative or a friend to do it instead.

The day of slaughter is considered a holiday and many relatives, friends, and neighbors are invited to partake in a feast. On the menu is Kazak-style meat, consisting of boiled mutton or horse meat with raw onions and greens. If the main dish is mutton, then the appetizers are horse heart, lung, and liver served with tea. The bulk of the meat, however, is stored for the long winter and spring. The flesh of fattened mares and especially tender colts is preferred for long-term storage. Meat is frozen for storage in wooden boxes outside the house, corned (preserved in brine), or dried. Smoked horse sausages containing meat and fat are prepared without fail. To smoke them, they are hung below the smoke hole of the family yurt. Horse fat is highly valued in winter, when it is easily assimilated to provide calories for warmth and energy. Horse meat is supposed to strengthen the human body during illness.

In addition to milk and meat, horses provide the people with useful skins. Hide is used extensively for vessels, clothing, and other things. To prepare it, a skin is first soaked in milk curds for about a month, after which it is cleaned of fat and dried. It is then softened and made more flexible with the aid of a notched wooden tool. In the spring skins are smoked over stone ovens by special craftsmen.

Various kinds of vessels for carrying *koumis* are made from horse skins: large ones for *koumiss* preparation, medium-sized ones for transporting it, and elaborately decorated flasks to hold individual portions of *koumiss*. Horse skin bags made from five hides are so big that a person has to be on horseback to churn the milk inside. Still bigger are those made from ten to twelve hides; these have to be hauled on carts when full.

The skin of camel necks is used in the production of nicely decorated vessels employed in mare milking. The Kazaks also use skin buckets to lift water from their wells. Bags for small items are produced from the skins of horse heads. During the last century a herdsman's shoes were often made from the skin of a horse's leg.

Horsehair is an extremely useful material in the steppes, serving as the primary raw material for making ropes, cords, and lassos. A simple kitchen knife is used to cut the hair. How the hair is cut depends on the sex and age of the horse. The hair of the manes and tails of yearlings is removed completely. The forelock is left alone on two-year-old mares and stallions, but the mares' tails are partially trimmed. Fortunately for the horses, the hair grows back.

In the past horse shoulder blades were hafted onto long wooden handles and used as scoops, skates were made from the cannon bones (metacarpals and metatarsals) of horse legs, and musical percussion instruments were made by tying two horse hooves together. Horse manure was one of the major sources of fuel for cooking and warmth, but has been replaced by wood and coal.

Folk Medicine

The Kazaks employ products from the horse, as well as some horse "magic," in folk medicine. In cases of prolonged illnesses, they wrap a sick person in a skin of a freshly slaughtered horse, a mare's skin for a man and a stallion's for a woman. If the treatment helps, the skin is sprinkled with flour and kept indoors for three days so that it will not be touched by the wind. Horse skins are used in this manner in the autumn, while sheep skins are utilized during the summer. Sometimes medicine men make a pure black horse jump over a sick person three times to drive out a "black spirit." In one ritual an illness or misfortune is transferred from the patient into the skull of a horse. A horse's hoof is also used for magical curing. During a difficult childbirth a mounted man is supposed to attack and beat the woman's yurt, fire his gun, and thrust a sabre or dagger into the ground while shouting, "Devil, go away."

In addition, the Kazaks use horse products in a more tangible way to treat illnesses. They believe in the power of horse sweat and use it against throat cancer, gastric diseases, ulcers, the plague, typhus, and other diseases. They also use horse bone, hair, fat, liver, kidneys, stomachs, and excrement for medicinal purposes. *Koumiss* is highly recommended for pulmonary diseases and chronic illnesses, as well as for nervous diseases. Medicine men use *koumiss* to treat tuberculosis, anemia, stomach ailments, and many other diseases.

Social and Religious Roles of Horses

The world view of these nomadic pastoralists is significantly affected by their reliance on the horse. Even their ways of expressing space and time reflect this dependence. Distance is measured by how far a horse can run at the races. A "foal's run" equals five kilometers (3 mi.), a "colt's run" is around ten to fifteen kilometers (6-9 mi.), and a "stallion's run" is thirty to forty kilometers (19-25 mi.). The distances between camps and pastures are gauged according to these units. To measure the passage of daylight, the Kazaks use mare milking activities, which the women perform about five times a day. A person might say that something will take place "at the time of the second mare milking" or "two intervals between mare milkings" (each interval being one to one-and-a-half hours). In the case of long trips, they measure time according to how many days it would take to reach their destination by horseback. The outstanding place horses have in the Kazak culture can be further demonstrated by their terms for "left" and "right," which are respectively "the side where the whip is kept" and "the side from which a horse is mounted."

Religious Beliefs

The Kazaks originally were animists but now are Sunni Muslims. They, however, retain many old beliefs. For example horses are thought to have a powerful, mysterious protector named *Kambar-ata*, the horse creator who teaches people how to make *koumiss*. The Kazaks also believe that horses are created from the wind. They esteem battle horses, and those that save their masters from danger and misfortune are the favorite characters of epics. It is forbidden to beat a horse, a sheep, or a camel on the head or to kick one. Their skulls and bones embody supernatural forces, so one should not tread on them. The skulls of horses are sometimes displayed on a pole or on top of a rock for ceremonial purposes. The Kazak belief system contains a whole hierarchy of sacrificial animals, surrounded by elaborate norms and sanctions. A white mare is sacrificed very rarely and only for extraordinary events, such as those relating to war and peace, or for the sake of the whole clan or tribe. At peace negotiations the important men from both sides have to dip their fingers into the sacrificial blood, which conveys a high level of responsibility.

Birth

The horse accompanies a nomad throughout his or her life and plays a role in all of the rites of passage. At childbirth southern Kazaks ask if the newborn is "a shepherd" (boy) or "a horse-herder" (girl), which refers to the fact that the daughter ideally will eventually receive forty-seven mares when she marries. The baby boy's umbilical cord is tied to a colt's mane or a ram's horn to symbolize male reproductive abilities—his source of wealth and prosperity. A very archaic custom that survives among some eastern Kazaks holds that a baby boy should be wrapped very tightly in cloth and passed through the right stirrup of a mounted person of great prominence so that the child will inherit his outstanding qualities. Traditional Kazaks put small pillows between the baby's knees and feet when swaddling him, so that his legs will grow in the correct shape for riding.

The first time a boy is seated in the saddle, at the age of three, is considered the most important event in his life. This act is performed at a ceremony of devotion to horses. Kazaks believe that the child's fate can be predicted through the first horse he mounts. During the ceremony the boy is blessed by respected old men of the community, who wish him fortune, glory, and happiness throughout his lifetime. By five years of age, a Kazak boy can mount and ride a horse by himself, and by seven he is able to assist his father in herding (figure 7).

Weddings

In traditional wedding ceremonies the horse serves as a symbol of wealth. Horses are the major components of the bride wealth (gifts given by the groom's parents) and the bride's dowry. Marriage negotiations can take as long as three years, during which time various payments are made between the bride's and groom's families. At the initial matchmaking ceremony up to forty-seven two-year-old mares might be given to the couple by the bride's parents as "wedding livestock." Two or three years later, the bride's parents receive many highly valued gifts, including between forty and fifty horses from the groom's family. The final payment by the groom's family to the bride's family consists of another thirty to fifty horses, as well as other valuables. The bride brings a dowry into the marriage that is composed of textiles, clothing, a yurt, various cooking and serving vessels, bedding, and, most important, several good horses.

According to tradition, the exchange between the two families means that several persons receive other gifts. The bride's father receives a fine horse with a valuable harness. The bridegroom has to present a horse to the owner of the yurt where he stays while visiting the bride's community. A horse-herder receives a horse for showing the herd to the matchmakers, and the list goes on. While meeting with matchmakers, the bride's father has to present an expensive gift to the groom's father. That gift includes a whole herd of horses and a special saddle horse. The matchmakers employed by the bride's family receive a gift when they first visit the bridegroom's community. They then transfer ownership of a horse from the bride's father to the groom.

On the eve of the wedding celebration, when almost all of the bride wealth and dowry have been paid, the bridegroom dresses the finest horse he can find with an expensive bridle and a good saddle and rides to visit the bride. Just outside the camp he dismounts and allows the horse to be taken in ahead of him by his friends. The friends hand the reins of his horse over to the bride's sister or close relative, who later receives a present from the groom for her duty of tethering the horse. Sending in the horse ahead of the bridegroom is an extremely meaningful symbol for the Kazaks, expressing both a devotion to and confidence in his hosts. This is understandable when put in perspective, since a person who finds himself in an alien camp without a horse in the middle of the steppes is essentially helpless. The bride's family stages an elaborate party for the groom and presents him with a horse. The wedding ceremony itself is arranged only after all of the bride wealth has been paid and the dowry is presented. To inform people of the completion of payment, the most beautiful woman of the community puts on the bride's wedding headdress and rides the groom's horse.

The matrimonial ceremony is held at the bride's home, where the bridegroom appears in his finest clothing, mounted on an ornately decorated horse. The man who presides over the ceremony stands holding a horsewhip tied with a piece of red silk, while singing songs that tease the couple. Another man enters with a horsewhip in his hand and joins in with his own song. The bride's veil is lifted by the groom with a horsewhip. As she curtsies, everyone joins round to see her face. There are many forms of entertainment during the wedding festival, of which horse races are a very important element.

Before leaving for the bridegroom's place of residence, the bride has to choose a horse from her father's herd. At parting, someone wraps a piece of meat in a scrap of cloth and waves it back and forth over the horse's head so that good fortune will accompany her. To show her hesitance in leaving her family's camp, the bride resists mounting her horse and pretends to fall off. Finally, the married couple departs and heads for the groom's home. There the young man's relatives and neighbors get acquainted with the girl and bestow numerous gifts upon her, a horse being the most honorable kind.

Polygyny to ensure many offspring was once widespread among wealthy persons. A traditional saying is, "If there are many mares, then there are many colts." The Kazaks, who are still patrilineal, value wives, and they place great significance on the bride's chastity. The young couple spend their first night in a white yurt. Adjacent to it a horse wearing an expensive harness is tethered and an oriental robe is hung beside it. If the groom is satisfied with his bride, he comes out and dons the robe, mounts the horse, and rides to her father with the good news. If not, he can rip open the horse's stomach, shred the robe, slash the yurt, and demand the bride wealth be returned.

Conflict and Crime

Generally, the violation of marriage rules can result in interclan enmity, once including horse stealing and armed clashes. In the past livestock were stolen from the offender in retaliation as a common means of finding justice and restoring the balance among the Kazaks. This practice of "an eye for an eye," known as *barymta*, demonstrated both strength and bravery. One could win prestige, glory, and great respect among his relatives and neighbors through horse stealing, and it was not considered a disgrace among highly respected people. To protect their own herds from these raids, horse-herders used peculiar wooden poles with bulb-shaped tips to fend off the robbers. In past times the theft of livestock was practically the only kind of stealing that took place. Therefore, a family could leave its yurt unattended for long periods with no fear of it being robbed. The Kazaks believed that in some cases livestock stealing could actually prevent misfortune or rescue a person from it. On the other hand, a *barymta* was often followed up with punishment in the form of another *barymta* or a bloody raid.

By the nineteenth century a large fine, greatly exceeding the price of the stolen livestock, was established to discourage stealing. As an example one thief had to turn over twenty-seven horses and a camel to his victim for the theft of just one horse. The majority of the compensation for killing an enemy was paid in horses—a murderer or his relatives had to pay 100 horses for the taking of a human life. If the murderer's clan agreed to pay this, a symbolic gift was first sent to the victim's clan. This present included various highly symbolic items, among them was a horse with its tail cut off. Usually, they did this to a horse whose owner had already died, since cutting off the tail of a man's horse was considered a serious threat upon his life. The act of cutting off the tail of a man's horse is treated as the equivalent of murder and penalties can be assessed accordingly. It is clear that the horse is the main subject of Kazak common law, whether it be the purpose for a crime or the principal part of the fine.

The most disgraceful and cruel punishment in the past was death by being torn into pieces by feral horses. A corpse of a punished person was sometimes tied to the tail of a horse that then dragged it all over the local area. For some minor crimes a person was covered with soot, forced to hold between his teeth a rope that was tied to a horse's tail, and made to run after the horse.

In forming alliances or making truces, ambassadors from different clans or tribes would meet in one group's village. The ambassadors would always send their horses in ahead of themselves as a sign of peace, since they would be highly vulnerable in the steppes without horses for transportation or as a means of escape. The resident khan would then send his personal horses out of the camp to where the ambassadors awaited. Thus, both groups could hold each other's horses hostage temporarily and good faith was shown on both sides.

Death

A Kazak man never parts with his personal horse while both are alive, and his horse continues to play an important role at the funeral ceremony. After a man's death, his personal riding horse is tethered to the mourning yurt, where its forelock and tail are trimmed. Then a messenger rides all around the camps crying and shouting, "Oh, my dearest." The funeral horse with its trimmed tail is the main feature of the funeral procession. The deceased person's saddle is put on it, his fur coat is draped over the saddle, his whip is fixed there, and his hat is put on it backwards. The horse is then driven past several mounted girls wearing men's hats, also put on backwards. The widow wears a black shawl and follows the horse. Then camel and horse herds are driven in the procession, followed by armed riders on horseback. Many mounted women surround the funerary caravan. An old proverb refers to carrying the deceased on a litter when it says, "Speak, my eloquent tongue, before you are taken away on the wooden horse." Following the ceremony the horse is herded with the rest of the horses for a year and then slaughtered at a special funerary feast. Several other horses and some sheep are also slaughtered for the feast, which is held near his grave. Horse races are organized so the deceased can listen to the thunder of hooves.

Equestrian Sports

Horse races of various kinds are extremely popular among the Kazak people. They are held at almost every public gathering, including annual holidays, markets, weddings, circumcision rites, funerals, and sacrifices. Men and women alike travel long distances to participate in and observe the races. Both long and short cross-country races are among the most popular equestrian competitions. These range from just 1,200 meters (3,937 ft.) to as much as fifty kilometers (31 mi.), and horses of particular age groups are chosen for certain races. The Kazaks claim that their best horses can cover sixty kilometers (37 mi.) in an hour. Special highly skilled trainers are assigned to prepare the horses for the races. Because a valuable prize is awarded to the winner, trainers never share their trade secrets with anyone else. In one case in the early nineteenth century, the first prize was 150 cattle plus a slave. Under those circumstances a winner could instantly become very wealthy from a single race, much like our lottery.

The famous equestrian sport *buzkashi*, meaning "to steal a goat," is popular among the Kazaks (figure 8), as well as other Turkic nomads all over Central Asia and Afghanistan (see chapter 6). It involves a contest over a goat carcass between two teams of riders who try to capture it and bring it to the goal. In their attempts to grab the carcass quickly, players often pull out tufts of hair and pieces of the goat's skin. The riders and horses crowd together as they struggle to get the carcass. As a result, the game can be extremely risky and often results in serious injuries to the players. White bandanas are often tied around the heads of all the riders to make them highly visible in order to avoid accidental blows to the head. Sometimes the goat is thrown at the doorstep of a yurt to bring the household good luck.

8. Kazak men playing buzkashi, or "steal the goat," in north-central Kazakstan. (Photo by Barbara Pitman)

Even more dangerous are fencing competitions that resemble medieval knights' tournaments. The rivals, carrying lances, are protected only by a light chain-mail suit and an oriental robe. The defeated rider, knocked down from his saddle, is often badly mutilated. Sometimes one or even both riders are killed. Women are known to occasionally participate in these tournaments.

The sport of wrestling on horseback seems outlandish, but is far less dangerous than fencing and many other competitions. In this sport each competitor tries to drag his opponent down from his saddle. Another game involves riders trying to pick up silver ingots or coins tied in scarves while riding at high speed to demonstrate their equestrian skills. The rider has to lean down with his head near the ground to pick up the scarf. Many of the riders fall off their horses and tumble head over heels, sometimes breaking a bone or two. One of the old traditional games involves a struggle in which two riders try to seize a plate of meat from each other. Pursuing a young woman on horseback provides another opportunity for a young man to show off his riding abilities. The young woman is given a head start on her own horse and the young man attempts to catch and kiss her. Further tests of skill include a complex program of equestrian sports—jumping, lassoing competitions aimed at pulling one's opponent to the ground, and horseback archery. All of these contests play a role in training young boys for the hard life as herders and, in the past, as warriors. Women once competed in many of these events alongside the men and also took an active part in defending their camps against armed raiders.

The Changing Kazak World

Modernization has severely affected the life-styles of these nomadic pastoralists, primarily because of forced sedentism inflicted on them in the past eighty years in Kazakstan and more recently in China. Despite all of the changes, the living attributes and symbols of their culture can still be observed today, especially in Mongolia and northwest China. Many of these Kazaks in China and Mongolia continue the old nomadic life-style described in this chapter, with only minor modifications. Those in China plant small plots of grain at the base of the Tian Shan Mountains and leave the elderly and a few adolescents to care for the fields while the rest of the people move their herds and their camps to fresh pastures in the mountains for the summer, using the traditional migration routes.

Today life is very different for those living in Kazakstan. Although they now have political independence, their land is divided into large privatized farms. Most Kazaks are completely sedentary and either work on the farms caring for livestock and raising crops or in industry in the cities. Small family groups are allowed to move the herds along parts of the traditional migration routes, however, and this practice may increase in the future. The horse is still extremely important in their lives, both economically and socially. The old traditions associated with rites of passage, like weddings and funerals, still persist and are actively carried out in some areas.

Contact between Kazakstan and China and Mongolia has strengthened in recent years, but this does not herald the return of nomadic pastoralism to Kazakstan, as might be expected. At the time of this writing, the Kazakstan government is providing economic incentives for neighboring nomadic Kazaks to move from China and Mongolia and resettle in Kazakstan. Because many of the state collective farms have been privatized and little land remains unclaimed, it is difficult for these new immigrants to earn a living according to their traditional nomadic life-style. In their new situation these self-reliant nomads are finding themselves in the unenviable position of being without herds or grazing rights and having to work as laborers for other people.

Reading List

Allen, T. B. "Xinjiang." *National Geographic* 189(3) (1996), 2-43.

Bacon, E. E. "Types of Nomadism in Central and Southwest Asia." *Southwestern Journal of Anthropology* 10 (1954), 44-68.

Dunn, S. P. and E. Dunn. "Soviet Regime and Native Culture in Central Asia and Kazakhstan: The Major Peoples." *Current Anthropology* 8(3) (1967), 147-208.

Forde, D. "The Kazak: Horse and Sheep Herders of Central Asia," in *Man in Adaptation: The Cultural Present*, ed. by Y. A. Cohen. New York: Aldine Publishing Co., 1968.

Hudson, A. E. *Kazak Social Structure.* New Haven: Yale University Press, 1938.

Jackson, W. A. D. "The Virgin and Idle Lands of Western Siberia and Northern Kazakhstan." *Geographical Review*, January 1956, 1-19.

Krader, L. *Peoples of Central Asia.* Bloomington: University of Indiana Press, 1963.

Olcott, M. B. *The Kazakhs.* Stanford, CA: Hoover Institution Press, 1987.

Pierce, R. A. *Russian Central Asia, 1867-1917.* Berkeley: University of California Press, 1960.

Tranquilla, J. "The Shepherds of Kazakhstan." *The Shepherd* 39(3) (1994), 10-12.

Tursunbayev, A. and A. Potapov. "Some Aspects of the Socio-Economic and Cultural Development of Nomads in the U.S.S.R." *UNESCO International Social Science Journal* 11(4) (1959), 511-24.

Winner, I. "Some Problems of Nomadism and Social Organization Among the Recently Settled Kazakhs." *Central Asian Review* 11 (1963), 246-67, 355-73.

Winner, T. G. *The Oral Art and Literature of the Kazaks of Russian Central Asia.* Durham: Duke University Press, 1958.

Eight

THE PROLIFERATION OF HORSE BREEDS

D. PHILLIP SPONENBERG

A breed is usually defined as a group of domesticated animals all of which are similar enough to be *logically* classified together and that, when bred to one another, produce offspring that are likewise similar to the original group. This is a genetically based definition and implies that each breed is at least somewhat genetically uniform and distinct from other breeds.

The history of horse breeds and breeding is a long and complicated story. Some breeds occur as isolated pockets of local horses that have evolved into distinct genetic pools. These are breeds in the narrow sense, but there are very few isolated breeds of horses. Most modern horse breeds are based on populations that have had varying and repeated introductions of outside horses. This interbreeding was brought about by increased human mobility made possible by the horse itself. These intercrossed breeds are much more common than the genetically isolated ones.

Basic Breed Groups

Horse breeds occur in several basic groups that were developed because humans need a variety of horses to perform different tasks. The largest and heaviest are the *heavy draft breeds*, which reached their peak of development as a consequence of the widespread use of horses in agriculture. Immense size and weight characterize this group of horses, which have a cobby (round and stout) conformation rather than the rangy (long and tapering) conformation of most riding horses. *Light draft breeds* were similarly developed for agricultural work but were also employed to haul loads. They resemble the heavy draft breeds but tend to be shorter and less massive in build.

Those horses bred specifically for use as carriage or road horses are usually called *heavy harness horses*. They are normally tall and less massively built than the draft horses, tending to be rangier and more angular instead of extremely cobby. This group of breeds, also called *warmbloods*, are increasingly being used for riding instead of for harness work. *Saddle horses* are lighter still and usually not as tall as the heavy draft horses and the heavy harness horses. These familiar horses, bred to be ridden, are today the largest and most varied group of breeds.

Ponies, while usually arbitrarily defined as shorter than horses, can also be cobby and tend to be used in harsh and somewhat deprived environments. Pony breeds used for riding are taller and rangier than those used as general purpose horses, which are cobby and short. *Miniature horses* are the truly tiny horses and ponies that are bred more for interest than for specific performance traits. (See the Appendix for a list of the major breeds and their basic characteristics.)

Facing page, 1. Brabant gelding. (Photo by Evelyn Simak)

Horse breeds of all categories have generally become more refined over the years. This is the result of horse breeders' conscious selection of horses that will produce offspring that are pleasing to the eye as well as functional.

Human society has changed over the centuries, and the relationship between people and horses has kept pace with these changes. As a result of cultural evolution that includes an acceleration of technology, the guiding philosophies and goals of horse breeding have been altered. These modifications have caused some breeds to change, others to disappear, and still others to become more common than in the past. (This process of change and loss has also been true, to a somewhat lesser degree, of other domestic livestock.) Organizations such as the American Livestock Breeds Conservancy have begun working with breeders of rare horses in North America to assure that these breeds do not become extinct. Some breeds that are currently rare may be needed in the future, even if they are not popular or appreciated today. If anything is certain, it is that our expectations and decisions will be different in the future from today, so it is important to have a great variety of breeds to fit specific and changing needs.

Draft Breeds

Draft horses were developed during the last 500 years or so in order to have large animals for heavy and demanding agricultural work. A secondary use of these horses has been to move heavy loads along roads. When roads were still deep mud tracks, oxen or packhorses worked better for transport than did wheeled vehicles drawn by large powerful draft horses. With better roads, however, the draft horse quickly superseded both the ox and the packhorse as a means to transport goods.

The current draft horse breeds of the world can be put into only a very few main breed groups. One of these is a group of numerous breeds that originated in western Europe. All of these breeds can be traced back in one way or another to horses from Belgium and all tend to be very massive. This is the main group that was used to improve heavy draft horse breeding throughout Europe. A second group contains only a few breeds from central Europe and springs originally from horses in the Alpine regions of Austria. A third small group of breeds comprises indigenous Nordic horses.

Western European Draft Horses

Development of the large western European group of draft horse breeds has proceeded for centuries. Although these breeds originally had close ties, many are now very distinct from one another. The most central to this breed group is the *Belgian Ardennais* horse from Belgium and neighboring areas of France. This horse is of moderate height but is extremely massive and very cobby and round. The usual colors are roan or bay, with chestnut occurring commonly as well. The Belgian Ardennais comes from an area of low hills and light soils where truly massive size was not needed for plowing. The same genetic pool that created the Belgian Ardennais gave rise to the *Brabant* horse (figure 1), a much taller and heavier horse in the lowland areas of Belgium, where heavy clay soils occur. A third and closely related breed is the *Flemish* horse, which is similar to the Brabant but more likely to be chestnut in color.

Old and important offshoots of the Belgian and Flemish horses include most of the other western European heavy draft horses. The British developed the *Clydesdale* (figure 2), *Shire* (figure 3), and *Suffolk* to be general purpose horses. The Scottish Clydesdale (named for the River Clyde) was used both as an agricultural horse and for hauling coal to Glascow. The breed dates to the 1830s. The Shire, developed in England in the 1700s, is more massive than its close relative the Clydesdale and at eighteen hands[1] is one of the largest horses in the world. It can pull five times its own weight, which can be as much as 1,524 kilograms (1.5 tons). Despite its size and strength this breed is gentle and tractable. Both the Shire and the Clydesdale have feathering (long hair) on their lower legs and are somewhat less stoutly built than the breeds from Belgium. Clydesdales are generally bay, while Shires tend to be black or gray. Horses of both breeds tend to have white marks on the head and legs. The Clydesdale's high step gives it a flashy appearance.

The Suffolk, the third of the British heavy draft horse breeds, is very different from the Clydesdale and Shire. Shorter and more massively built, it was used more in agriculture than for road haulage. This horse is always some shade of chestnut color and lacks feathering, and breeders discourage white markings. Suffolks were developed as a practical horse that could withstand long, hard hours of strenuous work with very little care and food. Although still very rare, the Suffolk is increasing in numbers because of a renewed appreciation of its qualities as a no-nonsense workhorse.

The French draft horses all fit into the western European grouping, and the *Percheron* horse is one that has had widespread international popularity. It is a tall, heavily built horse that was originally used primarily in agriculture, although lighter types were also employed in hauling loads on the road. The Percheron is black or gray, generally with little white on it. It is characterized by a very finely shaped head, reputed to have come from some Arabian influences. This breed was originated to pull the large French stagecoaches known as "diligences." Because it was very popular for its farm work, the Percheron contributed heavily to the early wave of draft horse breeding in America in the late 1800s and early 1900s. It is still highly valued as a good heavy draft breed, although its popularity in the United States has lagged behind that of the American Belgian.

2. *Clydesdale mare. (Photo by Evelyn Simak)*

The western European group of breeds became the common "improver" of farm horses throughout most of Europe. As a result most of the heavy draft breeds in Europe are fairly uniform. This is the case primarily because most of them had large-scale introductions of Brabant, Belgian Ardennais, Clydesdale, Shire, or Percheron breeding fairly recently. Together these improver breeds have remained distinctive within this large western European group of breeds.

American breeders have developed only one draft horse breed, the *American Cream Draft Horse* (figure 4), having imported all others directly from western Europe. All American Creams are descended from a foundation

1. A hand is a unit of measure equal to ten centimeters (4 in.).

3. Shire Horse. (Photo by D. Phillip Sponenberg)

mare called "Old Granny" that was born in 1900. Unfortunately, this breed was expanding in the Midwest in the twenties and thirties just as farm mechanization was beginning to occur, so it never had a chance to become very popular as an agricultural power source. Of moderate size compared with the other heavy draft breeds in the United States, it is still powerful and massively built. As the name implies, this horse is light cream in color and generally has pinkish skin and amber eyes.

All of the imported American heavy draft breeds are in the western European group with origins in or ties to the Belgian Ardennais horse. The *American Belgian* horse is a direct offshoot of Belgian and Flemish horses brought to the United States in the 1800s. It differs from its European ancestors, however, in that it is generally chestnut or a very typical blond sorrel color with white mane and tail and, although it is heavy, it is less cobby in build. Despite its size it is very gentle and has a relatively small appetite. Though introduced into the United States later than other heavy draft horse breeds, American Belgian horses have slowly supplanted the others to become the most popular heavy draft horse breed in America today. As tractors eliminated the dependence on draft animals in the 1950s, the American Belgian's numbers plummeted but have been steadily increasing since the 1970s.

The six draft horse breeds that have been used in the United States are the American Belgian, Percheron, Clydesdale, Shire, Suffolk, and American Cream, somewhat in that order of popularity. Valued in their own right, these large horses were also crossbred with western range horses to provide what were called *farm chunk* horses. Farm chunks were generally around fifteen hands and 680 kilograms (1,499 lb.). Horses of this size were usually preferred for working on most American farms, but it took a heavier stallion from the draft horse breeds to produce such horses from the light western mares. Because of this crossbreeding, the lighter versions of the heavy draft breeds, like the Belgian Ardennais itself, were never imported from Europe. The six most popular breeds in America are among the heavier and more massive of the draft breeds known around the world, partly because of this historic use in crossbreeding and not necessarily because horses needed to be heavy for effective work on most American farms.

Alpine Draft Horses

The second important type of draft horse is the Alpine, consisting of the *Noriker* of Austria and a few other breeds closely related to it. The Noriker (figure 5) is a horse of moderate height (about fifteen hands) that weighs about 680 kilograms (1,500 lb.). Norikers originated in the Alpine regions of Austria and have a long history of maintaining the same form throughout their existence. They are powerful but less massive than most breeds in the western European group and tend to have longer backs. Their colors are commonly bay, black, or chestnut and occasionally roan. Some have an unusual and distinctive leopard pattern. Norikers are important horses in central and eastern European draft horse breeding, although all of the breeds based on the Noriker type have been influenced by the horses of the western European group as well. The Noriker is still common in its homeland, where it is highly regarded for both agricultural work and road haulage.

Nordic Draft Horses

As old breeds that tend to be isolated from the other two groups, the Nordics include the *North Swedish Horse* and the *Finnish* draft or *Finnish Universal.* These horses are about the same size as the Alpine draft horses, but there is a tendency to produce within these breeds a more massive type for farm work as well as a lighter type for trotting competitions. Nordic horses are strong and serviceable. They are usually bay, black, or chestnut with other colors appearing more rarely. Although in build and style they resemble the Noriker than they do the western European draft breeds, Nordics are genetically distinct. (The Norwegian *Dole Gudbrandsdal* is sometimes included in this group, but more often is considered with the ponies.)

4. American Cream Draft Horse. (Photo by D. Phillip Sponenberg)

Heavy Harness or Warmblood Breeds

The heavy harness or warmblood breeds are interesting in terms of their historic importance as well as their present popularity. The term *warmblood* (formerly crossbred, half-bred, or three-quarter-bred) was coined in the 1960s to distinguish these somewhat intermediate horses from the draft horses (coldbloods) and the lighter saddle horses (hotbloods). It is unfortunate that *warmblood* connotes a mixing of two types, since warmbloods are in reality a separate type of horse. Some of the warmblood breeds were originally closely related to the original coldblood horses, from which the heavy and light draft breeds were developed. Other members of the warmblood breed group, at least originally, represented a branch of the family tree of horses that is totally distinct from both the draft horses and the lighter riding horses.

For centuries warmblood horses were used for general purposes. They were big enough to work effectively as farm horses, energetic and dependable enough for work in harness on roads, but also durable and athletic

5. Noriker mares. (Photo by Evelyn Simak)

enough for use as cavalry mounts. Their prime use, however, has been as harness horses. Currently, their function and breeding are changing after centuries of use as carriage and light farm horses to their present widespread use as riding horses. The popularity of warmblood horses is growing for performance or sport riding, including dressage events, cross-country events, and jumping competitions. This trend is changing the selection goals for this group of breeds.

Warmblood breeds are becoming the most genetically homogeneous group of horses. These breeds all began as isolated genetic populations that were strongly and proudly associated with their areas of origin. In the era after World War II, however, communication and transportation greatly improved, leading to considerable intercrossing of the various warmblood breeds. In contrast, the individual breeds of heavy draft horses have become very distinct from one another because the original three types underwent centuries of isolation. This isolation is particularly true of the large Ardennais-related western European group.

Several of the warmblood breeds were once restricted to specific geographic regions but are now popular internationally. These include the *Trakehner, Oldenburg, Holstein, Hanoverian, Austrian Warmblood, Swedish Warmblood, Swiss Warmblood,* and *Friesian* (figure 6). All were originally carriage or light draft horses. In the past restrictive breeding policies in which mares could only be served by licensed stallions limited the choice of stallion as well as the direction of selection within the breeds. Breeding was usually run by a governmental or quasi-governmental committee that used very strict rules for selection, testing, and licensing.

Today the trend for most of these breeds is increasingly for licensed stallions to include representatives of other warmblood breeds as well as *Thoroughbreds* and even occasionally *Arabians.* This current direction has reduced the differences among these originally distinct breeds. Recent breeding has also moved away from the tall, heavy, rugged originals toward a still tall but somewhat rangier, lighter, and more-refined style. The present warmbloods remain larger than most other saddle horses but are generally smaller than they once were. The original style of warmblood horse still persists, however, in most of these breeds as minority types (especially the Groninger type of *Dutch Warmblood* and the *Kladruby* [figure 7]). There is a tendency to mate heavier individuals in most warmblood breeds with lighter ones in order to narrow the overall weight range. Warmbloods are commonly gray, bay, black, or chestnut, but some interesting duns, palominos, and paint patterns also occur at least occasionally in most of the breeds.

Against this backdrop of an increasingly homogeneous population of sport horses are some warmbloods that remain unique. Two of these are the *Cleveland Bay* from England and the *Irish Draught* horse. These both are old, tall,

6. Friesian horses. (Photo by Evelyn Simak)

rugged, lighter strains that represent the ancestral coldblood horse but are included in the warmblood classification because they lack the very round, cobby conformation typical of the present draft breeds. Both perform adequately in harness and in sporting events like dressage and show jumping. Prince Philip, for example, had a team of Cleveland Bays that he used in international driving competitions. Their major use, though, is in crossbreeding to produce sport-event horses. The usual cross is a Thoroughbred sire with a Cleveland Bay or Irish Draught mare. Because the crossbred foals are worth much more than the purebred foals, these two breeds

7. *Kladruby stallion. (Photo by Evelyn Simak)*

have become endangered as distinct genetic resources. The Cleveland Bay and Irish Draught horses are examples of how breeds that are ideal for crossing can become rare because of the low numbers of pure foals being produced. Breeders are taking steps to counter this trend, with the Irish Draught breeders having more success than those of the Cleveland Bay. Cleveland Bays, as the name suggest, are always bay in color and white marks are very much discouraged. The Irish Draught horse is commonly gray or bay, but some sport rarer colors such as dun and roan.

Light Horses / Saddle Horses

As with the draft and warmblood breeds, it is possible to divide the light horses into major groups by virtue of their genetic and historic relationships. There are only a few light horse breeds that are truly unique genetically. Many are combinations of the more distinct original strains, the primary ones being the Spanish and the Arabian (figure 8). There are a few other isolated pockets of

8. *Arabian mare. (Photo by Evelyn Simak)*

unique horses worldwide, but most breeds have been strongly affected by either Spanish or Arabian horses.

The Spanish horse has produced a variety of present-day breeds. Some recent archaeological evidence has been interpreted as suggesting that horse domestication was undertaken independently in Iberia, and this may be a reason that these horses appear different from the more eastern Arabian light horses (but see chapter 4). The most characteristic trait of Spanish horses is a convex nasal profile that sometimes extends into the forehead region.

9. Argentine Criollo gelding.
(Photo by Evelyn Simak)

They also have sloping croups (rumps), and low-set tails, although there is some variability in these traits.

The Spanish horse was an important export for Iberia as far back as Roman times. Following the Roman era there are two versions of the history of horses in Iberia. One is that the Moslem conquerors of this peninsula brought with them Barb (see below) and Arabian horses, but this theory is difficult to prove by historic documentation. The other is that the Moslem invaders actually availed themselves of an already superior Iberian horse and exported them back to Arabia and North Africa. Whichever version is correct, the Spanish horse does, indeed, appear to be different in conformation and character from the Arabian.

In the fifteenth and sixteenth centuries, the Spanish horse was used widely in Europe to crossbreed with various local strains in an attempt to improve them. Spanish horses were also traded far and wide, appearing as early as A.D. 1000 in Wales. In addition, the Spanish (and Portuguese) horses were taken to the New World by explorers and colonists to become the predominant horse throughout most of that hemisphere. While the numerous breeds derived from this base share some common characteristics, their differences are also interesting. These variations arose because of the specific selection goals of the breeders in the locations where the horses were raised for the intervening centuries.

The current horses in Spain and Portugal have been selected to be large, strong, handsome riding horses with a great aptitude for dressage. Uniformity of these traits is greatest in the Spanish *Andalusian.* Andalusians are usually fifteen to sixteen hands high. Today most are gray, but occasionally individuals are bay or black. This is in great contrast to the wide variety of colors present in this breed in the past. The Portuguese *Lusitano* is a closely related breed, but is somewhat more varied in color and slightly smaller than the Andalusian. The Lusitano is probably closer to the original Iberian horse, in part because of the Portuguese tradition of mounted bullfighting. This custom has preserved many of the original traits that allow Lusitanos to outperform other horses. A rare contemporary Spanish breed type is the *Sorraia,* a primitive pony (see "Ponies" below) that probably closely resembles the original Spanish horse soon after it was domesticated. Sorraias are generally zebra dun or grullo in color. They have the characteristic head, croup, and hip conformation that is so consistent across all Iberian breeds.

A major European offshoot of the Spanish horses is the *Lipizzaner,* which has become a central and eastern European general purpose horse. This breed has a long history of use as a high school dressage horse, most notably in the Spanish Riding School of Vienna (see chapter 6). The breed is fairly widespread in central Europe, where it serves as a light draft horse in addition to its riding uses. Lipizzaners are usually about fifteen hands. Their foals are dark at birth, but by their eighth year nearly all have lightened to gray. Other colors occur rarely. Lipizzaners mature much slower than other breeds but have great longevity. Many reach thirty-five years of age. They are closely managed and bred in six to eight different lines, depending on the stud. Some are the old, classic baroque horses with the amazingly convex heads. Others have a more moderate head conformation. Some have tails set on high, while others are more-typically Iberian with low-set tails. These variants are kept within the breed by maintaining the various distinct sublines. Because breeders periodically mate mares back into their own ancestral line, certain characteristics are concentrated within each lineage.

Another breed that is usually considered along with the Spanish group is the *Friesian* of the Netherlands. This breed is probably intermediate between the warmbloods and the Iberian horse. It is used in the Netherlands the way a warmblood would be, being both ridden and driven. Friesians today are uniformly black with very minor white marks on the head or feet and are also one of the few light horse breeds to have extensive feathering on the legs. Friesians are powerfully built horses about fifteen hands high with Spanish head and hip conformation.

10. Spanish Mustang. (Photo by Marye Ann Thompson)

In the Western Hemisphere the Iberian horse, introduced by the conquistadors in the sixteenth century, has persisted in a variety of breeds, one of which is the *Criollo* (figure 9) of Chile, Argentina, Uruguay, and Brazil. These horses are stocky, somewhat short (around 14.2 hands), and very durable. They come in a wide variety of colors, although duns and blue roans tend to be favored. The duns have a dorsal stripe and zebra-striping on the legs, much like the Przewalski horses. Some have a smooth lateral gait (running walk), although most have the diagonal trot common to most breeds, where the hind- and forelegs on opposite sides move forward simultaneously. Horse races in South America are often grueling endurance tests over hundreds of miles that have contributed to breeders' selection of horses with considerable stamina. Criollos have long been praised as ideal for nearly any task requiring hard use in riding.

Another important South American group of breeds that comes from the Spanish horses consists of the Peruvian *Paso* and the *Paso Fino* in Colombia, Brazil, and the Caribbean islands. Some exchange of bloodlines—usually from Peru to the other countries—occurs. These horses are small (fourteen hands high) but durable with a Spanish conformation. The paso, the gait for which these breeds are named, is a running walk with a smooth, four-beat lateral gait, as opposed to the diagonal, synchronous, and rougher trot of most horses. The uniformity of Paso breeds reflects the long history of selection for their gait and smooth, elegant conformation. They also have very good endurance for hard use and long rides. Most Pasos are dark in color, because this trait is generally favored by breeders. Some lighter or more unusual colors, however, do persist as minorities within these breeds.

The North American remnants of the Spanish horses are more variable, particularly in color, than the South American breeds. These *Spanish Mustangs* (figure 10) are small (13 to 14.2 hands high) and are generally finely built, durable, and wiry. Just as in the original imports from Iberia, the full range of horse colors occurs. The Spanish Mustangs are a combination of feral,[2] Native American tribal, and rancher strains that are all fairly similar in appearance and durability. Some are gaited like the Pasos from farther south. Of all the Spanish breeds Mustangs are the least standardized and have the least controlled breeding. As a result they provide an interesting look into what the Iberian horses must have been like five hundred years ago.

Intermediate between the Spanish and the Arabian horse is the *Barb* of North Africa, which shares many conformational characteristics with the Spanish horses. The Barb is light, somewhat small, and very rugged. It has the convex head, sloping croup, and low-set tail of the Spanish horses. Barbs are usually gray, although other solid colors also occur. The Barbary Coast, for which the Barb is named, has produced these horses for 2,000 years. Barbs were the horse of the Moors, who invaded Spain in the eighth century A.D. Because Barb mares are usually crossed with Arabian stallions, Barb horses are becoming very rare. This crossbreeding is changing the old-type Barb into something very similar to the Arabian.

Light horses in the Arabian group differ from Iberian horses in that they have a concave forehead and a straight nasal profile. They also tend to have flatter croups and tails with a higher set. The *Arabian* breed itself (figure 8) is the best known of this group. It is a highly refined, small horse (standing fourteen to fifteen hands high) that historically has been regarded for its durability. Arabian horses occur worldwide. While typical in the Arabian Peninsula and Egypt, important purebred herds also occur in Spain, England, Russia, Poland, and the United States. Their colors are generally gray, chestnut, and bay, or more rarely brown or black. Although spots are discouraged, some Arabians do possess them. Arabian horses are trotters with little or no tendency for an amble or the pacing gait that is so common in the Spanish breeds. The Arabian is valued for its beauty and purity, as well as for its movement and endurance. Its contributions to worldwide horse breeding is very important because of its use as a pure breed in crosses with large numbers of native breeds. As a result of the Arabian's growing popularity, the Spanish breed group has become increasingly rare.

Other eastern types related to the Arabian do persist, but none has an international distribution like the Arabian. One of these other breeds is the *Caspian* pony. This is a rare but important breed from northern Iran that is extremely small (only 9.2 to 11.2 hands high) but very horselike. These ponies are usually bay, gray or chestnut. Resembling miniature Arabians, they may be a very old version of the original strain of oriental horse. Some believe that they were the breed used in Mesopotamia from the third millennium B.C. until the seventh century A.D., when they disappeared from the records.

Another ancient and important breed related to the Arabian is the *Akhal-Teké* (figure 11) from the Turkmenistan area of Central Asia. These horses are larger than most Arabians and tend to be somewhat less smooth and elegant. Their heads are long and narrow; their limbs, very long and slender. They occur in the usual dark colors but also come in bright metallic shades of palomino and buckskin. The Akhal-Teké has been used for both racing and dressage.

At least some strains of the hardy Akhal-Teké are very similar to the famous horses used for millennia by nomads and warriors in the deserts of Central

---

2. A feral horse is one that has escaped from domestication and has become established in the wild.

Asia. These ancient horses were able to travel for three days across the desert without drinking water. Horses of the steppes of Central Asia were widely sought after for centuries as items of trade to both the East and the West. Consequently, the Akhal-Teké and related types have provided a prolonged and extensive base for horse breeds in both Asia and Europe. The Akhal-Teké is all that remains of this original fountainhead of breeds since the Soviet program of horse breeding involved crossing the various local light breeds with the Arabian and Thoroughbred, as well as with other breeds. This breeding program was undertaken to make the indigenous horses more refined and acceptable in international commerce. Only small pockets of the less-improved (but more-authentic) foundation strains still persist.

Almost equal in importance to the Arabian, because of its widespread use in crossbreeding, is the English *Thoroughbred* (figure 12). The Thoroughbred is a large riding horse originally based on a preponderance of eastern (Arabian) breeds. It emerged from breeding Arabian, Turk (perhaps similar to the Akhal-Teké or the Arabian), and possibly North African Barb stallions with English mares to increase the speed of local racehorses. The Thoroughbred is, therefore, highly developed for racing and riding. It continues to be crossbred with other breeds to foster their ability in these areas. The Thoroughbred has ultimately had more impact than either the Spanish or Arabian horses since it is bred with both the large warmblood horses and the small, light breeds of horses and ponies.

Abundant and widespread, Thoroughbreds exhibit some minor variations. In areas where selection is for a short-distance racer, their muscling tends to be shorter and blockier than in strains selected for racing ability over longer courses. Thoroughbreds all tend to have powerfully built rear quarters and a smooth elegant conformation. The combination of athletic ability and good looks is one of the major reasons that the Thoroughbred has been used so widely in breeding programs. Thoroughbreds never have gaits different from the usual walk, trot, and canter/gallop. They are the expected dark colors—bay, chestnut, gray, and black—with very rare exception. Their popularity derives from their success as riding and racing horses.

The ancestry of most other saddle horse breeds can be traced in varying degrees to Spanish, Arabian, or Thoroughbred breeding. The *American*

11. *Akhal-Teké stallion. (Photo by Evelyn Simak)*

12. *Thoroughbred stallion. (Photo by Evelyn Simak)*

Quarter Horse (figure 13) is one of the most numerous of these breeds in the United States. The name refers to its racing prowess over quarter-mile courses. The American Quarter Horse is a general-purpose riding and short-course racing horse that was originally based on a blend of English and Spanish horses from the East Coast of the United States. The major early influences on the American Quarter Horse shifted, however, when northern European settlers began to move west. As Spanish horses were encountered on the western frontiers, their genetic input increased and became predominant. Varying amounts of Morgans (see below), draft horses, and especially Thoroughbreds were bred with the predominately Spanish stock to develop the present-day American Quarter Horse.

Today's American Quarter Horse is generally fairly stocky, but within the breed there is considerable variation that includes individuals with a build similar to the Thoroughbred. American Quarter Horses are usually fifteen to sixteen hands high. Color varies, but body spots are not allowed. In addition to the usual dark colors are dun, grullo, palomino, buckskin, and roan. American Quarter Horses are popular because they are generalists that are bred to behave and appear differently depending on their intended use. Within the American Quarter Horse breed can be found individuals that excel at a variety of functions—racing, working cattle, rodeo events, pleasure riding, and sporting events.

The *Appaloosa* (figure 14) and the *Paint* are two breeds from the western United States that are closely related to the American Quarter Horse both historically and genetically. Both were originally based on Spanish Mustangs but now reflect a mix of influences similar to the American Quarter Horse. The Appaloosa breed was started in the American Northwest by the Nez Percés, Native Americans who lived in the Appalouse Valley of Washington. Both breeds differ from the American Quarter Horse in the desired color patterns. Appaloosa horses have a wide variety of symmetrical patterns generally centered over their hips. These patterns include mottling, white scleras, and striped hooves as minimal expressions, as well as varnish roans, blankets, leopards, and snowflakes (see the Appendix for definitions). The Paint horses, in contrast, are marked with asymmetric patterns, including tobiano and overo. The latter can be further split into frame overo, speckled overo or sabino, and splashed white. These color patterns, which were present in the original Mustangs, found favor among various Native American tribes. Both the Appaloosa and the Paint are used for the same wide range of functions as the American Quarter Horse.

A recent development in Mexico is the *Azteca* breed, a cross between the American Quarter Horse and the Andalusian that has resulted

13. American Quarter Horse stallion. (Photo by Evelyn Simak)

in an attractive and useful animal. This new breed combines the strengths and conformation of both parent breeds. This is an interesting concept given their common ancestry, even though the relationship is in the distant past.

Other saddle horse breeds are more distantly related to the common base of American Quarter Horses so widely used in America. Several of these breeds are gaited, meaning that they replace the usual trot of horses with a variety of closely related smoother gaits such as the amble, running walk, fox trot, and plantation walk. These breeds were originally based on Spanish horses, from which they, like the Paso breeds, inherit the tendency to be gaited. To the original Spanish base have been added other breeds to increase size and change appearance.

One of these gaited horses is the *Tennessee Walking Horse*. It is a large horse that has a spectacular "big lick" running walk, a four-beat gait intermediate between walking and running. Tennessee Walking Horses are taught to accomplish this exaggerated gait, although even without training they have an inherently comfortable running walk. Usually referred to as the plantation walk, their gait was developed to afford owners of large estates a comfortable ride while overseeing their lands. Tennessee Walking Horses are normally black, bay, or chestnut. *Missouri Fox Trotters* have a somewhat similar but less extreme gait. They are smaller, tougher, and more variable than the Tennessee Walking Horse and are favored for endurance riding. Missouri Fox Trotters come in a wide variety of colors and occasionally have curly hair.

One of the most highly developed gaited saddle horses is the *American Saddle Horse*, sometimes referred to as the *Saddlebred*. This is a large horse with a smooth conformation and flat croup. Some individuals have very long heads with convex profiles, similar to those of some Spanish horses. Saddle Horses have a gait called the rack, which has four beats with very high action. They are usually conservatively colored (bay, brown, chestnut, or black), but a few have brighter colors or are wildly spotted. Saddle Horses are popular at shows because of their flashy movements.

14. *Appaloosa mare with a varnish snowflake pattern. (Photo by Evelyn Simak)*

With the rising popularity of gaited horses, many new breeds and associations have been started. This is especially true in the Midwest and Appalachian areas, where breeds like the *Plantation Walking Horse* (or the plantation-style Tennessee Walking Horse), *Kentucky Mountain Saddle Horse, Mountain Pleasure Horse, Single-Footing Horse, Racking Horse,* and *Rocky Mountain Horse* have been developed. There are even *Walkaloosa* and *Tiger Horse* associations for horses of Appaloosa color that have a lateral gait rather than a trot. At least one of these breeds, the Rocky Mountain Horse, is the missing link in the chain from the Spanish horses to the rest of the gaited group. This breed commonly sports an unusual chocolate color with a light mane and tail.

In contrast to the gaited breeds are most other breeds that simply trot. The trot, which is the normal intermediate gait of horses, has been specially selected in a family of breeds that are raced as trotters and pacers. Trotters move the diagonal limbs together in their gait, while pacers move the limbs on one side of the body forward together at the same time. Trotters and pacers usually occur in the same breeds and are registered together. Both are generally raced in front of a small, fast cart called a sulky, although in Europe these horses are raced under saddle as well (see chapter 6).

The premier trotting breed in the world is the *American Standardbred* (figure 15). This successful breed was originally based largely on Thoroughbred bloodlines, although it has had many genetic influences. American Standardbreds are usually darkly colored or gray (with an occasional roan thrown in) and tend to be somewhat more coarsely conformed than the Thoroughbred. Because the American Standardbred is faster than any other trotting breed in the world, it has had a profound effect on other breeds like the French Trotter. A few other old trotting breeds, including the original Orlov Trotter and the Nordic draft breeds, still exist separately from this faster Standardbred group. All of the Nordic draft breeds have a lighter version used for racing at the trot. These breeds are raced only in competitions among members of the same breed, so there is no need to cross-breed them in order to increase their speed.

The *Hackney* is a trotter developed for driving light carriages rather than for racing. A number of different breed influences on the Hackney have resulted in a medium-weight carriage horse with an exaggerated trotting action. It carries its head and tail high as it arches its neck, creating a very showy look. Although Hackney horses tend to be dark in color, they also usually have much white on the legs and face. This coloration combines with their flashy action to make an elegant performance in driving competitions. They tend to be flat crouped and powerfully, but splendidly built.

The *Morgan* is a distinct American breed that began as a member of a small group of breeds from the Northeast. Originally Morgans were general-purpose farm, riding, and race horses in New England that were similar to a small light draft horse. The exact bloodlines of the founder stallion, owned by Justin Morgan, are the subject of much conjecture. The original Morgan was a small, somewhat cobby, chunk-type horse (fourteen to fifteen hands high) that was light enough to be very athletic. Today's Morgans vary from this original cob, popular for driving, to a refined, elegant, and spirited riding horse. Morgans tend to be very dark, although some are palomino or buckskin. In the past it was the colors that varied in Morgans, whereas currently it is their body style and movements that range from the characteristics of the older strains to those of the more-refined modern type.

The *Canadian Horse* is fairly close in build to the original Morgan. Also a small farm chunk, it possesses a good combination of riding, driving, and farm abilities. Canadian Horses tend to come in dark colors. They have not been modified to the same extent as some Morgan strains, thus they are more consistent with the original farm horses of the Northeast and Canada. Because they have become much rarer than they were in the past, they are fairly closely monitored.

Some horse breeds are based around colors rather than conformational or familial similarities. Included in this group is the *Pinto,* which is spotted similarly to a Paint but is allowed to vary more in body type than the Paint is. The Pinto sometimes has the American Quarter Horse conformation but may resemble the American Saddle Horse, Arabian, and others.

The *Palomino,* similarly, is a breed built around a color more than around a specific conformation or lineage of horse. Palomino horses have a range of conformational types, but they must be as close in color to a gold coin as possible. Their gold bodies are set off by nearly white manes and tails, making them very attractive indeed.

Yet another breed defined by its color is the *Buckskin.* This horse must be some shade of line-backed dun, including zebra dun, grullo (mouse dun), and red dun. Its conformation is usually one of a western stock or American Quarter Horse rather than of a more-refined conformational type, since tough range horses are generally preferred over flashy show animals.

The *American Albino, American White,* and *American Cream* are, as the names suggest, white or nearly so. True albinism, however, has not been reported in horses, and these breeds vary from truly white normally with dark eyes to cream colored with blue eyes. All have pink skin. They are general-purpose riding horses, unified primarily by their pale colors.

15. American Standardbred mare. (Photo by Evelyn Simak)

Another breed based on an external trait is the *American Curly* horse (figure 16). In the past it was called the *Bashkir Curly* since it was thought that the original horses were similar to Bashkiri horses in Russia. However, the curly horses from Central Asia are from the Lokai breed, not the Bashkiri breed. Curly horses have occurred worldwide in an array of breeds, including the Percheron and Missouri Fox Trotter. The American Curly has most of its foundation in feral herds from the western states, especially Nevada. In this breed the hair is very long and curly in the winter and less so in the summer. Some individuals have very wavy manes and tails, and many shed the mane and tail hair along with the body hair in the spring. American Curly horses, which are reputed to be docile yet tough, come in a wide variety of colors.

16. American Curly foal with a bay overo coat. (Photo by D. Phillip Sponenberg)

Ponies

The term pony really has two definitions. One is any horse under 14.2 hands in height at the withers. This definition includes many horses that are simply smaller than their cousins. The other definition incorporates conformation and behavior as well as size. Ponies by this second definition are generally of cobbier conformation and of somewhat more placid temperament than most horses. There are exceptions, but these characteristics certainly come into play when most people separate ponies from horses. Arabians, for example, are rarely considered to be ponies even though many of them do, indeed, qualify as such based on their height.

Ponies are an interesting group of small, useful breeds that have been selected primarily to fill specific local transportation and draft needs. Because ponies were locally produced and used, many small, regional breeds developed. To counter this trend, there was a move toward improving ponies that began around the beginning of the twentieth century. As a result of incorporating genes of Arabians and other breeds into pony stock, many local pony breeds that once were distinct now share similar characteristics.

A few unique pony breeds still do exist, although some are very rare. One of them is the *Sorraia* (figure 17) of Spain, which, as previously discussed, was the remnant of the original Iberian horse. Another primitive breed is the *Dülmen* of Germany. Although the Dülmen has a somewhat mixed gene pool, it still possesses predominantly primitive northern traits. These ponies are somewhat coarse and are generally some shade of line-backed dun or mouse dun. The *Konik* of Poland and the reconstructed *Tarpan* are also primitive. These both are supposedly close to the original wild European horse or Tarpan that went extinct in 1918. The modern Tarpan was reconstructed by interbreeding a variety of primitive Polish ponies, most notably the Konik, and persists now in forest reserves in Poland. These are small, cobby, and generally mouse dun with a dorsal stripe.

Another virtually indestructible and relatively unimproved breed is the *Mongolian Pony*. It is descended from the ponies that made the nomadic warring tribes of Asia such a threat throughout long periods of history. Although coarsely conformed by today's standards, the Mongolian Pony is very durable and strong and can work hard with very little care. Some Mongolian ponies have lateral gaits, which add to their usefulness as long-distance mounts.

17. Zebra-dun Sorraia stallion. (Photo by Evelyn Simak)

Nordic ponies form an interesting group that contains several breeds considered to be either small horses or large ponies. All these ponies tend to be selected for both riding and draft use. The *Norwegian Fjord*, the most widespread of these breeds, is always some shade of line-backed dun, usually pale zebra dun. Its trimmed, upright mane and its coloration make this breed look truly primitive. The Fjord is, in fact, a highly selected and successful general-purpose horse. Some strains of the Fjord horse are heavy enough to be considered almost light draft horses; others are much lighter and refined and are used solely for riding.

The *Gotland* is a small riding pony of Nordic strain derived from the island of the same name in the Baltic Sea. These were the horses of the Vikings. Gotlands were distributed around the whole Baltic area during the time when the Hanseatic League controlled trade throughout Denmark, Norway, Sweden, and to some extent London (from the 1100s through the 1400s). Occurring in a wide array of colors, Gotlands are the target of conservation efforts in Sweden as well as in America.

18. *Icelandic Horse stallion.* *(Photo by Evelyn Simak)*

One of the oldest and most unusual of the Nordic ponies is the *Icelandic Horse* (figure 18), which is between a true pony and a horse in size. The Icelandic has been bred in isolation and was traded to Britain to work in coal mines until the twentieth century. As a result it has contributed to horses from Scotland, Ireland, and the Isle of Man. In Iceland easy gaits have been highly treasured, so Icelandic ponies are highly selected to have a running walk in addition to the racking gait. It is interesting to see these traits in a Nordic line of horse, since the easy gaits are usually associated with breeds having a Spanish influence. While selection in Iceland has greatly favored particular gaits, it has disregarded color. As a consequence Icelandic ponies come in most of the colors known to occur in horses.

The British Isles have also been the source of many pony breeds. All these breeds were originally very distinct, but recently selection has favored a more-uniform conformation converging on that of the Arabian. One old-style pony is the *Shetland* (figure 19), which is cobby, hairy, and very small. In its native islands its toughness makes it useful for a variety of farm-related tasks. In America the Shetland has been used for showing and carriage driving, which favored selection of a larger, more flashy and elegant conformation than that of the ponies in the native islands. The *American Shetland*, a recognized breed in its

19. *Shetland ponies. (Photo by Sandra Olsen)*

own right, has some contributions from the Hackney pony, a refined driving pony from Britain that has been influenced by a variety of other breeds. Now both the original type and the show type of Shetlands are raised in the United States. Color varies widely in these ponies.

Like the Dülmen, Konik/Tarpan, and Sorraia, the Exmoor pony is a truly primitive breed. *Exmoor* ponies are raised on free range in the moors of southwestern England, and many are rounded up only once a year. In color they range from light seal brown to dark dun and have the lighter areas on the muzzle and belly that characterize most wild equids like the Przewalski horse. They are now very rare, but ongoing breeding programs are closely monitored to assure

20. *Connemara pony mare. (Photo by Evelyn Simak)*

21. *Welsh Mountain Pony stallion. (Photo by Evelyn Simak)*

that this unique resource does not become extinct.

The *Connemara* (figure 20) of Ireland is another old breed. Originally these ponies were rugged and somewhat heavy, but current selection favors the more-refined, tapered conformation. Both conformational types still exist side by side within the breed. The *Highland* pony of Scotland similarly varies from the original heavier, general-purpose conformation to a more-refined type. Dun is typical in the original, whereas gray is common in the modern ones. Many with the original conformation still persist today.

The Welsh ponies and cobs form an interesting concept in breeds. The *Welsh Stud Book* is divided into sections by conformation and height. The smallest breed, the *Welsh Mountain Pony* (figure 21) (Section A in the stud book), is probably the truest to the original. It is 12 hands or less in height and tends to be primitive. The *Welsh Pony* (Section B) shows the most refinement as a riding pony and is the result of crossing Spanish, Arabian, and Thoroughbred stallions with mountain ponies over the course of several centuries. (Wales was an active trading center even in the eleventh century, with horses being imported from Spain.) The Welsh Pony varies in height from 12 to 13.2 hands and comes in a wide variety of colors, although spots of white on the body are discouraged and in some countries even disallowed. The *Welsh Pony of Cob Type* (Section C) is a heavier driving pony. It has been influenced by a variety of heavier horses and can be a maximum of 13.5 hands in height. Finally, the *Welsh Cob* (Section D) is a heavy, sometimes tall (over 13.2 hands), general-purpose horse that easily fits in with other general-purpose light draft horses and cobs.

Historically, horses registered in one section of the stud book have been allowed to contribute to horses in other sections through interbreeding. The Section A ponies and the Section D cobs are probably more genetically isolated than the ponies in Sections B and C, but genetic material has moved among all of the sections. Although this movement is currently being discouraged, past breeding practices have resulted in a useful and handsome group of ponies and cobs. In some areas of Wales the local horses are a great source of pride, and good-natured local rivalry in shows and other competitions helps maintain their excellence.

Other British pony breeds like the *Dartmoor, New Forest,* and *Dale* are rarer than the ones already discussed. These all tend to vary between heavy and light conformational types depending on their desired uses, and solid colors are always preferred.

The United States has also contributed a few unique pony breeds to the worldwide array. The *Pony of the Americas* is a small version of the Appaloosa horse. Not surprisingly, bloodlines in this breed can generally be traced both to the Appaloosa and to pony breeds. A few are entirely of Welsh Pony breeding, since occasional leopard-patterned animals will appear in Welsh Ponies and other breeds. Ponies of the Americas, founded in the 1950s and used for small riders, are dependable, unpretentious mounts that incorporate willing hearts and flashy appearances in a very neat package.

22. Haflinger stallion. (Photo by Evelyn Simak)

With some breeds there is a problem of whether to classify small cobs as horses or ponies, much as has already been discussed regarding the Fjord and the Welsh Cob. One breed that falls right at the boundary between ponies and horses is the *Haflinger* (figure 22) of the Alpine region of Austria and Switzerland, with a related breed in Italy. Haflingers are always chestnut or sorrel, and often have very light manes and tails. They are used extensively for both riding and driving and are increasing popular as general-purpose cobs.

The smallest ponies are usually classified as miniature horses. Selection has given miniatures a more horselike appearance rather than the cobby conformation of ponies. The main breed of this group is the *American Miniature Horse,* which comes in a wide variety of colors. These are tiny animals (from nine down to even six hands in height) that are strong enough to be used for driving. The *Falabella* of Argentina is another extremely small strain that has been used extensively in some American Miniature bloodlines.

Summary

The wide array of horse and pony breeds in the world today is a consequence of the long and intimate association of horses and humans. Each breed is the result of human action and choice, along with some accidents of history. Each breed is tailored to meet a specific human need, and variation in breed types assures that these needs will always be met. Condensing the breeds into fewer and fewer conformational, behavioral, and size types and genetic strains is a modern trend. Such a trend, unfortunately, runs the risk of losing some of the rarer but still interesting breeds and conformational types.

Reading List

Clutton-Brock, J. *Horse Power.* Cambridge Mass.: Harvard University Press, 1992.

Edwards, E. H. *A Standard Guide to Horse and Pony Breeds.* New York: McGraw-Hill Book Company, 1980.

Goodall, D. M. *Horses of the World.* New York: MacMillan Publishing Co., Inc., 1965.

_____. *A History of Horse Breeding.* London: Robert Hale, 1977.

Heise, L., and C. Christman. *American Minor Breeds Notebook.* Pittsboro, NC: The American Minor Breeds Conservancy, 1989.

Hendlicki, Bonnie. *An International Encyclopedia of Horse Breeds.* Norman: University of Oklahoma, 1995.

Loch, S. *The Royal Horse of Europe.* London: J. A. Allen, 1986.

Sponenberg, D. P., and B. V. Beaver. *Horse Color.* College Station: Texas A&M University, 1983.

Nine

THE
ADVANCEMENT
OF EQUINE
MEDICINE

CORINNE RAPHEL SWEENEY

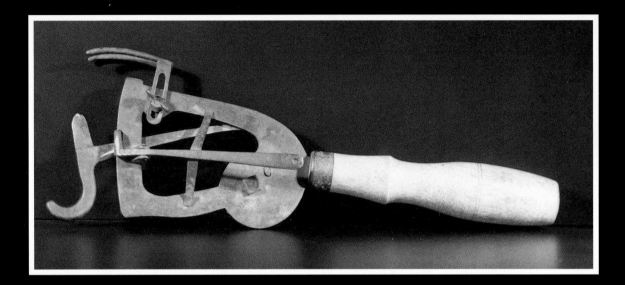

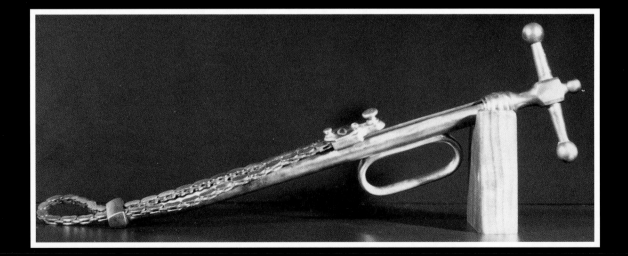

*R*eferences to the practice of veterinary medicine are found in the oldest records of civilization. The Babylonian code of Hammurabi (about 2000 B.C.) clearly stated the tasks of the "doctors of oxen and asses" and specified the fees that could be collected. The oldest written record of veterinary procedures is contained in the Egyptian papyrus of Kahun (about 1900 B.C.), a long medical treatise with a veterinary section. Surviving fragments show three incomplete prescriptions for animals. This inclusion of veterinary matter in the medical treatise indicates that veterinary medicine was highly regarded at that time.

The Early History of Veterinary Medicine

The most complete early writings about veterinary medicine survive from the Vedic period of India (about 2000-1800 B.C.). These documents show the high esteem that the ancient Hindus had for animal life and indicate that veterinary medicine flourished along with human medicine.

At this time in India, specialization in practice, a high level of professional ethics, and laws regulating veterinary services existed. The most celebrated veterinarian was Salihotria. For centuries, in deference to his reputation, veterinary practitioners were designated as Salihotria. About 250 B.C., during the reign of King Asuka, the first permanent veterinary hospitals were built in India. Today remnants of these hospitals, as well as all the edicts of Asuka relating to the treatment of animals, still survive.

Records of veterinary medicine in early western civilization are scant. Human medicine, however, did flourish in ancient Greece. By the sixth century B.C., when speculative philosophy developed, medicine had begun to move from the realm of magic and mysticism toward science. Diseases and their causes were studied and described, and the structures of organisms were investigated. In conjunction with the development of human medicine in Greece and Rome came veterinary medicine, with a focus primarily on the horse. A veterinary practitioner in ancient Greece was referred to as *hippiatros*, whereas the Romans called him *equarius medicus* (doctor of horses). Later the doctor of animals was designated as *veterinarius*, from the Latin word *veterinus*, pertaining to a beast of burden like an ox. From this comes today's noun *veterinarian*.

As a means of transportation for their armies, the horse was an important animal to the Romans (see chapter 5). Veterinarians accompanying the cavalry into Asia Minor conducted a high level of practice during the late Roman Empire. During this time, historians have conceded, veterinary medicine forged ahead of human medicine. The classic work *Hippiatrika*, a book about the diseases of horses, was written then. Many of the methods of diagnosis and treatment for the diseases of horses specified in it are still in use in one form or another.

Facing page, 1. The fleam (top), a modified version of a lancet, was used to make small incisions. It was designed so that it could not penetrate the body beyond a given depth, thus preventing injury to underlying organs. The fleam was commonly used to perform phlebotomies (bloodlettings). This particular fleam dates to around 1850. (Photo by Donna Woodall, courtesy of the International Museum of the Horse) The ecraseur (bottom) was an instrument used for castrating colts. One manufacturer's promotion claimed "no clamps, no firing nor twitching, nor any trouble afterward." This ecraseur dates to between 1885 and 1890. (Photo by Donna Woodall, courtesy of the International Museum of the Horse, Lexington, Kentucky)

In the fourth century A.D., Apsyrtus of Constantinople taught veterinary medicine to cavalrymen and wrote with some accuracy on contagious and infectious diseases of horses. At this time Roman blacksmiths fitted and forged the first iron horseshoes (chapter 5, figure 4). They also turned to the treatment of diseases in horses, learning their medical skills through apprenticeship, and for many centuries thereafter veterinary medicine became synonymous with farriery, the craft of the blacksmith.

The end of the fourteenth century ushered in the Renaissance, a 200-year period that was one of the most revolutionary and stimulating in mankind's history. While human medicine was making remarkable advances, veterinary medicine did not keep stride. Veterinary medicine remained in the hands of farriers until the latter half of the eighteenth century, when great animal plagues in Europe made reforms in the system of veterinary education necessary. It was realized then that the system of apprenticeship training for farriers could not meet the demand for well-trained veterinary practitioners. The first veterinary school, established at Lyons, France, in 1762, devoted most of its attention and resources to the diseases of cattle. The second school, built at Alfort, France, became known as the National Veterinary School and focused on equine diseases. Other European countries soon recognized the value of university-level education for veterinarians and also began to establish schools.

The History of Equestrian Medicine in America

Care for the health of horses in the United States is a very recent phenomenon compared with Europe and Asia. In the early history of the United States, trained horse doctors were virtually nonexistent. There were no graduate veterinarians in America until the early 1800s. Instead, as in early Roman days, farriers, trained in home remedies and treatments for lameness, cared for horses with medical problems. The first record of the American Congress paying a farrier for treating a horse was in 1775, when George Washington hired one to attend two ailing geldings that had recently been castrated.

Horses in the Military

On the fateful Christmas night of 1776, when George Washington led 5,000 men across the Delaware to Trenton, the troops were accompanied by hundreds of horses. Many of the horses were unshod and thus slipped on the ice. The number of dead horses at Valley Forge was so great that the soldiers could not bury them fast enough. The grim scene caused Washington to be concerned for the health of the camp as a whole. At that time the Revolutionary army had no farriers in its employment, and the lack of medical care greatly increased the number of horse casualties. On January 16, 1777, Washington ordered that forty blacksmiths be recruited to work in a shop in Pennsylvania to serve the military.

Prior to 1835 the American army had no official regulations regarding the veterinary care of their horses. Before the U.S. cavalry moved to Carlisle, Pennsylvania, in 1838, soldiers furnished their own horses, and either the quartermaster hired civilian farriers or the soldiers had to pay for shoeing and medical care of their own horses.

On March 3, 1863, an act was passed stating that "each regiment shall have one veterinary surgeon with the rank of regimental sergeant-major, whose compensation shall be $75.00 per month." Recruiting was difficult, however, since most veterinarians regarded the salary, rank, and social position to be too low. It was 1916 before the first army veterinarian was promoted to a commissioned officer.

The cost in lives of horses during the Civil War was vast. In just eight months in 1864, the cavalry of the Army of the Potomac required 40,000 replacement horses. Farriers were in big demand because an estimated 500 horses had to be shod in the Union Army every single day.

Veterinary Practice Through the Years

The kinds of diseases that struck horses most frequently in the early years of our country were glanders (a disease causing fever, swelling, and pneumonia), yellow fever, encephalitis, tuberculosis, and tetanus. Horses with leg fractures were put down, because there was little hope that they would ever be capable of carrying out their assigned functions. Farriers used a variety of home remedies of herbs and roots based on prescriptions developed in Europe blended with considerable superstition. Bloodletting, purging, and blistering were some of the more adverse forms of treatment. Another less severe treatment involved wrapping a piece of paper with mysterious lettering on it over an abscess.

By 1850 fewer than two dozen veterinarians had immigrated from Europe to America, and there still were no veterinary schools in the United States. During the last quarter of the nineteenth century, however, the number of veterinarians in the United States increased. Some were European immigrants, others came from schools in Canada, and for the first time there were graduates from schools in this country. The horse was the animal that received the greatest attention from U.S. practitioners during the first three quarters of the nineteenth century, since it supplied most of the power needed for transportation and farming. As the disease rate among livestock soared, however, the profession began to devote more of its attention to farm animals. Despite the increase in livestock veterinary practice, there was much concern in the profession when the bicycle, automobile, and tractor began to replace the horse. Some individuals actually feared the profession might become extinct.

By the end of the nineteenth century, veterinary school graduates were becoming more common in the United States, and proper medical treatments were becoming preferable over home remedies. A few of the doctor's instruments that might have been seen in a vet's office around 1900 are the oral speculum, the fleam, the ecraseur (figure 1 on page 176), the balling gun, tooth floats, tooth extractors, and the "humane horse-killer." The oral speculum was an instrument that allowed the mouth to be opened safely for examination. The fleam was a bloodletting device that eventually dropped out of use when people came to realize that draining blood did not cure people or horses. The balling gun shot large pills into the horse's throat. (Today pills are usually ground up, or the medication is given in liquid form through syringes.) Tooth floats are still used to file the horse's teeth to make them even. A tooth extractor, as the name implies, was employed to pull out a badly aligned or diseased tooth. The "humane horse-killer" preceded modern-day injections for putting down a horse with an incurable problem. The instrument was held with the end pressed tightly against the forehead of the horse and a bullet was then fired directly into the head, causing instant death.

Veterinary Education Through the Years

Several prominent persons in Philadelphia during the late 1700s and early 1800s tried in vain to set up a school of veterinary science. Dr. Benjamin Rush (1746-1813), one of the signers of the Declaration of Independence, lectured to his medical students at the University of Pennsylvania about the need to monitor the health of domestic animals. He recognized the risks of diseases spreading from the livestock to people. In 1792 Dr. James Mease, also a physician in Philadelphia, was the first to describe the outbreak of yellow fever in horses in America that led to the death of thousands of horses in Pennsylvania alone. Mease strongly advocated the development of veterinary science in this country to replace the self-taught farriers. Despite their struggles they did not succeed in opening a school.

Veterinary medical education in North America actually began with the establishment of private schools. From the mid-nineteenth century until 1927, they played an important role. Although the quality of private institutions varied greatly, it is estimated that nearly 10,000 veterinarians received their degrees from them. The first substantial veterinary schools in North America were founded in Canada. In 1862 the Ontario Veterinary School opened at Guelph, and in 1866 the Montreal Veterinary College was established. One of the strongest private schools in the United States was the American Veterinary College, organized in 1875 in New York City by a French veterinarian. In 1889 this school merged with the New York College of Veterinary Surgeons to form the New York-American Veterinary College. In 1913 it became a state institution known as the New York State Veterinary College of New York University until it closed in 1922. A private school that survived for thirty-seven years—from 1883 to 1920—was the Chicago Veterinary College, which awarded the M.D.C. (Medical Doctor Comparative) degree. Some other private colleges with a substantial number of graduates were the Kansas City (Missouri) Veterinary College, McKillip Veterinary College (Chicago), Indiana Veterinary College (Indianapolis), the Grand Rapids (Michigan) Veterinary College, and the Saint Joseph's Veterinary College (Saint Joseph, Missouri). The last of the private veterinary schools was the United States College of Veterinary Surgery in Washington, D.C. It was organized in 1894 and suspended in 1927.

In addition to the private schools there were a few early veterinary schools connected with universities, but they did not survive beyond 1918. The most notable were the schools of veterinary medicine at McGill University (Montreal) and Harvard University, and George Washington College of Veterinary Medicine (Washington, DC).

There were also the "quack" schools. These often had only one or two faculty members, and in some cases the requirements for a diploma were the reading of a book and the payment of fees. In addition, some offered a correspondence course leading to a degree. Naturally, these "schools" were a source of embarrassment to the developing profession.

Although private institutions made a contribution to the country's growing need for trained veterinarians, it was obvious that the future of veterinary medical education had to come through schools that were an integral part of established universities. Between 1862 and 1895 seven schools, still in existence today, were established. The first was the Ontario Veterinary College, affiliated with the University of Toronto, in Guelph, Canada. In 1879 the Division of Veterinary Medicine was created at Iowa State College. It was followed closely by the Veterinary Department of the University of Pennsylvania, created in 1884. Then came schools at Ohio State University (1885), the University of Montreal (1886), Cornell University (1894), and finally Washington State University (1895).

In 1885, a year after the University of Pennsylvania founded the School of Veterinary Medicine, it opened a veterinary hospital. Since horses were the primary patients, a blacksmith shop was attached to the hospital. In those early days many outpatients were treated without charge, and others remained in the hospital for only a nominal boarding fee. The fee structure for hospitalized animals in 1888 was one dollar per day for horses and mules, fifty cents per day for donkeys and dogs, and a quarter per day for cows, sheep, pigs, cats, and birds. This included the cost of medicines. A full set of shoes for a horse cost three and a half dollars. Until the advent of the automobile, the hospital provided two horse-drawn ambulances, one for large animals and the other for small ones. Among the horses seen at the clinic, the most common diagnoses were fistulous withers, chronic arthritis, quittor, azoturia (Monday morning sickness), colic, influenza, contracted hooves, and various dental problems.

Current Equine Veterinary Practice

Clinical equine medicine in the 1990s has become predominately a practice for companion and sport animals. The horse, formerly a beast of burden and a source of power, now serves as a leisure-time partner. Horse racing is a multi-billion-dollar industry. Trotting, jumping, and exhibition horses are of substantial public interest for spectators. Riding horses are now clearly in the category of companion animals.

In 1955, when public interest was minimal and the horse population of the nation was about three million, there were fewer than 100 equine practitioners in the entire country. By 1992 a survey of the American Association of Equine Practitioners showed an active membership of 4,500, 43 percent of whom practiced exclusively on horses. This growth can be ascribed to demand for medical services for a horse population that had grown to exceed 6.6 million, constituting an industry valued in excess of 15 billion dollars.

Equine practitioners are currently located throughout the country. Many operate excellent modern veterinary hospitals, while others serve as resident veterinarians on large breeding farms. The majority, however, provide service by transporting all required supplies and equipment to the horse in specially designed motor vehicles. They serve not only as medical practitioners, but also as consultants and advisors in preventive medicine and management.

The basic professional education of equine practitioners is customarily identical to that of other veterinarians. Specialization in the clinical practice of horses usually comes after formal postgraduate study, internship, or practice. Some veterinarians limit their practice specifically to horse breeding farms, racehorses, horse shows, or particular breeds of horses like Thoroughbreds or Standardbreds. Clinical services may also be restricted to a specialty such as equine internal medicine, surgery, or reproduction. In the 1980s and continuing into the present, there has been further development of specialization within each

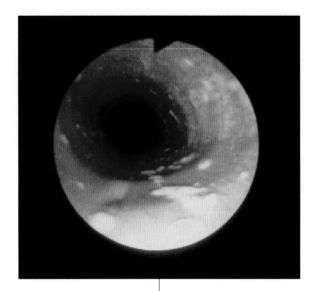

2. View through an endoscope of the trachea of a horse with exudate (mucus). (Photo courtesy of Corinne Sweeney)

of these fields. Currently, equine veterinarians specialize in areas such as cardiology, pulmonology, neonatology, ophthalmology, neurology, gastroenterology, critical care, soft tissue surgery, and orthopedic surgery. Equine reproduction veterinarians may even specialize in fertility problems of the mare or the stallion. The majority of equine veterinarians, however, engage in general equine practice, providing clinical services for all breeds of horses with all types of medical problems.

It is obvious that equine medicine has advanced greatly since the early days of Salihotria. The following descriptions of the advances over the last twenty years demonstrate that the practice of equine medicine has reached the cutting edge of modern technology.

Endoscopy

An endoscope is an instrument for internal examination. In the 1980s, the flexible fiberoptic endoscope was introduced to equine medicine and has advanced to a stage where its use has become a routine procedure performed many times on a daily basis. A fiberoptic endoscope is a system used to transmit light and images through long, thin fibers of optical glass. Because a single fiber cannot transmit a whole image, thousands of fibers are bundled together. These fiber bundles are fitted into a tube approximately nine millimeters (0.35 in.) in diameter. In horses, a meter-long (3.3 ft.) endoscope enables the veterinarian to examine the upper respiratory tract (figure 2), the upper part of the esophagus, the uterus, and the bladder. In order to examine the lower part of the esophagus, lungs, and stomach of the horse, the endoscope needs to be approximately two meters (6.6 ft.) long.

Because the endoscope is flexible, it is readily passed up the horse's nose for examination of the throat and then passed either into the trachea (windpipe) or esophagus. Mild restraint, but no sedation, is usually necessary for such procedures. The majority of the flexible endoscopes used in horses have a bending section that allows the end that enters the patient to be turned in four directions (right, left, up, and down), greatly increasing the field of view. The endoscope most commonly used by equine practitioners has an eyepiece at the end that the veterinarian uses for viewing. Videoendoscopy, a technology available in equine medicine since the mid-1980s, replaces the eyepiece with a video monitor. This allows the horse owner or trainer, as well as the veterinarian, to see the area under examination.

Endoscopes are widely used in equine medicine today. In one case endoscopic examination was applied to a horse that tired readily when ridden and made an audible respiratory noise. The endoscope revealed a problem in the upper respiratory tract that could be corrected surgically. Another horse with blood-tinged urine was found to have bladder stones when endoscopy was used. Endoscopic examination spotted a thorny twig blocking the airway of a lung in one horse with a history of chronic coughing over several months. Endoscopy of the stomach uncovered ulcers in a horse that experienced mild colic every time it ate its grain. Finally, the endoscope was used to discover problems in the uterus that caused a history of infertility in a broodmare.

Imaging

The 1980s brought to veterinary medicine numerous imaging techniques including ultrasound (figure 3), nuclear scintigraphy, and CAT scans. The use of ultrasound allows the equine veterinarian to detect numerous medical problems like renal calculi (kidney stones), heart valve conditions, bile duct stones, and pleuritis. The large equine heart, with its valves and chambers, can be watched in motion with the use of an echocardiogram. This technique assists equine veterinarians, for example, in determining the reason for a heart murmur or an irregular heart rhythm. Nuclear scintigraphy displays or maps functions of different organs by measuring the individual scintillations in radioactive emission. As an example, scintigraphy of the lungs can determine if an area of the lung is receiving inadequate blood flow (perfusion) or inadequate air flow (ventilation).

Evaluation on a Treadmill

As with the human athlete the equine athlete is prone to develop injuries associated with the stress of exercise, particularly racing. Equine disorders that would not impair a horse's usefulness as a beast of burden or means of transportation might have an effect on its performance at maximum speeds. Horse races are

3. An equine patient having its jugular veins examined with ultrasound to determine the presence of a thrombus (blood clot). (Photo courtesy of Corinne Sweeney)

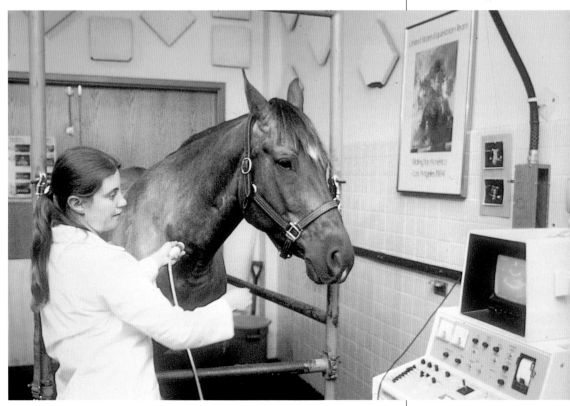

won by fractions of a second, and problems like a slight disorder of the respiratory tract could be responsible for a poor racing career. In an effort to detect what could contribute to a horse's poor racing performance, the equine veterinarian has traditionally relied on careful examination of the horse at rest and observation of the horse during exercise. Today, it is common to examine the equine athlete on a high-speed treadmill that can simulate the speed and effort of a horse during a race. Many areas of the horse, particularly the heart and lungs, can be evaluated while the horse is exercising at racing speeds on the treadmill (figure 4).

Lasers

The term laser, an acronym for Light Amplification by Simulated Emission of Radiation, has become as familiar in equine clinical circles as it is in human medicine. Laser light is a single, colored, highly organized, and highly directional beam. This intense, pure light, available in a wide range of wave lengths and power levels, may be used in continuous waves or incredibly short, powerful pulses. These characteristics allow the light to be used for a variety of purposes including welding, drilling, cutting metal, heat treating, taking measurements, and reading bar codes. In medicine lasers can be used for everything from diagnosis and cancer therapy to genetic engineering and tissue welding.

In equine medicine lasers were introduced during the 1980s. The one most frequently used for equine surgery is the Neodymium: Yttrium-aluminum-garnet (Nd: YAG). Because the Nd: YAG laser has a flexible light beam, it can be passed through an endoscope. This allows the laser to be used in various body cavities of the horse for surgery of the upper respiratory, urogenital, and gastrointestinal tracts.

The most frequent use of the laser in the horse is to remove tissue causing severe obstruction to the flow of air through the upper respiratory tract. The purpose of removing this tissue is to allow greater air flow, so the horse can breath normally and perform up to its ability. Prior to the use of laser surgery, most surgeries of the upper respiratory tract required the horse to be completely anesthetized. This resulted in an increased health risk to the equine patient, greater expense, and a longer recovery time. With the use of laser surgery, many surgical procedures can be done while the horse is standing and lightly sedated. The animal can be brought to the hospital immediately prior to surgery and returned home within an hour of completing the surgery.

The goal of laser surgery is to reduce the complications and the convalescent period associated with conventional surgery. Many horses are able to return to competitive work within one to two weeks following surgery. In the future, as new technology is available and more research is completed, lasers may be used on horses to enhance wound healing, ease pain, and hasten repair of strains and sprains. Lasers of the future may include ones that can cut below the skin without cutting the skin itself.

Arthroscopy

An arthroscope, developed in its modern form in the 1950s, is a slender, pencil-shaped optical instrument that permits the surgeon to look into the joint without opening it. Orthopedic surgeons working on humans adopted it

widely as a diagnostic tool in the mid 1970s and it was quickly transferred to veterinary medicine. Beginning in 1982, the University of Pennsylvania School of Veterinary Medicine, New Bolton Center began using the arthroscope on horses, and now approximately 200 arthroscopies (surgeries using the arthroscope) are performed there yearly. Prior to the development of this instrument, major surgery was necessary to remove bone chips or debris. The joint had to be opened widely, involving major trauma to the surrounding tissues. The traditional procedure also required a lengthy recovery time for the equine patient.

The arthroscope is inserted into a joint through a small, protective, ridged tube. Fiberoptics within the arthroscope illuminate the joint's interior, while a camera attached to the instrument allows the clinician to examine the area. The lens is at an angle so that rotation of this scope permits a wide viewing area. The incision for the arthroscope is very small, since the instrument is only four millimeters (0.16 in.) in diameter. When arthroscopy is performed, the joint is kept filled with sterile fluid to keep the soft tissues from collapsing into the joint space. The fluid runs constantly to keep the space cleaned of blood and to maintain distention of the joint. When other "grabbing" instruments are needed, they are inserted through a second small incision. These long, narrow instruments are specifically designed so that they can be manipulated into the tight joint space under arthroscopic visualization. The surgeon, who must be trained in the interior anatomy of the joints, needs bimanual dexterity.

In veterinary medicine arthroscopy is used primarily in horses. Following arthroscopic surgery, the horse is more comfortable and can return to training or racing sooner than with traditional arthrotomy (joint surgery).

4. An American Standardbred horse on a high-speed treadmill having its upper respiratory tract examined with an endoscope. (Photo courtesy of Corinne Sweeney)

185

Equine Reproduction

Theriogenology, or the study of animal reproduction, has made rapid advances in the last twenty years. Today's equine veterinarian has numerous diagnostic and therapeutic techniques available to increase the fertility rates of broodmares. Management practices on the farm, in conjunction with administration of medications, cause mares to begin their estrus cycles earlier than normal and on a more regular schedule, increasing the likelihood of pregnancy. Artificial insemination is also commonplace for many breeding farms.

Routine veterinary monitoring of the mares following breeding includes palpation and ultrasound examination of the uterus and ovaries. Within two weeks of conception, the equine practitioner can detect the fetus with ultrasound examination and determine if there will be twins. In the later stage of pregnancy continued ultrasound examination, in combination with blood tests and amniocentesis, allows the equine practitioner to determine if the pregnancy is proceeding normally or if medical intervention is needed. Postfoaling evaluation of the uterus and treatment with uterine washings (lavage) improve the chances of another pregnancy after a brief interval.

Embryo Transfer in Mares

The normal gestation period for the horse is eleven months: thus a mare can produce only one foal per year. The use of technology to allow embryo transfer in horses is helping horse breeders increase the number of offspring produced by superior mares. The estrus cycles of the donor mare (the superior mare that is bred) and the recipient mare (the mare that carries the foal) must be synchronized so that they are at the same stage. Each mare is examined daily to determine her receptivity toward the stallion. To determine the precise time both mares ovulate, their reproductive tracts are palpated and ultrasound is used. The mares are bred through artificial insemination just prior to ovulation. Seven days after ovulation, the donor mare's uterus is flushed. After the flushing, the embryo, no larger than a pinhead, is located and transferred into the recipient mare's uterus. After being flushed, the donor mare may return to competition or normal breeding, or be brought to cycle again and rebred for another transfer. In this way it is possible for one mare to produce two or even three foals during a single breeding season.

Critical Care

In recent years critical care for large animals has made numerous advances. A better understanding of disease processes, improved surgical techniques, and a commitment on the part of veterinarians and owners regarding the care of these critically ill patients have been vital to a successful outcome. At the University of Pennsylvania School of Veterinary Medicine, New Bolton Center, the Connelly Intensive Care Unit and Graham French Neonatal Section have been dedicated to the care of these critically ill, large animal patients and to meeting their special needs. The surgical/medical intensive care unit (ICU) provides care for adults, while the Neonatal Intensive Care Unit (NICU) services the foals. The adult wing has facilities to hoist "down" animals in a special sling lifted and lowered by a chain hoist attached to the ceiling. This apparatus is linked to an electric monorail that can transport disabled patients to and from a swimming pool for physical therapy. Each stall in the ICU is equipped with its own special air-flow system, compressed medical gases, oxygen, vacuum, and emergency call system.

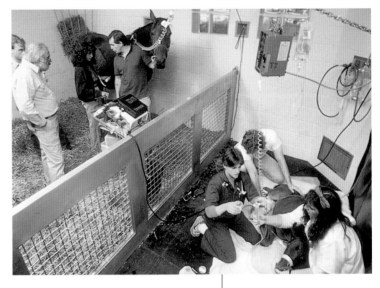

Patients can be monitored from a centralized nursing station that is staffed twenty-four hours a day by certified animal health technicians with intensive nursing care experience. The New Bolton Center treats approximately 800 critically ill patients each year. Although most of the patients are horses, other animals such as cattle, sheep, goats, pigs, and llamas are also treated. Varied problems that are treated include colic, renal failure, pleuritis, botulism, spinal cord trauma, and endotoxemia.

5. *View of the University of Pennsylvania, New Bolton Center Neonatal Intensive Care Unit. The broodmare (left) is receiving intravenous fluid while having a sonogram of her heart performed. The neonatal foal (right) is receiving intensive treatment. (Photo courtesy of Corinne Sweeney)*

Neonatology

During the 1980s many veterinarians believed that more could be done to improve the survival rate of sick and premature foals. Veterinarians realized that technology that was successful in saving human infants could be translated to the treatment of equine patients.

One of the newest and busiest units at the New Bolton Center is its Neonatal Intensive Care Unit (figure 5). Like the adult intensive care section, the NICU is equipped to provide fluid and oxygen, along with other sophisticated monitoring devices. Radiant-heat coils in the NICU floors assure adequate warmth, while custom-designed wall mats provide protection from self-inflicted trauma by recumbent patients. Padded rubber floors contribute to patient comfort, as well as facilitating hygiene. It is the round-the-clock people power, however, that is the key ingredient. Sick foals need constant attention, so staff veterinarians, house officers, and student volunteers assist the nursing staff in these labor-intensive tasks. By nature the foal is designed to stand up within the first hour of life. Any disease or musculoskeletal problem that keeps the foal recumbent longer than that puts it at risk for a number of secondary complications. There is an increased risk of pneumonia, the joints and tendons do not develop normally, and the foal often does not digest its food normally. The New Bolton Center NICU is prepared to treat equine patients suffering from a variety of disorders like prematurity and neonatal infections.

Another innovative equine program that is available at New Bolton Center identifies high-risk mares, monitors their pregnancies, and helps raise the odds of their delivering healthy foals. Conditions having a profound affect on the newborns' health and survival include lack of oxygen before or during birth, infection caused by bacteria or viruses, and inadequate delivery of nutrition to the unborn fetus resulting in abnormal development. Mares at risk for problem pregnancies are hospitalized and wear a special monitor that transmits a signal to a

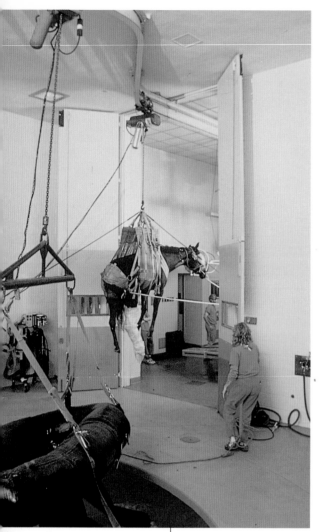

6. A horse hoisted in a sling being moved to the rubber raft for recovery from anesthesia in the pool. (Photo courtesy of Corinne Sweeney)

remote pocket pager whenever the mare lies down. Foaling stalls are equipped with closed circuit television monitors. The broodmare can be monitored with transabdominal ultrasound to check the activity and heart rate of the unborn fetus. If there are signs of fetal distress, delivery can be induced, or a Caesarean section can be performed to try to prevent the death of the fetus. Additionally, foals at risk can be aided from the moment they are born. Early intervention programs, like the high-risk pregnancy program for broodmares, have increased the survival rate for newborns at risk from 50 percent to 80 percent.

Recovery from Anesthesia

Bringing a horse out of anesthesia without injury is particularly tricky when the animal has severe bone fractures. Equine orthopedic surgeons may work four or more hours to repair a fracture successfully only to see their work undone by the horse as it tries to get back on its feet in the recovery stall. The weight of the horse alone can crack or snap the newly repaired fractured leg. A revolutionary concept for helping a horse through recovery is in place at New Bolton Center. A still unconscious 1,000-pound (454-kg) horse is hoisted from the operating table, slipped into a rubber raft designed to fit his contours, and then lowered into a pool of warm, moving water (figures 6 and 7). Suspended, the horse remains in a normal, upright position as it floats in the raft while recovering from anesthesia. Not only does this prevent him from banging into anything like a stall wall, but the water's resistance inhibits any violent movements that could cause reinjury. This special recovery pool is the core of New Bolton Center's orthopedic and rehabilitation center. The facility housing the pool includes an operating room with a special system of air movement and filtration that was one of the first of its kind in either human or veterinary orthopedics.

Fluid Therapy

As in humans, particularly infants, dehydration is a serious complication of severe diarrhea in the horse. Because of a horse's large size and the tremendous amount of body fluid lost during severe diarrhea, the horse is often incapable of drinking enough water to replace this loss. Intravenous fluids are, therefore, frequently required. A horse with a moderate to severe diarrhea will need the equivalent of twelve gallons of intravenous fluids a day. The use of intravenous fluids in the last twenty years has significantly helped horses with colic and shock.

Nutrition

Horses survive on nothing more than hay, grain, and water. Often, when a horse becomes ill, its appetite diminishes and it rapidly begins to lose weight. Its nutritional needs at this time are actually greater than normal, however, because its body needs additional nutrients due to the illness. Supplemental food can be given to the horse either by inserting a stomach tube and administering a liquid diet or by providing intravenous feeding (parenteral nutrition). Both liquid diets and intravenous feeding enable the horse to maintain its weight despite its poor appetite and illness.

Neurologic Diseases

In the last fifteen years several new diseases of the equine nervous system have emerged. A disease of the spinal cord that affects the horse's ability to walk is equine protozoal myeloencephalopathy. Although the disease has been recognized since the mid 1970s, it was only in the 1990s that the organism that causes the disease was identified. This information may lead to more rapid advances in either the successful prevention or treatment of the disease.

7. *A horse floating in the rubber raft in the pool as it recovers from anesthesia following orthopedic surgery. (Photo courtesy of Corinne Sweeney)*

Botulism, regarded by many as a form of food poisoning from spoiled meat, is seen relatively frequently in equine patients. The spores of the bacillus *Clostridium botulinum*, which causes botulism, are found in about 20 percent of soil samples from the mid-Atlantic states and Kentucky. These spores are dormant in the soil, but under the right conditions become active, producing a toxin so potent that a tiny amount can cause death. The organism can only grow in areas with limited oxygen (anaerobic conditions). The intestines of the young, puncture wounds, improperly canned foods, and spoiled forage and grains may provide the right environment in which the spores can become active and produce toxin. Botulism strikes all mammals, but young ones are most susceptible. People are exposed to the toxin primarily through improperly canned foods. Horses usually come into contact with the toxin through spoiled feed. Equines with botulism have difficulty swallowing and standing because the botulism toxin paralyzes the muscles. In severe cases the muscles responsible for breathing are paralyzed. When the disease was first recognized, in 1981, the mortality rate was nearly 75 percent, because there was no known prevention or treatment. Research at the University of Pennsylvania has been instrumental in the development and testing of an antiserum that can be administered once the condition is recognized. The use of the antiserum has reduced the morality rate to approximately 20 percent.

In the early 1990s equine motor neuron disease was discovered and was found to have many similarities to amyotrophic lateral sclerosis, or Lou Gehrig's disease, in humans. Horses with equine motor neuron disease tremble, lose weight, and have muscle weakness. Investigations into this disease in the horse may also shed light on the human disease.

Animal Behavior

The study of horse behavior and ways to resolve behavior problems is a rapidly expanding part of modern veterinary medicine. The veterinarian, as the primary source of health care for horses, is the ideal person to fulfill this need. The horse is a highly social animal, and studies have been done on the social structure of horses in both feral[1] and domestic herds living in a variety of environments. Common behavior problems in horses include stabling vices, traveling problems, and aggression. Veterinarians also attend to problems in the sexual behavior of mares and stallions, as well as maternal, developmental, resting, and feeding behaviors.

Tomorrow's Trends in Equine Medicine

The direction of equine veterinary medicine suggests that in the future veterinarians will conduct more sophisticated procedures and fewer routine hands-on tasks such as administration of worming medications and vaccinations. They will still provide advice on the routine procedures, but will train owners and farm employees to perform them. Although the equine practitioner will still serve as an unbiased advisor to management on all aspects of equine care, husbandry, and health, more of the veterinarian's efforts will be devoted to reproduction, neonatology, nutrition and nutritionally related diseases in sports medicine. Complex surgical procedures and new, less-invasive techniques like laser surgery will be practiced on horses when the cost can be justified. Modern radiologic and ultrasonographic imaging devices will continue to improve diagnostic capabilities. Equine sports medicine should move quickly toward prevention of injury and assessment of athletic ability.

Reading List

Martin, J. E. *A Legacy and a Promise: The First One Hundred Years, 1884-1984*. Philadelphia: Trustees of the University of Pennsylvania, 1984.

---

1. A feral horse is one that has escaped from domestication and has become established in the wild.

THE LIVING
RELATIVES OF
THE HORSE

SUSAN L. WOODWARD

Close relatives of the horse persist in the wild today in several parts of the Old World. Taxonomic interpretations vary, but most experts place them all in the genus *Equus* and recognize three species of zebras, two species of Asiatic asses, and one species of African wild ass. The continued survival of most of these fascinating and spectacular species is threatened. Despite the establishment of sanctuaries, many populations are faced with diminishing ranges and decreasing numbers. More widespread, but not necessarily more secure, are the horse relatives that are the product of domestication: the domestic donkey, the donkey/horse hybrids (mules and hinnies), and the feral[1] burro.

Extant wild relatives of the horse inhabit either grasslands or deserts. The digestive system of all equids is designed to extract energy and nutrients from coarse, low-quality forage by permitting passage of large quantities of plant matter through a long hindgut. The intestines of asses and Grevy's zebras are eleven to twelve times the body length; the intestines of mountain zebras and plains zebras are seventeen times the body length. The equid digestive system preadapts these animals to life in habitats dominated by grasses and shrubs. There are strong indications, however, that equids were not always restricted to such marginal habitats as they occupy today. During the Pleistocene (1.6 million to 10,000 years ago) some now-extinct North American species inhabited forested regions. Primarily grazers, most of these animals continue to exhibit considerable flexibility in diet and browse forbs, shrubs, and small trees. The seasonal and geographic variations in forage quantity and quality and in water availability typical of arid and semiarid environments cause most wild equid populations to be migratory.

In body form all equids are quite similar. They are specialized for running and for grazing on siliceous grasses, which rapidly wear down the teeth. Species can be differentiated, however, on the basis of qualitative and quantitative characteristics of the skull, tooth morphology, and length and robustness of the metapodials (foot bones). There are also variations in size, color, color patterning, hoof size and shape, mane length, presence or absence of a forelock, tail hair length and distribution, number and size of chestnuts, and vocalizations.

One reason all equids are vulnerable in the face of hunting pressures and habitat loss is that they reproduce slowly. Gestation lasts eleven to thirteen months, depending upon the species, and almost always only one foal is dropped each season. Although all equids have a foal heat seven to fourteen days after parturition, most researchers report that mares foal only every other year. Sexual maturity occurs at age two in females and age three to five in males. Life spans can extend twenty or more years.

Facing page, see figure 1.

---

1. A feral species is one that has escaped from domestication and has become established in the wild.

Equids are gregarious animals and are rarely seen alone. Two basic types of social behavior that seem to correlate with both lineage and habitat have evolved. The first social system, exemplified in the horse itself, is based on a harem. Two to six mares form small, permanent family bands (harems). They and their immature offspring are herded and defended by a mature stallion. Breeding is usually limited to the herd stallion. As young mares become sexually mature, they leave the harem of their own volition or are abducted by other stallions. Young mares may either join established harems or become the nuclei of new harems. Yearling males are driven from their maternal band and congregate in bachelor groups of two to twenty individuals until about five years of age, when they try to acquire harems of their own. In most instances the home ranges of bands overlap; and when forage and water conditions are optimal, aggregations totaling thousands of individuals are possible. Of the horse's living relatives, only the plains zebra and the mountain zebra have harem-based social systems.

The other social system exhibited by equids is based on a territory. Stallions defend a piece of prime land, at least during the breeding season. Mares come onto the territory, which usually can provide good forage and adequate water. Females may be attracted to the territory for mating and foaling because of the food and water resources and because the territorial male runs off other males that might be a threat or nuisance to the foal and nursing female. Most breeding probably occurs on the territory with the territorial male.

The only long-term bonds between individuals in the territorial social system are those established between mares and their foals during their first year. Yet these animals are gregarious and, except for mature stallions, are seldom seen alone. Two or more mares and their foals form small, loosely structured bands in which the actual individuals making up each band are continually changing. As in the harem system, young males travel in bands with other young males and occasionally with young, nonbreeding females. The composition of these bachelor groups also changes frequently. In desert habitats large numbers of individuals may congregate at water holes during the dry season. Grevy's zebras, Asiatic wild asses, African wild asses, and feral burros all seem to have territorially based social systems.

Zebras

The handsome striped equids of Africa fall into three distinct species: Grevy's zebra (*Equus grevyi*), the plains or Burchell's zebra (*Equus burchelli* = *Equus quagga*), and the mountain zebra (*Equus zebra*). Of these, the Grevy's zebra is most distinct. Taxonomically it is placed in the subgenus *Dolichohippus*, whereas the plains and mountain zebras are placed in the subgenus *Hippotigris*.

Grevy's Zebras

The Grevy's zebra is the largest of the wild equids and is usually considered the most primitive morphologically. Adults attain shoulder heights of 140 to 150 centimeters (55-57 in.) and may weigh 400 kilograms (880 lb.) or more. Its very narrow and closely spaced stripes make the Grevy the most strikingly beautiful of the zebras (figure 1). The stripes extend all the way to the broad hooves, leaving only the belly white. A broad black dorsal stripe is set off by a narrow zone of white on either side. Grevys are long legged and rather slenderly built with a long head. The black-tipped mane is relatively long and erect; their ears are very large and rounded. Grevy's zebras bray in a manner similar to a donkey.

Grevy's zebras are essentially confined to the semidesert of northern Kenya east of the Great Rift Valley and north of the Tana River. Their range extends into neighboring parts of Ethiopia and Somalia. During the rainy season mature stallions establish territories onto which mares come to foal and probably to breed. Gestation is thirteen months, longer than any other equid. Once the foals are born, the mares stay within two kilometers (1.2 mi.) of water and are almost always with the territorial stallion. Foals do not drink water until they are three months old and—unlike any other equid—are left in "kindergartens" frequently guarded by the territorial male while their mothers go to water. Grevy foals begin to forage much earlier than do feral horse foals: a six-week-old Grevy's zebra will graze as often as a five-month old horse. This accelerated development of feeding capability allows the young Grevy foal to become independent of its mother at a relatively early age.

Grevy's zebras are under continuing pressure from human encroachment on their habitat. During severe East African droughts in recent years, pastoral peoples have blocked the zebras' access to vital water holes and mortality rates have been high.

1. Grevy's zebras. (Photo by D. C. Gordon, courtesy of American Society of Mammalogists)

Plains Zebras

African equids for the most part replace one another geographically. There is a zone of overlap, however, between the Grevy's zebra and the plains zebra on the floodplain of the Ewaso Nyiro in northern Kenya. Here the two species form mixed grazing herds, but there is no record of interbreeding.

The plains zebra (figure 2) is the most abundant and widespread of extant wild equids, occurring throughout the tropical grasslands of East and southern Africa. It is quite stout in comparison with the Grevy's zebra. Shoulder height varies from 120 to 140 centimeters (47-55 in.), and a mature male may weigh 300 kilograms (660 lb.). Broad vertical stripes on the sides bend on the flanks to become horizontal across the rump. Stripes extend down the rather short legs to broad hooves. The stripes on the sides continue into the short, erect mane and meet under the belly. Stripes become less distinct on subspecies in the more southerly parts of

2. Plains zebras in Kenya. (Photo by Sandra Olsen)

its range. The plains zebra has a "bark" quite unlike the neigh of a horse or the bray of a donkey.

The pattern of stripes on all zebras is unique to each individual, with the variation greatest in the shoulder region. This has helped researchers identify and follow individuals over the course of long-term studies and may aid foals and adult zebras of a given harem in identifying each other in the large grazing herds.

The plains zebra has differentiated into several subspecies, two of which are now extinct. The Grant's zebra *(Equus burchelli boehmi)* is the most common of the plains zebra subspecies. With broad black stripes on a white background (Africans, reportedly, see white stripes on a black background), this subspecies is the zebra most frequently seen in zoos and circuses around the world. In the wild its distribution extends from southern Sudan through East Africa south to the Zambesi River. There may be some 300,000 left in the wild; on the Serengeti-Mara Plains alone there are an estimated 150,000 plains zebras. During the rainy season in Serengeti, aggregate herds of up to 10,000 individuals may form, part of one of the last great wildlife spectacles in the world.

The Chapman's zebra or the Damara zebra *(Equus burchelli antiquorum)* is a subspecies of plains zebra occurring from Angola and Namibia across northern South Africa to Transvaal. It is characterized by a pattern of broad, dark stripes alternating with thin, light shadow-stripes. The stripes fade into the brownish color of the body on the hindquarters and are absent altogether on the legs.

Another southern subspecies of the plains zebra, the Burchell's zebra *(Equus burchelli burchelli)*, now extinct, lacked stripes on the hindquarters. Its basic body color was reddish-yellow. Burchell's zebra existed from southern Botswana into the Orange Free State of South Africa. As European settlement spread northward from the Cape to colonial Southern Rhodesia, this subspecies was hunted to extinction. The wild herds had disappeared by 1910, and the last known individual died in the Berlin Zoo in 1918.

The southernmost subspecies, the quagga *(Equus burchelli quagga)* of South Africa, is also extinct. It occurred in large numbers south of the Orange River at the beginning of the nineteenth century, but Boer settlers decimated the population for meat and hides. The quagga disappeared from the wild by 1878, and the last zoo specimen died in 1883. All that remains today are nineteen pelts, a few skulls, three photographs, and a few paintings. The quagga was yellowish-brown with stripes that were confined to the head, neck, and forebody. DNA from one of the pelts has been retrieved and analyzed, establishing that the quagga was, indeed, a variant of the plains zebra and not a separate species as previously believed. There is currently an experimental breeding program in progress in South Africa to try to reconstruct the quagga from the Chapman's subspecies. The goal is to reproduce the quagga (its phenotype, or physical appearance) by 1998!

The Grant's zebra is the best studied of the plains zebras, and much of what we know of the behavior and biology of the species comes from work done with this subspecies in the wild and in zoos. Plains zebra have a harem-type social organization.

Mountain Zebras

The third zebra species is the mountain zebra. The most diagnostic feature of both mountain zebra subspecies is a square flap of skin or dewlap on the throat, best developed on males. Mountain zebras never form the large herds characteristic of plains zebras, but do exhibit a harem-type social system. During the winter they move up to twenty kilometers (12 mi.) from a water source. Where they are hunted, they water at night; where they are unmolested, they water at any time.

Two subspecies are recognized. Hartmann's zebra (*Equus zebra hartmanni*) occupies the rugged, broken terrain at the edge of the African Plateau east of the Namib Desert. Its habitat grades from an open woodland with a diverse, grassy understory in southern Angola and Namibia to the succulent steppe of the Karroo in South Africa. In the 1950s mountain zebras numbered between 50,000 and 75,000 and were regarded as vermin by an expanding livestock industry. Especially in drought years zebras competed with cattle for forage and water, and stampeding zebras occasionally tore down fences. By 1960 only 10,000 were left; and in 1973 Hartmann's zebra was considered an endangered species, with approximately 7,000 head remaining.

Hartmann's zebras have broad black stripes on an off-white body. The stripes extend down the legs to narrow hooves, but do not meet on the belly. These animals stand from 118 to 132 centimeters (46-52 in.) high. This subspecies seeks shade and rests during the hottest parts of the day and has been demonstrated to orient its body with respect to the sun. At midday zebras present the least amount and lightest parts of their bodies to the direct rays of the sun, thereby decreasing potential heat load. The vocalizations of the Hartmann's zebra are similar to the neigh of a horse.

The Cape mountain zebra (*Equus zebra zebra*) is the smallest of the extant zebras—with a shoulder height of about 120 centimeters (47 in.)—and the most restricted geographically. Its broad black stripes are closely spaced on a pure white body. Overall it is stockier than the Hartmann's zebra, has longer ears, and has a larger dewlap. The Cape mountain zebra formerly inhabited all the mountain ranges of the southern Cape Province of South Africa. By 1922, however, only 400 were believed to survive. To counteract the continued decline, Mountain Zebra National Park was established in 1937 on acacia veld near Cradock, South Africa, but its small population of Cape mountain zebra became extinct in 1950. That same year reintroductions from nearby remnant populations began. Eleven animals were donated from a nearby farm in 1950, and in 1964 another small herd was added. By the late 1960s the total Cape mountain population was only 140 but grew to 200 by 1979, with 75 percent of the animals in Mountain Zebra National Park. In 1984 the population was back to 400 head. Since then a few zebras have been reintroduced to the Cape Point Nature Reserve.

Asiatic Asses

Ass-like equids, sometimes referred to as half asses, occur in arid and semiarid environments across Asia from Iran to India, from the Caspian Sea to Tibet and Mongolia. There is disagreement as to whether one or two species exist, but here the kiangs of the Tibetan Plateau are considered a species distinct from the dziggetai, kulans, khurs (ghor-khars), and onagers of the lower elevation steppes and deserts.

Kiangs

Kiangs *(Equus kiang)*, the largest of the Asiatic asses, inhabit the cold steppe of the Qinghai-Xizang Plateau of Tibet (China) and Ladakh (India) at elevations between 4,100 and 4,800 meters (13,500-15,500 ft.). Their mean shoulder height is 142 centimeters (56 in.). Adult mares weigh 250 to 300 kilograms (550-660 lb.), whereas males may reach 400 kilograms (880 lb.). Kiangs are well adapted to the severe environment of their high-elevation habitat, where the growing season may be only two to three months long. The plateau where they live is dissected by barren mountain ranges into high plains twenty-five to thirty kilometers (15-20 mi.) wide. Kiangs concentrate on the plains, feeding on sharp, coarse grasses and swamp plants. Their hard, thick lips and horny palate equip them to graze on grasses that would tear the mouths of other equids. During August and September, when forage production is at its peak, kiangs accumulate a thick layer of insulating fat for the long winter. Adults may add thirty to forty kilograms (65-85 lb.) of fat during these months. August and September are also the breeding season, when kiangs may aggregate in herds of 300 to 400 individuals.

The kiang's summer coat is short, sleek, and bright reddish-brown with a dark dorsal stripe. Light patches create a disruptive pattern. The underparts are white as are the lower legs, throat, and muzzle; the mane is dark and erect. In winter the coat becomes thick and long, and the color turns to brown. Molt begins in April and is not completed until late July. Kiangs have been observed swimming, and it is believed that this activity aids in shedding their winter coats.

Kiangs are differentiated into two subspecies. In China *Equus kiang holdereri* occurs in Qinghai, northwest Sichuan, and a small portion of Gansu Province. *Equus kiang kiang* is found on the western part of the Qinghai-Xizang Plateau in Tibet and in Ladakh, India. Kiangs still exist in large numbers in China; a 1984 survey estimated that there were over 200,000 individuals. The Indian population numbers about 1,500. Tibetans reportedly revere and protect these animals and the Chinese have afforded them full protection, but encroachment from cattle-herders and heavy losses from poachers seeking meat and hides make continual monitoring of population sizes desirable.

Onagers

The other species of Asiatic ass is *Equus hemionus*, known locally by a variety of common names and categorized by taxonomists into at least five subspecies. As a group they may all be referred to as onagers. Onagers (figure 3) are similar in appearance to kiangs but are shorter in stature with proportionately longer and more slender limbs. They have smaller heads with narrower snouts and longer ears, and the mane is shorter. Body color is less red in summer and lighter in winter than kiangs' pelage, and the spring molt proceeds more quickly and in a different sequence along the body.

What may have been a nearly continuous range for *Equus hemionus* across Asia has in the twentieth century become fragmented into isolated segments as a result of human encroachment and usurpation of water holes. Onagers survive in Mongolia, China, Turkmenia, India, and possibly Iran.

The largest onager is the subspecies with the most northerly distribution. The dziggetai *(Equus hemionus hemionus)*, with a shoulder height of 130 centimeters (51 in.) and a weight at maturity of 260 kilograms (500 lb.), is disjunctly distributed in China in northwest Inner Mongolia and Gansu and in northwest Xinjiang. In the western part of the range, the dziggetai displays disruptive coloration with patches of reddish hair on the head and body. The border between the dark head, shoulders, and flanks and the white underparts is sharply drawn. There is also a very broad (55-77 mm., or 2-3 in.) dorsal stripe. The eastern population is sometimes recognized as a separate subspecies, *(Equus hemionus luteus)*, the Gobi wild ass. Its coat is lighter in color with a more subtle gradation of browns into the white of the underparts. After reductions in range and numbers during the 1970s, a 1982 estimate placed the total number of onagers in China at 2,000 head. About 350 of these are on the Kalamali Mountain Wildlife Reserve in Xinjiang.

The semideserts and deserts of Turkmenistan, Uzbekistan and Kazakstan were home to kulans *(Equus hemionus kulan)*. Kulans were protected in 1919 in what was to become the Soviet Union, but the population in Kazakstan became extinct following the severe winter freeze of 1935-1936. This wild ass stands about 120 centimeters (47 in.) at the shoulder and has a yellowish-brown coat grading gradually into white on the underparts. The broad dorsal stripe is set off by parallel bands of white. In winter, when temperatures reach ten to thirty degrees centigrade (4°-22°F), the kulan develops a thick coat, also yellowish-brown. Its habitat is open steppe with shrubs and pistachio trees and lies at 760 meters (2500 ft.). A small population of about 400 head is preserved in Badchys Reserve, Turkmenistan. The total population in 1977 was estimated to be about 1,000. Kulans in the Badchys Reserve have been shown to have a territorial social system. They reportedly migrate from 500 to 600 kilometers (310-375 mi.) between their summer and winter ranges.

3. Onagers. (Photo by Sandra Olsen)

The only known wild population of the Indian wild ass, the khur or ghor-khar *(Equus hemionus khur)*, is in the Little Rann of Kutch Desert on the Kathiawar Peninsula, Gujarat, India. Khurs once extended over an area from the Thar Desert of India into Iran. The Little Rann of Kutch is a saline desert, which summer rains convert to a grassy meadow with saline pools. Khurs graze on sedges and grasses and browse on shrubs, including exotic New World mesquites planted specifically to improve their habitat. The khur differs from the kulan in color and skull shape. Its summer coat is darker and reddish-gray with white reaching higher up the flanks. The winter coat is gray to pale chestnut and not appreciably different in length from its summer pelage. The khur appears to have the same social system as the kulan. Large herds form during the summer monsoon, which is the mating and foaling season. After the rains they disperse into small groups and wander about looking for forage. In the dry season, when temperatures may reach forty-four degrees centigrade (110°F), khurs have been reported to eat the shrubby halophytic plant known as seablite, presumedly as a source of water.

The population of khurs in India had dwindled from some 3,000 to 5,000 in 1946 to about 860 in 1962. Rapid decline continued and by 1967 only 362 individuals remained. The high mortality rates were attributed to a protozoan disease transmitted from encroaching domestic livestock. A 5,000-square-kilometer (1930-sq.-mi.) Wild Ass Sanctuary was established in 1973, and mesquite was planted at a rate of 800 hectares (2,000 acre) per year. By 1976 the khur population had increased to 720, and in 1983 a census revealed 1,989 head on the reserve. Human encroachment, however, continues to threaten the khur population as people cut wood for fuel and fodder. People have also introduced dogs, which harass the wild asses and sometimes disturb their breeding.

The Persian onager *(Equus hemionus onager)* once existed in large numbers in the deserts of Iran, spending summer months in high mountain valleys and descending to lower elevations in the winter. A relict population of 300 head had rebounded during the 1960s to about 1,000 animals.

The Syrian wild ass or achdari *(Equus hemionus hemippus)* was the smallest of the subspecies, with a shoulder height of 100 centimeters (39 in.). Most likely the wild ass of the Bible, it is now extinct. The last known specimen died in a zoo in 1929.

African Wild Ass

Africa is home to the true ass *(Equus africanus)*, the most endangered of wild relatives of the horse and ancestor of the domestic donkey. The British explorer Samuel Baker, who sought the source of the Nile, remarked:

Those who have seen donkeys in their civilized state have no conception of the beauty of the wild and original animal, far from the passive and subdued appearance of the English ass, the animal in its native domain is the perfection of activity and courage; there is a high-bred tone in the deportment, a high actioned step when it trots freely over the rocks and sand, with the speed of a horse as it gallops over the boundless desert.[2]

2. From S. W. Baker, *Exploration of the Nile Tributaries of Abyssinia* (San Francisco: F. Dewing, 1868).

The only surviving subspecies of African wild ass, the Somali ass (*Equus africanus somalicus = E. africanus somaliensis*) (figure 4) occurs in two small relict areas in Ethiopia and Somalia. Its average shoulder height is 129 centimeters (51 in.). The body and large head are a uniform light gray, while the muzzle, rings about the eyes, and underparts are white. The erect mane and long ears are tipped with black, and the tail ends in a tuft of dark hairs. Between knee and hock on both fore- and hindlegs, irregular dark bands circle the legs. There is a thin, faint dorsal stripe and sometimes a faint shoulder stripe.

The hot, stony, mountainous desert of the Horn of Africa from Danakil, in Eritrea, Ethiopia, to Webi Shebeli, in Somalia, was the original range of the Somali wild ass. The distribution area extended westward to the Ethiopian Highlands, where it overlapped with that of the Grevy's zebra. In the 1960s about 200 asses survived in Wadi Nogal in northern Somalia, but they were considered on the verge of extinction. The situation has been somewhat better in Ethiopia, where 2,000 to 3,000 wild asses were believed to remain in central Danakil as late as 1986. Somali asses are legally protected in Ethiopia, but Eritrea has been engaged in a long civil war with the government in Addis Ababa and has been effectively beyond the control of Ethiopian law. Indeed, war threatens the existence of the Somali ass in both Ethiopia and Somalia. In addition, nomadic herdsmen and their sheep, goats, cattle, donkeys, and camels displace asses from their pastures. Wild asses relinquish the plains to domestic herds during the day, finding refuge on the rocky hills. At night, when the livestock is corralled, they come down to graze and to water. Road construction may exacerbate the situation by altering traditional migration patterns of the herdsmen nomads and opening the most remote areas to livestock grazing.

The deserts of Danakil lie in the great fan-shaped valley at the northern terminus of Africa's Great Rift Valley. The Awash River flows across the nearly barren plains to disappear in marshes and salt lakes. At elevations of 600 to 900 meters (1,970-2,950 ft.), purplish-black lava beds and bare lava peaks interrupt the dry grassland on which annual grasses appear after rains. In the dry season the plants wither as temperatures soar to 50 degrees centigrade (122°F). In the west and to the south, aridity is less severe and acacia trees dominate the landscape. In both these regions wild asses are associated with oryx, Soemmering's gazelle,

4. Somali asses. (Photo by Sandra Olsen)

gerenuk, lesser kudu, and ostrich. Farther east the plains dip to 375 meters (1,230 ft.) above sea level and the habitat is drier. Only Soemmering's gazelle, Dorcas gazelle, and the ostrich occur with the wild ass. The desert reaches its extreme in the Danakil Depression at 75 meters (250 ft.) below sea level. There the only wild mammal reported is the Somali ass.

Until the 1950s there were still scattered reports of sightings of a second subspecies of African ass, the Nubian ass *(Equus africanus africanus)*, which is now presumed extinct. Somewhat smaller than the Somali, the Nubian ass stood 122 centimeters (48 in.) at the shoulders and was distinguished by a clear dark dorsal stripe, a distinct shoulder stripe, and the absence of leg stripes. This was the magnificent animal described by Samuel Baker. African wild asses were hunted in the Eastern Desert of Egypt by prehistoric peoples and were still hunted in Upper Egypt by Tutankhamen and Ramesses III around 1100 B.C. In the nineteenth century, however, when the Nubian ass became known to western science, it was restricted to a relatively small area in Sudan and a very small part of northern Ethiopia. The last Nubian asses—seen by Europeans, at least—were shot in the 1920s and 1930s.

The disappearance of the Nubian subspecies is believed to be more a consequence of genetic swamping with domestic donkeys—which have shared the range of their wild ancestor for some 5,000 years—than a result of direct persecution. It has apparently long been the custom of local peoples to tether estrous domestic mares away from the villages where they would be bred by wild stallions. It is likely that domestic mares, and stallions also, frequently wandered off and joined wild breeding populations.

Domestic Asses or Donkeys

There is consensus that the most probable ancestor of the domestic donkey *(Equus asinus)* is the Nubian subspecies of African wild ass; however, the history of its domestication is poorly known. The earliest known remains of the domestic donkey date to the fourth millennium B.C. from a site at Ma'adi, Lower Egypt. Domestication of Africa's only contribution to the world's major livestock species came long after the domestication of sheep, goats, and cattle in Southwest Asia (eighth and seventh millennia B.C.). It is probable that cattle-raising peoples in Nubia, in the distribution area of the Nubian wild ass, first developed the domestic donkey as a beast of burden. The donkey was to supplant the ox—which had the singular disadvantage of requiring a rest period in which to ruminate—as the chief pack animal. The tame donkey was easily led by any type of halter available and could be trained to follow a route on its own. Early effects of donkey domestication were increased mobility of pastoral peoples and perhaps true nomadism, in which whole families rather than just the men could follow their flocks from pasture to pasture.

Donkeys were vital in developing long-distance trade through the Egyptian deserts. Before the first pyramids were raised, pack trains wended their way down Wadi Hammamat from the Nile Valley to the Red Sea to trade with Arabia.

Donkeys were kept in great herds in ancient Egypt. In the tombs of the Dynasty IV (ca. 2675-2565 B.C.) are indications that wealthy and powerful people possessed droves of over a thousand head. In addition to their use as a pack animal, donkeys were employed to tread seeds into the fertile Nile floodplain and to thresh the harvest. Elsewhere, mares were kept as dairy animals. Donkey's milk, higher in both sugar and protein content than cow's milk, was used as food, as medicine, and as a cosmetic to promote a white skin. Donkey meat has also provided food for various peoples.

The donkey was dispersed out of the Nile Valley and eventually reached all habitable continents. Donkeys were in Southwest Asia by the end of the fourth millennium B.C. By 1800 B.C. the center of ass-breeding had shifted to Mesopotamia. Damascus, known as the city of asses through cuneiform writing and a center of the caravan trade, became famous for its breed of large, white riding ass. At least three other breeds were developed in Syria: another saddle breed, one with a graceful easy gait for women, and a stout breed for plowing. In Arabia the Muscat or Yemen ass was developed. This strong, light-colored donkey is still used in caravans and also as a riding animal.

The donkey was brought to Europe by the second millennium B.C., possibly accompanying the introduction of viticulture. In Greek mythology the ass is associated with Dionysus, Syrian god of wine. The Greeks brought the vine and the donkey to their colonies along the north coast of the Mediterranean, including those in Italy, France, and Spain. Romans later continued the dispersal in Europe to the limits of their empire.

A supply ship to Christopher Columbus on his second voyage brought the first donkeys to the New World in 1495. Four jacks (males) and two jennies (females) were among the inventory of livestock delivered to Hispaniola. They would produce mules[3] for the conquistadores' expeditions onto the American mainland. Ten years after the conquest of the Aztecs, the first shipment of twelve jennies and three jacks arrived from Cuba to begin breeding mules in Mexico. Female mules were preferred as riding animals, whereas the males were used as pack animals along the trails that tied the Spanish empire together. Both mules and hinnies were used in the silver mines. Along the frontier each Spanish outpost had to breed its own supply of mules, and each hacienda or mission maintained at least one stud jack.

The main influx of donkeys into the western United States probably came with the gold rushes of the nineteenth century. Many of the prospectors were Mexican and the burro was their preferred pack animal (see "Feral Asses or Burros" below). The lone prospector and his donkey became a symbol of the Old West. However, donkeys were also important in mining operations in the deserts. They carried water, wood, and machinery to the mines; hauled cartloads of ore and rock out of the mine tunnels; and brought sacks of ore to the mills, where other donkeys turned the mills that ground the ore.

The end of the mining boom coincided with the introduction of the railroad in the American West. The age of the burro had come to an end. When the mines shut down and the prospectors left, their animals were of little value and were often turned loose. Having originally evolved in the Eastern Desert of

3. Breeding a male donkey to a female horse produces a mule, whereas breeding a male horse to a female donkey produces a hinny. See the next section, "Mules and Hinnies."

Egypt, these hardy beasts had little problem in the American deserts (figure 5). Populations of free-roaming (or feral) burros remain to this day.

Everywhere the donkey was a hardy work animal able to be maintained at low cost on poor forage. It could be ridden, used to pull plows and carts, or packed with a load weighing up to 100 kilograms (220 lb.). In many parts of the world, the donkey was not replaced by the horse, largely because of its negligible cost and maintenance requirements. Instead, it became—and remains today—the work animal of the world's poor.

Improved breeds of ass were developed in Europe and later in America when mule-breeding became important (see below). The marvelous long-haired Poitou ass, which has a shoulder height of 154 centimeters (61 in.), has been bred in southern France since 1016. It is powerfully built and has an exceptionally large head, but what makes this ass unique is its long black hair that, when uncombed, reaches the ground in great unique mats and ringlets. Poitou numbers declined after World War II, when motorized vehicles replaced mules. Today the breed is extremely rare with only about forty individuals in the entire world, many of which are in zoos.

On the Iberian Peninsula, Catalonia and Andalucia each developed a large breed of ass, putting Spain in the forefront of the mule-breeding industry. Exportation of Spanish jacks was prohibited until 1813. However, the King of Spain presented George Washington with a large black jack in 1785. This animal, "Royal Gift," is considered the father of the mule industry in the United States.

George Washington, along with Henry Clay and others, developed an American donkey breed for mule-breeding purposes. They crossed a number of European breeds, including the Andalusian, the Majorca, the Maltese, and especially the Catalonia, to produce what has become known as the American Mammoth Jackstock. Mammoths, with a shoulder height of 142 to 152 centimeters (56-60 in.) and a weight of 450 to 530 kilograms (1,000-1,160 lb.), are the largest breed of ass in the world. They are renowned not only for their size but also for their style. Most are black, but as the large red mules produced from Belgian mares have become popular, the red-colored jack has become more and more common. The American Mammoth Jackstock suffered a rapid and serious decline in numbers, however, when the tractor replaced mules in American agriculture. The population is currently estimated at about a thousand animals. A resurgence in interest in large mules for show and competition may help preserve this only truly American breed of ass.

Today improved, specialized breeds account for only a small minority of the donkeys in the world, including the United States. The most common donkey everywhere is gray-dun with a light belly, muzzle, and eye-rings; reddish brown backs to the ears; a conspicuous black dorsal stripe; and a bold shoulder stripe. Yet everywhere there are also black, brown, red, white, and spotted domestic asses. In the United States three common types are recognized by the major breed registry:

5. Feral burro in California. (Photo by Susan Woodward)

the Standard, the Large Standard, and the Miniature. The Standard, measuring 91 to 122 centimeters (36-48 in.) at the shoulder, is the most common. The Large Standard reaches 122 to 137 centimeters (48-54 in.) at the withers. Miniatures stand only 71 to 91 centimeters (28-36 in.) high and weigh 115 to 205 kilograms (250-450 lb.). Miniatures originated separately on the islands of Sicily and Sardinia, and most in the United States are probably a mix of these two breeds.

Today donkeys are becoming increasingly popular in the United States and Canada as recreation and companion animals. They are ridden or used to pull wagons and still function as pack animals in wilderness adventures. On ranches they are used to halterbreak calves. A new role for the donkey is developing as a guard animal, defending flocks of sheep from dogs and coyotes.

Mules and Hinnies

Under conditions of domestication it is possible to obtain hybrids between equid species. There are records of onager/ass, onager/horse, and zebra/horse (zebroids) crosses, but the cross that has been most significant in human history is the one between horses and donkeys. Breeding a male donkey to a female horse results in a mule; breeding a male horse to a female donkey produces a hinny.

Offspring from either cross, although fully developed as males or females, are almost always sterile. Hence, a line of horses and a line of domestic asses must be maintained to perpetuate mule or hinny production.

Generally speaking the hybrid offspring has a head and forebody resembling its male parent, while the tail and hindquarters is like its mother. Body size is larger than a donkey and sometimes larger than a horse. Thus, a mule has a large head, long ears, erect mane, strong hindlimbs, and a tail with long hair down its entire length. Hinnies have small heads and short ears and a tail that ends in a tuft of hair.

The mule in most circumstances has been the preferred product of the horse/ass cross. (The breeding is also easier to manage.) The mule has greater endurance and is stronger and less excitable than a horse. Depending on the need, different breeds of horses can be used to produce fine riding mules, heavy draft mules, or medium-sized pack animals. In Medieval Europe, when horses were bred large to carry armored knights, mules were the preferred riding animal of gentlemen and clergy. Mules were once used to pull fire-fighting equipment and were often employed by armies to pull artillery and to remove the wounded from the battlefield. The twenty-mule team that hauled borax from Death Valley and other mining centers in the West has become part of American legend. Indeed, some western towns were originally laid out with extremely wide streets (well adapted to today's vehicular traffic) to allow the mule teams to turn around.

The main mule-breeding centers in the United States developed in Tennessee, Kentucky, and Missouri to provide work animals for the cotton fields of the Old South. After the American Civil War and the development of tenant farming throughout the South, the mule continued as the major draft animal in American agriculture. "Forty acres and a mule" was all one needed for self-sufficiency. The importance of the mule declined rapidly in the 1940s and 1950s, however, as gasoline-driven tractors became widespread, and mules all but disappeared from the American scene.

Today there is renewed interest in mules for recreation and competition. In the Southeast mules are used for nighttime raccoon hunting, and the mules' ability to jump over fallen trees or fences is exploited in jumping competitions. Pulling contests using heavy draft mules have created a new demand for large mules. Particularly popular are large red mules produced by crossing American Mammoth Jackstock with Belgian mares.

Feral Asses or Burros

Domestic livestock, when liberated from the control of humans and able to establish free-roaming breeding populations, are referred to as feral. Feral ass populations have probably existed for as long as there have been domestic populations. In the United States the Spanish name burro has been adopted to distinguish feral donkeys from domestic ones. Burros, as described above, are the descendants of work animals abandoned at the close of the mining boom era and the beginning of the railroad era in the late nineteenth century.

The burro has an average shoulder height of 120 centimeters (47 in.). Most are gray with white underparts, muzzles, and eye-rings and distinct dorsal and shoulder stripes. Many have stripes circling the legs. Generally burros are sleeker than their domestic relatives with a quickness and high step reminiscent of the ancestral African wild ass. In some populations there is a high frequency of dark brown or black individuals; white, red, and spotted burros also occur.

Feral burros were reported in the Grand Canyon as early as 1884, and dozens roamed the vicinity of Organ Pipe Cactus National Monument, Arizona, by 1910. By the 1920s and 1930s burros occurred in most western states, and the growth of their populations was causing concern among natural resource managers. Burro control began in the Grand Canyon in 1924; in Sitgreaves National Forest, Arizona, in the late 1920s; and in Death Valley, in 1939. In addition to federal agencies' attempts to control or eradicate burros, private citizens also participated. Ranchers decimated herds believed to be threatening cattle range in the Southwest. State wildlife management personnel shot hundreds in attempts to eliminate possible competition for forage and water and to preserve dwindling populations of native desert bighorn sheep. Entrepreneurs were trapping and shooting burros for human consumption and pet food or for redomestication as pets and pack animals.

In the early 1950s the California Fish and Game Department, believing burros threatened some native plant and animal species, openly encouraged the hunting of burros. The campaign only served to arouse a public that was already enamored with the appealing, free-spirited inhabitants of their deserts. Public protest led to the enactment of a temporary provision for complete protection of the burro. In 1957 the law became permanent, and feral burros were made the property of the state of California. For the first time they came under the protection of game laws rather than livestock regulations.

Meanwhile in Nevada, Velma Johnston was waging a one woman battle with the federal government to enact laws requiring the humane treatment of feral horses. She began with an effort designed to prohibit the use of aircraft in horse roundups. After a massive publicity campaign such a law was passed in 1959. The feral burro was, almost as an afterthought, included in the legislation. Mrs.

Johnston continued to agitate for increased protection for all feral equids. She again aroused public sentiment and Washington was deluged with letters. In December 1971 the United States unanimously passed Public Law 92-195:

> Be it enacted by the Senate and House of Representatives of the United States of America in Congress assembled, that Congress finds and declares that wild free-roaming horses and burros are living symbols of the historic and pioneer spirit of the West; that they contribute to the diversity of life forms within the Nation and enrich the lives of the American people; and that these horse and burros are fast disappearing from the American scene. It is the policy of Congress that wild free-roaming horses and burros shall be protected from capture, branding, harassment or death; and to accomplish this they are to be considered in the area where presently found, as an integral part of the natural system of the public lands.

This full-protection law pertained to burros on public lands administered by the Bureau of Land Management (BLM) and the United States Forest Service. At the time of enactment there were an estimated 14,400 burros on these lands, with the major concentrations in the lower Colorado River Valley and in southeastern California. Because of strong public sentiment, removal efforts in national parks, national wildlife refuges, and military reservations were also suspended. Neither ecologists nor Mrs. Johnston herself saw complete protection as the solution to the burro problem. Some type of management was necessary to maintain viable populations and viable ecosystems. In the two decades since the enactment of the federal law, there have been many adjustments to policy and practice. Burros have been removed or are scheduled to be removed from lands in the National Park system, where there is a mandate to remove all exotic species of plants and animals. China Lake Naval Weapons Center in California, the military base with the largest burro population, has reduced its herd to a tiny remnant in efforts to improve range quality. The Bureau of Land Management has developed comprehensive management plans that include burro population control in its various districts and even outright eradication of burros from ecologically sensitive areas. At present Mojave Desert National Park is planning to remove several of the largest concentrations of feral burros from BLM jurisdiction and thereby remove their federal protection. Ironically, burro populations and their total distribution area have decreased since burros were afforded federal protection.

Feral asses are also known in various parts of the world outside the United States. Feral populations occur in the central massifs of North Africa, west of the Nile in Sudan, on the island of Sokotra off the Horn of Africa, on Ogurchinsky Island in the Caspian Sea, on the Galapagos Islands in the Pacific off the coast of Ecuador, on high-elevation grasslands in Argentina, on the Caribbean islands of Saint Thomas (U.S. Virgin Islands) and Bonaire (Netherlands Antilles), and in Australia. The Sokotra population may be thousands of years old and is of interest because of the diminutive size of the animals. Feral asses are viewed as a major ecological problem on the Galapagos Islands, in Sudan, and in Australia.

Summary

The wild living relatives of the horse are few in number and rare in occurrence. The world is probably witnessing the end of most of these beautiful, still poorly known species. The zebras of Africa, the asses of Asia, and the ass of

Africa all are experiencing the alteration of their habitats and the fragmentation and decimation of their populations. Their survival cannot be assured without the dedication of vast tracts of land for their conservation.

The domestic relative, the donkey, will probably hold its own worldwide. The failure of the world economic system to bring real development to the people of the Third World means that this hardy, easily maintained work animal will keep its niche in rural and urban systems. What are in real danger of being lost are the old specialized domestic breeds, particularly those developed for mule breeding. The Poitou is almost extinct; the American Mammoth Jackstock, highly vulnerable to extinction.

Feral asses will probably persist in the Third World, where they are continually replenished by domestic stock. Island populations may disappear as native species conservation efforts increase. On the mainland United States and in Australia, where the largest feral populations have occurred, efforts to eradicate them will undoubtedly continue.

The conservation of any species—wild, domestic, or feral—is a multifaceted problem with no simple or single solution. Survival and extinction are ultimately determined by human values, needs, and activities. Throughout the world all species are members of the greater human ecosystem. Only if this global ecosystem can be managed in a sustainable fashion that provides social and economic well-being and cultural expression for the diverse human species is there hope for the continuing survival of the living relatives of the horse.

Reading List

Becker, C. D., and J. R. Ginsberg. "Mother-Infant Behavior of Wild Grevy's Zebra: Adaptations for Survival in Semi-Desert East Africa." *Animal Behaviour* 40 (1990), 1111-18.

Fox, J. L.; C. Nurbu; R. S. Chundawat. "The Mountain Ungulates of Ladakh, India." *Biological Conservation* 58 (1990), 167-90.

Gao, X., and J. Gu. "The Distribution and Status of the Equidae in China." *Acta Theriologica Sinica* 9 (1989), 269-74. [English summary]

Grzimek, B., editor. *Grzimek's Animal Life Encyclopedia*, vol. 12. New York: Van Nostrand Reinhold Company, 1972.

Heise, L., and C. Christman. *American Minor Breeds Notebook*. Pittsboro, NC: The American Minor Breeds Conservancy, 1989.

Joubert, E. "Habitat Preference, Distribution and Status of the Hartmann Zebra *Equus zebra hartmannae* in South West Africa." *Madoqua* 7 (1973), 5-15.

Klingel, H. "A Comparison of the Social Behavior of Equids," in *The Behavior of Ungulates and Its Relation to Management*, vol. 1, ed. by V. Geist and H. Walther. Morges, Switzerland: IUCN, 1974. Pp. 124-32.

____. "Observations on Social Organization and Behaviour of African and Asiatic Wild Asses." *Zeitschrift für Tierpsychologie* 44 (1977), 323-31.

____. "Soziale Organization und Verhalter freilebender Steppenzebras *(Equus quagga)*." *Zeitschrift für Tierpsychologie* 24 (1967), 590-624.

McKnight, T. L. "The Feral Burro in the United States: Distribution and Problems." *Journal of Wildlife Management* 22 (1958): 163-78.

Penzhorn, B. L. "A Long Term Study of Social Organization and Behaviour of Cape Mountain Zebra *Equus zebra zebra*." *Zeitschrift für Tierpsychologie* 64 (1984), 97-146.

Smielowski, J., and P. P. Raval. "The Indian Wild Ass—Wild and Captive Populations." *Oryx* 22 (1988), 85-88.

Woodward, S. L. "The Social System of Feral Asses *(Equus asinus)*." *Zietschrift für Tierpsychologie* 49 (1979), 304-16.

Appendix

General Information on the Horse

Scientific Classification of the Domestic Horse

Kingdom Animalia
　Phylum Chordata
　　Subphylum Vertebrata
　　　Class Mammalia
　　　　Order Perissodactyla
　　　　　Suborder Hippomorpha
　　　　　　Family Equidae
　　　　　　　Subfamily Equinae
　　　　　　　　Tribe Equini
　　　　　　　　　Genus *Equus*
　　　　　　　　　　Species *Equus caballus*

Skeleton of the horse.
(Drawing by Sandra L. Olsen)

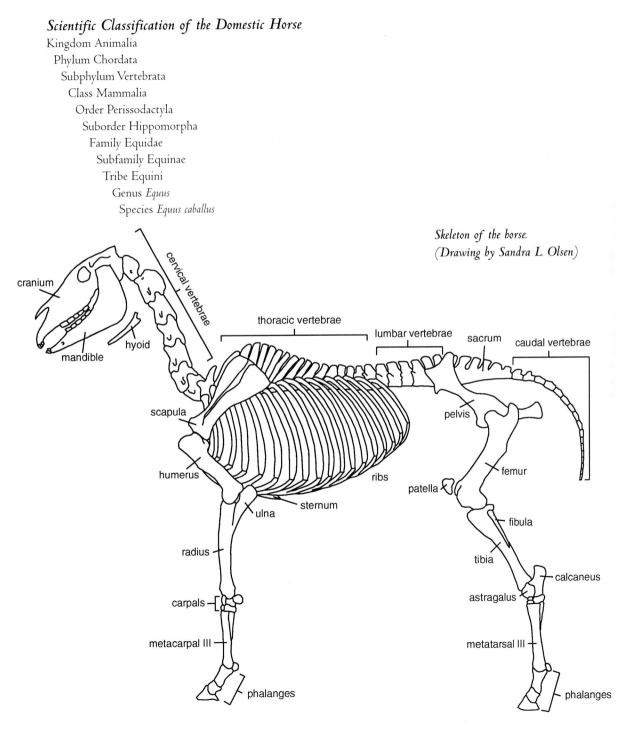

Table 1. Major Horse Breeds and Their Characteristics

Breed	Height in Hands[1]	Weight in Kilograms (lbs.)	Colors
Draft Horses			
American Belgian	15.2-18	860-1000 (1,900-2,200)	Sorrel, chestnut, rarely roan
American Cream Draft Horse	15.2-17	725-905 (1,600-2,000)	Light cream with white points and sometimes white markings
Belgian Ardennais	14.2-15.2	635-725 (1,400-1,600)	Bay roan, bay, chestnut, blue roan
Brabant	15-18	815-1090 (1,800-2,400)	Red roan, bay, chestnut, blue roan
Clydesdale	16.1-17	725-815 (1,600-1,800)	Bay, brown, black, rarely chestnut, with white face and legs
Døle Gudbrandsdal	14.2-15.2	545-635 (1,200-1,400)	Black, brown
Finnish Universal	16.2-18	680 (1,500)	Bay, black, chestnut, brown
Noriker	14.2-16	680 (1,500)	Bay, chestnut, black, roan, leopard
North Swedish Horse	15.3-16.2	680 (1,500)	Any solid color
Percheron	16-17.2	860-955 (1,900-2,100)	Black, gray
Shire	16.2-18	770-1225 (1,700-2,700)	Bay, black, also brown, gray, with white markings on head and legs
Suffolk	16-17	770-860 (1,700-1,900)	Chestnut, with white markings discouraged
Heavy Harness Horses/ Warmbloods			
Cleveland Bay	16.2	545-680 (1,200-1,500)	Mahogany bay with no white markings
Dutch Warmblood	16-17	545-590 (1,200-1,300)	Usually any solid color, sometimes spotted
Friesian	15-16	455-590 (1,000-1,300)	Black
Hanoverian	16.2	545-635 (1,200-1,400)	Any solid color, with white markings on face and legs permitted
Irish Draught	16-17	590-680 (1,300-1,500)	Usually solid colored
Oldenburg	16.2-17.2	545-680 (1,200-1,500)	Usually solid colored
Trakehner	16-17.2	545-680 (1,200-1,500)	Usually solid colored
Light Horses/ Saddle Horses			
Akhal-Teké	14.2-16	410-545 (900-1,200)	Gold with metallic sheen, also gray, bay, black, with white marks permitted on head and feet
American Albino	14.2-15.2	455 (1,000)	White or cream colored, with blue eyes and pink skin
American Quarter Horse	14.2-17	455-590 (1,000-1,300)	Any solid color
American Saddle Horse (Saddlebred)	15-16	455-545 (1,000-1,200)	Bay, brown, chestnut, black, palomino, sometimes spotted
American Standardbred	15.2	545 (1,200)	Bay, brown, chestnut, black
Andalusian	15.2	455-545 (1,000-1,200)	Gray, also bay, black
Appaloosa	14.2-15.2	455-590 (1,000-1,300)	Leopard complex colors including blanket, varnish roan
Arabian	14.2-15	410-500 (900-1,100)	Gray, bay, black, chestnut, rarely others
Barb	14-15	410-500 (900-1,100)	Any solid color
Criollo	14-15	365-455 (800-1,000)	Dun, also chestnut, gray, roan, palomino, bay, black
Hackney Horse	~15.3	410-545 (900-1,200)	Any solid color
Lipizzaner	15.1-16.2	410-545 (900-1,200)	Gray, rarely bay, brown
Lusitano	15-16	455-545 (1,000-1,200)	Gray, most other colors
Morgan	14.2-15.2	410-545 (900-1,200)	Any solid color, dark colors preferred
Orlov Trotter	15.2-17	455-590 (1,000-1,300)	Gray, black, bay
Paso	14-15.2	410-500 (900-1,100)	Any solid color
Selle Français	16	455-545 (1,000-1,200)	Any solid color
Spanish Mustang	12.2-14.2	365-455 (800-1,000)	Wide variety, including cremello, paint, white, appaloosa, some speckled

1. A hand is equal to ten centimeters (4 in.).

210

Table 1. Major Horse Breeds and Their Characteristics *(Continued)*

BREED	HEIGHT IN HANDS[1]	WEIGHT IN KILOGRAMS (LBS.)	COLORS
Tennessee Walking Horse	15-15.2	410-635 (900-1,400)	Black, bay, chestnut, palamino, spotted
Thoroughbred	16-17	455-590 (1,000-1,300)	Usually bay, chestnut, gray, or black, rarely others
Welsh Cob	14.2-15.2	455-590 (1,000-1,300)	Any solid color
PONIES			
American Miniature Horse	6-9	90-225 (200-500)	Any color
Caspian	10-12	270 (600)	Gray, brown, bay, chestnut
Connemara	13-14.2	365-455 (800-1,000)	Gray, bay, black, dun, brown
Dülmen	~12.3	320-365 (700-800)	Dun, sometimes brown, black or others
Exmoor	<12.3	270-365 (600-800)	Mealy brown or mealy bay, no white markings
Falabella	≤8	70-180 (150-400)	Any color, including spotted
Haflinger	<14.2	590-680 (1,300-1,500)	Chestnut or sorrel, often with white markings
Highland	13-14.2	455-635 (1,000-1,400)	Gray, dun, black, bay
Icelandic Horse[2]	12-14	320-410 (700-900)	Any color
Norwegian Fjord	13-14.2	545-635 (1,200-1,400)	Dun
Shetland	9.5-10.6	135-270 (300-600)	Black, also other colors except piebald or skewbald
Sorraia	12-13	270-340 (600-750)	Dun, grullo, red dun
Welsh Mountain Pony	<12	180-320 (400-700)	Any solid color
Welsh Pony	12-13.2	205-340 (450-750)	Any solid color
Welsh Pony of Cob Type	<13.5	270-455 (600-1,000)	Any solid color

1. A hand is equal to ten centimeters (4 in.).
2. Horse is the correct designation, despite its small size.

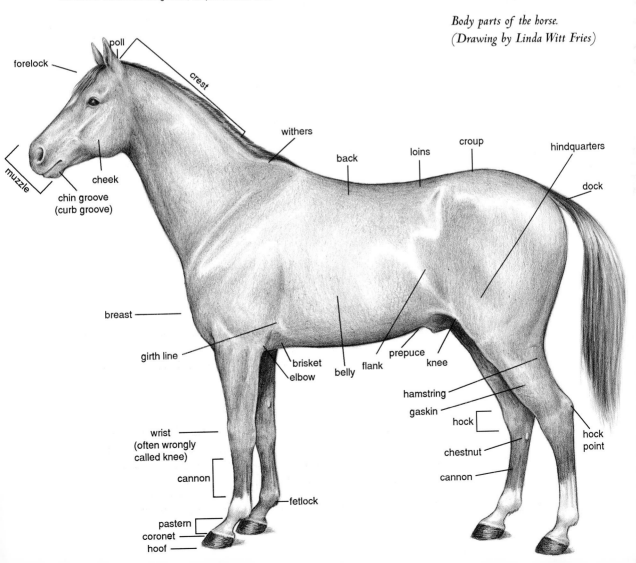

Body parts of the horse.
(Drawing by Linda Witt Fries)

poll
forelock
crest
muzzle
cheek
chin groove (curb groove)
withers
back
loins
croup
hindquarters
dock
breast
girth line
brisket
elbow
belly
flank
prepuce
knee
hamstring
gaskin
hock
chestnut
cannon
hock point
wrist (often wrongly called knee)
cannon
fetlock
pastern
coronet
hoof

Horse Colors and White Patterns

Colors

Albino: white body, white points,[1] and blue eyes. These are not truly albino in the strict biological sense, in which case the eyes would be red.

Bay: reddish body with black points. Bay coats range from a light shade that is nearly yellow to a dark shade that is almost black.

Black: black body and black points.

Brown: light- to dark-brown body with no red. Points are black.

Buckskin: yellow with black points, but lacking the primitive markings (dorsal stripe, withers stripes, and zebra striping on legs) of a dun coat.

Chestnut: medium- to dark-red body with nonblack points.

Cremello: cream-colored body and points and blue eyes.

Dappling: a network of dark areas overlying lighter areas on the body. Dappling can occur on any color of horse and may be more prominent in the spring or fall when the horse is changing its coat.

Dun: light- to dark-yellow coat that may also have some red or gray with black points. Primitive markings are common and include a dorsal stripe, withers stripes, and zebra stripes on fore- and hindlegs.

Gray: dark-colored coat with white hairs mixed in. The quantity of white increases with each year's change of coat. Dappling is common. Compare with "Roan" under "White Patterns."

Grullo: slate-colored body with black points and dark or black head. Also known as mouse dun.

Mealy muzzle: See Pangaré.

Mouse dun: See Grullo.

Palomino: metallic gold or yellow body with flaxen or off-white with points.

Pangaré (also known as "mealy muzzle"): lighter colors on the muzzle, around the eyes, on the inside of the legs, and in the flanks. Pangaré is a primitive color pattern seen in many depictions of horses in the Pleistocene cave paintings of Europe and the Przewalski horse, as well as in many modern breeds.

Perlino: cream-colored body with slightly red or blue points and blue eyes.

Sorrel: generally a light, clear-red body with nonblack points.

White: white body and points, pink skin, and brown or blue eyes.

Zebra dun: Dun (see above) with primitive striping on legs.

White Patterns

Bald-faced: a wide blaze in which the white runs up to or around the eyes or nostrils and over most of the upper lip.

Blanket: symmetrical pattern of white that can cover just the croup and hips or spread over most of the body.

Blaze: extensive white marking covering the forehead, nasal bones, and the area between the nostrils.

Frosty (also known as "skunk-tail"): a very rare pattern in which white hairs are distributed in the mane, down the back, over the hips, on the hocks, and at the base of the tail.

Leopard spotting: symmetrical pattern on a white horse or a horse with a blanket in which there are small colored spots in the white area.

---

1. The term *points* refers to the ear rims, mane, lower legs, and tail.

Medicine hat paint: asymmetrical pattern in which the horse is predominantly white, but has color on the ears and/or around the eyes and colored patches on the chest, flank, and base of the tail.

Mottled: small points of white on the muzzle, around the eyes, and on the genitalia.

Overo: asymmetrical pattern in which white areas with ragged margins are distributed somewhat horizontally below the topline on the sides, neck, and belly. The head also frequently has considerable white, and the eyes may be blue.

Paint: any asymmetrical patterns of white on a base color, including overo, piebald, sabino, skewbald, splashed white, and tobiano. Also known as pinto.

Piebald: a general term for any asymmetric pattern of white on a black horse.

Pinto: See Paint.

Rabicano: a pattern in which there is a concentration of white hairs at the base of the tail and an array of white hairs mingled with colored ones spreading out from the flank.

Race: a long, straight, narrow white mark on the forehead or nasal bones that wanders off to one side.

Roan: a pattern in which individual white and colored hairs are evenly distributed over the body, normally exclusive of the head and points. Unlike the gray color, this pattern is stable through the horse's life. Roans are distinguished by their base color, such as bay roan and sorrel roan, or by their blended color, such as blue roan, strawberry roan, or honey roan.

Sabino: asymmetrical pattern often confused with overo. Sabino horses have white flecks and/or patches that may or may not be distinct. Much of the head is usually white, but the upper lip is normally colored. Some or all of the legs are usually white, and patches normally cover the belly.

Skunk-tail: See Frosty.

Skewbald: general term for any asymmetrical pattern of white on a nonblack horse.

Snip: white mark between, near, or running into the nostrils.

Snowflake: symmetrical pattern of small white spots beginning when the horse is young and increasing in number with age. Sometimes the pattern stabilizes at a certain age; other times the horse eventually becomes nearly all white.

Splashed white: asymmetrical pattern in which the white patches have cleanly defined edges. The four legs, most of the head, and some of the belly are usually white.

Star: white mark on the forehead.

Strip: narrow mark along the nasal bones.

Stripe: long, straight, narrow mark made by connecting a star, strip, and snip.

Tobiano: asymmetrical pattern in which the white marks have cleanly defined edges. All four legs are typically white, the topline has at least one white area, and the head is colored like normal, unspotted horses.

Varnish roan: pattern in which the white hairs are dispersed on the head, as well as the body. Darker hairs are more concentrated over the bony eminences of the face, withers, shoulders, knees, stifles, and pelvis.

War-bonnet paint: asymmetrical pattern in which the horse is nearly all white, with color mostly limited to the ears.

White sclera: white ring around the eyeball.

For further information on horse coloration, see D. P. Sponenberg and B. V. Beaver, Horse Color *(College Station: Texas A&M University Press, 1983).*

A

Abri Montestruc (France), *51*

Achdari or Syrian wild ass, 200

Adaptation
to cold environment, 68, 135, 136
and evolution, 17-18, 22
to grasslands, 25-27, 28-29, 37, 41-42
to running, 17-18, 22, 24
See also Dentition; Diet; Evolution

Africa, fossil record in, 32

African wild ass, 200-02

Age, estimates from teeth, 4, 66, 73-74

Age of Chivalry, 6, 110-11

Akhal-Teké (breed), 164-65

Alexander the Great, 88, 108

Alpine draft horses, 158-59

American Albino (breed), 169

American Association of Equine Practitioners, 181

American Belgian (breed), 158

American Cream Draft Horse (breed), 157-58, *159*, 169

American Curly (Bashkir Curly) (breed), 169

American Livestock Breeds Conservancy, 156

American Masters of Foxhounds Association, 120

American Miniature Horse (breed), 173

American Quarter Horse (breed), 165-66, *166*

American Saddle Horse (breed), 167

American Shetland (breed), 171

American Standardbred (breed), 125-26, 168, *169*, *185*

American White (breed), 169

Americas, domestic horses in the, 99-100, *101*

Amu Darya River site (Afghanistan), 62, *63*

Anatolia, 61, 71-72

Anatomy
equid, 65-66, 193, *209*, *211*
foot, 17, 24, 29

Anchitheres, 23-24

Anchitherium, 24

Andalusian (breed), 162, 166

Appaloosa (breed), 166, *167*

Apsyrtus of Constantinople, 178

Arabian (breed), 97-98, 160, *161*, 164

Arcelin, Adrien, 44

Archaeological sites
Bronze Age, 65, 93
of cave art, 42, *46*, 47-52, 69
Copper Age, 65, 67-68, 70-82
Eurasian, *60* (map), 72; Amu Darya River site (Afghanistan), 62, *63*; Botai (Kazakstan), 75-76, 79; Cave Ignatiev (Russia), 51; Davlekanovo (Russia), 75; Dereivka (Ukraine), 63, 72-75, 77-81; Kapovaia (Russia), 51; Maikop (Caucasus Mtns.), *65*; Mullino II (Russia), 75; Pazyryk (Siberia), 92-93; Pirak (Baluchistan), 62; Scythian sites, 61-62, 91-93; Sergeivka (Kazakstan), 79; Sredni Stog culture sites, 72-75, 77-81; Sungir (Russia), 52, *53*; Utyëvka VI (Russia), *74*
European, *40* (map); Abri Montestruc (France), 51; Bédeilhac (France), 53; Combe Grenal (France), 41; Duruthy (France), 53; Ekain (Spain), 48, *49*; Erberua (France), 42; Gabillou (France), *46*; Gönnersdorf (Germany), 52; Gouy (France), 51; Isturitz (Spain), *52*; La Bastide (France), 42; La Grotte des Eyzies (France), 42, 47; La Madeleine (France), 42, *54*; La Marche (France), 52; La Pileta (Spain), 50; Lascaux (France), 49, 50, 51; Les Trois Frères (France), 51; Lourdes (France), 53; Mas d'Azil (France), 53; Niaux (France), 50; Pech-Merle (France), 49; Pincevent (France), 42; Saint-Michel d'Arudy (France), 55; Solutré, 43-47; Taillebourg (France), 50; Tito Bustillo (Spain), 48; Vogelherd (Germany), *51*, 53
with horse remains: Bronze Age, *74*; Copper Age, *65*, 72-82; Upper Paleolithic, 41-47
Magdalenian period, 42-43
of mobile art, 51-55
Near Eastern: Ma'adi (Egypt), 202; Malyan (Iran), 77; Mesopotamia, 61-62; Tell Brak, 77
Neolithic, 75
Paleolithic, *40* (map); Middle, 39-41, 52; Upper, 41-56
See also Cave art; Fossil localities

Aristides, 124

Armor, knights', 96, *99*, 110

Art depicting horses, 47-56, *65*, 85-86, *87*
Afghanistan, 62, *63*
Chinese (Tang Dynasty), 94, *95*
Egyptian, 86
on Greek vases, 89, 108
Mesopotamian, 62
Qin Shi Huang effigies, 93-94
Roman, 109
Scythian, 91
Upper Paleolithic, 42, *45*, *46*, 47-54, 69; *bâtons-de-commandement*, 52, *54*, 55; cave art, *46*, 47-55, 69; *contours découpés*, 52; as evidence for horse husbandry, 54-55; horse-head pendants, 52; mobile art, 51-55

Art of Horsemanship, The (Xenophon), 5, 87-88

Assateague Island feral horses, 66

Asses, 32, 197-208
African, 200-02; Nubian, 202; Somali, 201
Asiatic, 197-200; achdari, 200; dziggetai, 199; half-asses, 197; khur or ghor-khar, 200; kiangs, 198; kulans, 199; onagers, 198-200
burros and other feral asses, 206-08
digestive system of, 193
donkeys or domestic asses, 85, 202-05
evolution of, 32
Pleistocene European, 51-52; Poitou, 204
true, 200-02

Assyria, 61, 85-86

Astrohippus, 29, 30

Austrian Warmblood (breed), 160

Azteca (breed), 166-67

B

Barb or Barbary horses (breed), 97-98, 164
Bars I, 125
Bâtons-de-commandement, 52, *54, 55*
Bayeux tapestry, 96, *97*
Bédeilhac (France), 53
Behavior, 45-46, 50, 190, 194
    champing at the bit, 8
    foraging, 67-68, 135, 136
    temperament and personality of wild horses, 67, 69
Belgian Ardennais (breed), 156
Bell Beaker Culture, 70-71
Betting, pari-mutual, 127
Bible, horses in, 86-87
Bit wear, 63, 75, 76-79, *80*
Bits, 8, 110
    in horse's mouth, 76-79, *80*, 110
Blacksmiths, 178
Bleeding or Bartlett's Childers, the, 98
"Blood-sweating" horses of Ferghana, 94
Bökönyi, Sandor, 65, 72
Botai site (Kazakstan), 75-76, 79
Brabant, *154*, 156
Breeds, 155-73, 210-211
    draft horses, 156-61; farm chunk horses, 158, 168;
        Nordic breeds, 159; Western European breeds,
        156-58
    heavy harness or warmblood, 159-61
    light or saddle horses, 161-69; Arabian breeds, 97-98,
        161-62, 164, 165; gaited breeds, 167-68;
        Spanish breeds, 161-64, 170; trotting breeds,
        168, *169*
    ponies, 169-73; American, 173; British, 171-73
    See also Kazak horses; names of breeds
Britain, 90, 96-99
Bronco-busting, 118
Bronze Age, China, 65, 93
Bucephalus, 88, 108
Buckskin (breed), 169
Buffalo Bill's Wild West, 116-17
Burial sites, horse, 71-75, 92-93
Burros, 203, *204,* 206-07
Butchering. *See* Food, horses as
Buzkashi, 115, *150,* 150-51
Byerley Turk, the, 98

C

Caballine horses, 32
Caesar, Julius, 90
Calippus, 29
Cam's Card Shark, *127*
Canadian horse (breed), 168
Carriages, Chinese bronze, 93-94
Caspian pony (breed), 164
Cave art, Upper Paleolithic, 42, *46, 47*-52, 69
Cave Ignatiev (Russia), 51

Cavendish, William, 112
Cenozoic Era, *15*
Chariot racing, Greek and Roman, 88, 89, 91, 106, 108-10
Chariots
    ancient, 85-89, 105
    antiquity of, 62-63
    Assyrian, 85-86, *87*
    Chinese, 93
    Egyptian, 86, *87*
    Greek, 87-89, 106
    in Old Testament, 86-87
    Roman, 91, 108-10
    war, 87, 90
    See also Vehicles
Chersky horse, 38
China, ancient, 93-95
Chivalry, Age of, 6, 110-11
Chromosome number, 64-65, 71
Cimmerians, 61
Circus, Roman, 108-10
Circus Maximus, 108
Cleveland Bay (breed), 160-61
Clichés involving horses, 4-8
Climate, 21-22, 28-29, 41
Clydesdale (breed), 157
Code of gallantry, 6
Cody, William F. ("Buffalo Bill"), 116-17
Coldblood heavy horses, 63, 65, 159, 161
Coloration, 169, 210-11, 212-13
    of Ice Age horses, 38, 48-49, 54-55
    of Kazak horses, 142
Columbus, Christopher, 99, 203
Combe Grenal (France), 41
Connemara (breed), 172
Contours découpés, 52
Copper Age sites, 65, 66-68, 70-82
Cormohipparion, 27, 28
Costillo Pocket (Colorado), 19
Cowboys, life of, 116-18
Crib-biting, 55, 69
Crinoline, 8
Criollo (breed), *162, 163*
Crusades, 97

D

Dale, (breed), 173
Dan Patch, *126,* 127
Darley Arabian, the, 98
Dartmoor (breed), 173
Darwin, Charles, 48-49
Davlekanovo (Russia), 75
"Dawn horses," 19-22
De la Broue, Solomon, 112
De la Guérinière, F. Robicon, 112, 113
De Pluvinel, Antoine, 112
De Preuilly, Geoffri, 110
De Saunier, Gaspart, 112

Death, season of, determined from teeth, 47
Dentition, 16, 22-29
Dereivka cult stallion, 72-79, *80*
Dereivka site (Ukraine), 63, 72-75, 77
Devonshire Flying Childers, the, 98
Diet, 5, *21*, 24, 25, 27, 37, 38, 193
    See also Dentition
Digestive system, 4-5, 193
Dinohippus, 30
Diseases, 179, 181, 187, 188-90
Djut, 134
DNA studies, 14, 64-65
Dog rituals, 72
Døle Gudbrandsdal (breed), 159
Domesticated horse, possible ancestors of, 63-65
Domestication, 54-55, 59-82
    and Bell Beaker Culture, 70-71
    and change in body size, 65-66, 70-71
    and Dereivka site, 72-76, 78-80
    evidence for, 62-82
    location of, 68-76
    reasons for, 68-69
    and reindeer herders, 69
Don Quixote, 7
Donkeys, 85, 200, 202-05
    and American gold rush, 203
    American Mammoth Jackstock (breed), 204
    domestication of, 202
    Egyptian use of, 202-03
    feral (burros), *204*, 206-07
    introduction of, to New World, 203-04
    as recreation and companion animals, 205
    Royal Gift, 204
    as source of food, 203
Draft horses, 155, 156-59
    See also names of breeds
Dressage, 6-7, 108, 111-14, *115*
    See also Xenophon
Dülmen (breed), 170
Duruthy (France), 53
Dutch Warmblood (breed), 160
Dziggetai, 199

E

Eclipse, 98
Ecology, 66
    and Kazak horse herds, 133-35
    and Miocene horse, 26-27
    and Pleistocene horse, 37, 41
Ecraseur, *176*, 177
Effigies, horse, 52, 93-94
Egypt, 86, *87*, 177, 202-03
Ekain (Spain), 48, *49*
Environmental change and evolution, 14-16, 19, 21-22, 28-29, 31-32
Environments
    Ice Age, 41

Kazakstan, 133-35
Eocene epoch, 14-15, 18-23
Epihippus, 22, 23
Equestrian sports. *See* Sports, equestrian
Equidae, 13, 14-19
Equids
    adaptation of, 17-18, 22, 24-29, 37, 41-42, 68, 135-36
    anatomy of, 16-17, 65-66, 193, *209*, 211
    digestive system of, 4-5, 193
    origin and evolution of, 13, 14-17
    reproduction of, 186-88, 193
    sexual dimorphism in, 20-21, 50
    social behavior of, 44-47, 194
Equinae, 24, 29
Equine horses, 24, 26, 29-32
Equine medicine. *See* Medicine, equine
Equipment. *See* Tackle
Equus, 29-32
    africanus, 200-02
    asinus, 202-05
    burchelli, 194, 195-96; ssp. *antiquorum*, 196; ssp. *boehmi*, 196; ssp. *burchelli*, 196; ssp. *quagga*, 196
    caballus, 32
    ferus, 65
    fossil species of, 29-33, 38
    grevyi, 194-95
    hemionus, 198-200; ssp. *hemionus*, 199; ssp. *hemippus*, 200; ssp. *khur*, 200; ssp. *kulan*, 199; ssp. *onager*, 200
    kiang, 198
    lenensis, 38
    origin and spread of, 29-33
    przewalskii, 32, 38, 48, 55, 64-65, 67, 69
    zebra: ssp. *hartmanni*, 197; ssp. *zebra*, 197
Erberua (France), 42
Eurasia, 28-29, 32, *60* (map), 62-63, 68-69
Europe, 18, 21-22, 37, *40*, 41-53, 65, 95-97, 110-11, 178, 203
    horse domestication in, 69-71
    See also individual sites
Evolution, 13-14, *15*
    of adaptations to grasslands, 21-22, 24-27
    of asses, 32
    and environmental change, 14-16, 19, 21-22, 28-29, 31-32
    of horses, 13-33, 37, 63-65
    of zebras, 30, 32
    See also Adaptation; Dentition; Diet; Fossil record
Evolutionary relationships, *17, 18, 26*
Exmoor (breed), 171-72
Extinctions, 24, *26*, 28, 31
    Cretaceous, 14
    Pleistocene, 31, 61, 99

F

Falabella (breed), 173
Farm horses, Middle Ages, 96
Farriery or blacksmithing, 178
Feral horses and burros, 46, 66, 67, 100, 204, 206-07
"Ferghana heavenly horses," 94

Finnish or Finnish Universal (breed), 159
Fleam, *176*, 177
Flemish (breed), 156
Folk medicine, Kazak, 145-46
Food
    domesticated horses as, 59, 67, 71; among Kazaks,
        142, 144-45; Paleolithic, 39-47; processing and
        preservation of meat, 41, 46-47, 145; wild
        horses as, 39-47, 71, 74-76
    other equines as, 70, 142, 203
    products from horses, Kazak, 143-45
Foraging by horses under snow, 135, 136
    See also Adaptation; Diet
Fossil Horses (McFadden), 14
Fossil localities
    Costillo Pocket (Colorado), 19-21
    Last Chance Creek (Yukon, Canada), 38
    Messel (Germany), 21
    Selerikan River (Siberia), 38
Fossil record, 13-33
    anatomy, 16-17
    anchitheres, 24
    dentition, 16, 22-29
    Eocene epoch, 14-15, 18-23
    Equidae, 13, 14-17
    Equinae, 24, 29
    equine horses, 27, 29-32
    Equus origin and spread, 29-32
    hipparionine horses, 27-29
    hippomorphs, *17*, 18-19
    hyracotheres, 19-22
    merychippine horses, 25-27
    Miocene period, 22, 24-30
    Oligocene period, 22, 24
    one-toed horses, 29-32
    Paleocene epoch, *15*, 16
    paleotheres, 17, 21
    parahippines, 24-27
    Pleistocene epoch, *15*, *29*, 30-32, 37-39, 56; Chersky
        horses, 38; distribution of horses, 37-38; frozen
        horse carcasses, 38; Selerikan River stallion, 38
        See also Archaeological sites
    Pliocene epoch, 30-31
    taxa: *Anchitherium*, 24; *Archaeohippus*, 24; *Astrohippus*, 29;
        Calippus, 29; *Cormohipparion*, 27, 28; *Dinohippus*,
        30; *Epihippus*, 22, 23; *Equus*, 29-32; *Equus caballus*,
        32; *Equus lambei*, 38; *Equus lenensis*, 38; *Equus simpl-*
        icidens, 30; *Equus stenonis*, 32; *Haplohippus*, 22;
        Hipparion, 28; *Hippidion*, 29, 30; *Hyracotherium*, 19-
        20, 22; *Merychippus*, 25, 28; *Mesohippus*, 22-23;
        Miohippus, 22-24, *28*, 31; *Nannippus*, 28;
        Neohipparion, 29; *Onohippidium*, 30; *Orohippus*, 22;
        Pliohippus, 29-30, *31*; *Propalaeotherium*, 21;
        Protohippus, 27, 29; *Pseudhipparion*, 28; *Radinskya*, 16;
        Systemodon, 20-21; *Tetraclaenodon*, 16
    three-toed horses, 22-29
Fox hunting, 118-20
French Trotter (breed), 168
Friesian (breed), 160, 163

G
Gabillou (France), *46*
Genetic studies, 64-65
Genghis Khan, 94-95
Gli ordini di cavalcare (Grisone), 112
Godolphin Arabian, the, 98
Gold prospecting, donkeys and, 203
Gönnersdorf (Germany), 52
Gotland (breed), 170-71
Gouy (France), 51
Grand Canyon, feral burros in, 206
Grassland adaptations, 21-22, 24-27
    See also Dentition; Diet; Environmental change and evolution
Great Panathenaea, 89
Greek Empire, 87-89, 106-08, 177
Grisone, Federico, 111
Grotte des Grotte des Eyzies (France), 42, 47

H
Hackney (breed), 168
Haflinger (breed), 173
Hambletonian, 125
Hammurabi, 177
Hand (measurement), 115
Hanoverian (breed), 160
Haplohippus, 22
Harems, equid, 194
Harness racing, 125-27
Haute école, 6-7, 105, 112-14, *115*
Head and hoof burials, 72-75
Heavy harness or warmblood horses, 155, 159-61
    See also names of breeds
Henry VIII, 97
Herodotus, 60, 92
Highland (breed), 172
Hinnies and mules, 205-06
Hipparion, 28
Hipparionine horses, 26, 27-29
Hippidion, 29, 30, 31, 32
Hippodromes, Greek, 106
Hippomorphs, *17*, 18-19
Hipposandals, 89
Hobgoblin, 98
Holstein (breed), 160
"Horse," definition and classification of, 14-19, 209
Horse breeding, Kazak, 137
    See also Kazak horses
"Horse" classification, 209
Horse family, origin of, 14-19
Horse hunting. *See* Hunting
Horse husbandry, Upper Paleolithic, 54-55
Horse Latitudes, 99
Horse products, Kazak, 145
Horse racing. *See* Racing
Horse sacrifices, ritual, 72-75, 91-92
"Horse sense," 5-6
Horse sweat, in Kazak folk medicine, 146

Horseback riding. *See* Riding, horseback

Horsepower, 6

Horses

in ancient civilizations: Assyria, 85-86, *87*; Bible, 59, 86-87; China, 93-95; Ancient Egypt, 86, *87*; Ghengis Khan's empire, 94-95; Greek Empire, 87-89, 106-08; Mesopotamia, 85; Roman Empire, 89-91, 108-10; Scythians, 91-93, 106

caballine, origin of, 32

compared with other livestock, 5, 67-68, 135, 136

digestive system of, 4-5, 193

farm, 96

frozen carcasses of, 38, 92-93

intelligence and instincts of, 5-6, 18

Kazak, 141-50

in Middle Ages, 6, 95-97, 110-11

in Upper Paleolithic art, 47-55

wild, 38, 42, 45, 48, 50, 67, 69-70, 77-78, 99

See also Fossil record

Horses (Simpson), 14

Horseshoes, original, 89

Hotblood horses, 159

Human burials, Scythian, 92

"Humane horse-killer," 179

Hunting, *87*

fox, 118-20

horses for food, 39-52, 55-56, 76

Middle Paleolithic, 39-41

onagers, *87*

Upper Paleolithic, 40-41, 41-47

using horses in, 86, *87*, 100, 108, 118-20, 142

weapons, 41, 52, *54*

See also Food, wild horses as

Hybrids, 85, 205

Hyoid bone carvings, 52

Hyracotheres, *18*, 19-22

Hyracotherium, 19-22

Hywel Dda, Welsh Laws of, 96

I

Ice Age extinctions, 31, 61, 99

Icelandic Horse (breed), 171

Indians. *See* Native Americans

Intelligence and instincts of horses, 5-6, 18

Irish Draught (breed), 160-61

Isturitz (Spain), 52

J

Jockey Club (England), 99, 123

Johnson, Velma, 206-07

Jousting, 110-11

K

Kahun papyrus, 177

Kapovaia (Russia), 51

Kazak

equestrian sports, 150-51

horses: breeds and breeding, 137, 141-42; equine veterinary practices, 142; food products from, 143-45; herd size as measure of wealth, 133; role at births and weddings, 147-48; role in death and burial, 149-50; role in folk medicine, 145-46; social and religious roles of, 146-47; stealing of, 148-49; tackle and equipment for, *141*, 143

people, *132* (map); adaptation to environment of, 133-41; clothing of, 140; economy of, 132-33; household and personal posessions of, 138-41; and livestock, 135; origin and modern distribution of, 131; seasonal migration of herds of, 136-38

Kazakstan

climate and soils of, 133-35

as location of horse domestication, 75-76

Scythian artifacts in, 60

and shift to pastoral nomadism, 62

See also Kazak

Kentucky Mountain Saddle Horse (breed), 167

Khurs, 200

Kiangs, 198

Kladruby (breed), 160, *161*

Knights, 6, *7*, 95-97, *99*, 110-11

Konik (breed), 170

Koumiss, 93, 143-44, 145

Kublai Khan, 95

Kulans, 199

L

La Bastide (France), 42

La Madeleine (France), 42, *54*

La Marche (France), 52

La Pileta (Spain), 50

Lascaux (France), 49, 50, 51

Last Chance Creek (Yukon, Canada), 38

Lath, 98

Laws pertaining to horses, 91, 96, 177

Le Cavalerice François (Pignatelli), 112

Le Maneige Royal (de Pluvinel), 112

Light or saddle horses, 155, 161-69

See also names of breeds

Lipizzaner (breed), 107, 113-14, *115*, 162-63

Lottery, 120

Lourdes (France), 53

Lusitano (breed), 162

M

Maikop (Caucasus Mtns.), 65

Man O'War, 124, *125*

Mas d'Azil (France), 53

Master of Foxhounds Association, 120

Mease, James, 180

Medicine, equine

American Association of Equine Practitioners, 181

Apsyrtus of Constantinople, 178

diseases, 179, 181, 187, 189-90
early history, 177-81
instruments (early), *176*, 177, 179
Kazak, 142
neonatology, 187-88
reproduction, 186
techniques, 181-82; anesthesia, 188, *189*; arthroscopy,
    184-85; CAT scans, 183; critical care of sick
    horses, 186-87; embryo transfer in mares, 186;
    endoscopy, 182-83; intravenous fluid therapy,
    188; laser surgery, 184; nuclear scintigraphy in,
    183; treadmill tests, 183-84, *185*; ultrasound,
    183, 186
in United States, 178-82
University of Pennsylvania, 180-81; New Bolton
    Center, *182, 183*, 185-89
veterinary education, 178, 179, 180-81
Merychippine horses, 25-27
Merychippus, 25, *26, 28*
Mesohippus, 22-23
Mesopotamia, 61, *62*, 85
Messel (Germany), 21
Messenger, 125
Middle Ages, 6, 95-97, 110-11
Migration of Kazak herds, 136-38
Miniature horses, 155, 173
Miocene epoch, *15*, 22, 23-30, *31*
Miohippus, 22-24, *28*
Missouri Fox Trotter (breed), 167
Mongolia, 94-95, 116
Mongolian Pony (breed), 170
Montestruc, Tarn-et-Gavonne (France), *51*
Morgan (breed), 168
Mountain Pleasure Horse (breed), 167
Mules and hinnies, 203, 205-06
Mullino II (Russia), 75
Muybridge, Eadweard, 125

N

Nannippus, 28
National Association of Trotting Horse Breeders, 125
National Trotting Association, 126
Native Americans, 99-100, 166
    as analog for Sredni Stog culture, 80-81
    use of horses by, 68, 80, 100, *101*
Neandertal scavengers and hunters, 39-41
Near East, 60-63, 71-72
Neohipparion, 29
Neolithic archaeological sites, 65, 69-71
New Forest (breed), 173
New World, 37, 38, 66, 99-100, 203-04
Niaux (France), 50
Nomadism, pastoral, 60-61, 62, 131-41
Nomads
    armies of, 95
    Kazak, 131-41
    Native American, 100

    pastoral, 60-61, 62, 131-41
    Scythian, 91-93
Nordic draft horses, 159
Norfolk Trotter (breed), 125
Noriker (breed), 158-59
North Swedish Horse (breed), 159
Norwegian Fjord (breed), 170

O

Oldenburg (breed), 160
Oligocene epoch, *15*, 22, 24, *28*
Olympic events, equestrian, 89, 106, 112, 122
Onagers, 85, 198-200
One-toed horses, 29-32
Onohippidium, 30, 31
Origin of Species (Darwin), 48-49
Orlov Trotter (breed), 125, 168
Orohippus, 22-23

P

Paint (breed), 166
Palomino (breed), 169
Paleocene epoch, *15*, 16
Paleolithic, Middle
    archaeological sites, 39-41
Paleolithic, Upper
    archaeological sites, *40* (map), 40-55
    art, *36*, 44, *45, 46*, 47-55, 69
    horse hunting, 40, 41-47
    horse husbandry, 54-55, 69
Parahippines, 24-26
Paso and Paso Fino (breeds), 163
Pastoral nomadism, 60-61, 62, 131-41
Pazyryk, frozen tombs of, 91-92
Pech-Merle (France), 49
Percheron (breed), 157
Perissodactyls, origin of, 16-19
Photography, in horse racing, 124-25
Pignatelli, Giovanni, 112
Pincevent (France), 42
Pinto (breed), 169
Pirak (Baluchistan), 62
Plantation Walking Horse (breed), 167
Pleistocene epoch, *15*, 29, 30-32, 37-39, 56
    Chersky horses, 38
    distribution of horses, 37-38
    extinctions, 31, 61, 99
    frozen horse carcasses, 38
    Selerikan River stallion, 38
Pliocene epoch, *15*, 30-31
Pliohippus, 29-30, *31*
Polo, 114-15
Polo, Marco, 95
Ponies, 155, 169-73
    See also names of breeds
Pony of the Americas (breed), 173

Propalaeotherium, 21
Protohippus, 27, 29
Proverbs about horses, 4-9
Przewalskii horse, 38, 48, *55*, 67, 69
    as ancestor of modern horse, 32, 64-65
Pseudhipparion, 28

Q

Qin Shi Huang tomb and terra-cotta horses, 93-94
Quadriga, 91, 106, 109
Quagga (Zebra), 32, 196
Quarterhorse, American (breed), 165-66
Quintain, 111

R

Races and racetracks, 122-25
Racing
    American, 123-25; Australia, 124; English, 122-23;
        Kazak, 150; Mongolian, 116
    chariot, 88, 89, 91, 106, 108-10
    maxims from, 7
    steeplechasing, 120-21, 122
    trotting and harness racing, 125-27
Racking Horse (breed), 167
Radinskya, 16
Riding, horseback, 60-63, 76, 78-82, 89, 110-12
    See also Buzkashi; Fox hunting; Haute école; Polo;
        Racing; Rodeo, American; Show jumping;
        Steeplechasing
Ritual sacrifices of horses, 72-75, 91-92
Rocky Mountain Horse (breed), 167
Rodeo, American, 116-18
Roman Empire, 89-91, 177-78
Roxana, 98
Running, adaptation for, 17-18, 22, 24
Rush, Benjamin, 180
Russia, 38, 51, *53*, 75, 92

S

Sacrifices, ritual, of horses, 72-75, 91-92
Saddlebred (breed), 167
Saddle or light horses, 155, 161-69
    See also names of breeds
Saddles. *See* Tackle
Saint-Michel d'Arudy (France), *55*
Salihotria, 177
Scythians, use of horses by, 60-61, 91-93, 106
Secretariat, 124
Selerikan River (Siberia), 38
Sergeivka (Kazakstan), 79
Sexual dimorphism, 20-21
Shetland (breed), 171
Shire (breed), 157, *158*
Show jumping, 121-22
Simpson, George Gaylord, 14

Single-footing Horse (breed), 167
Sir Barton, 123
Solutré horse-kill site (France), *36*, 43-47
Solutré, ou les Chaseurs de Rennes de la France Centrale, 44
Somali ass, 201
Sorraia (breed), 162, 170
Spain, domesticated horses in, 70-71
Spanish Mustang (breed), 163-64
Spanish Riding School of Vienna, 6, 107, 112-14, *115*
Spear thrower, antler, 52-53, *54*
Sports, equestrian
    American rodeo, 116-18
    boar hunting, 108
    buzkashi, 115, 150
    dressage, 111-12
    flat racing, 122-25
    fox hunting, 118-20
    Greek, 106-08
    haute école, 6-7, 105, 112-14, *115*
    Kazak, 150-51
    medieval jousting and tournaments, 110-11
    Mongolian, 116
    in Olympic competitions, 89, 106, 112, 122
    polo, 114-15
    Roman, 108-10
    Scythian, 106
    show jumping, 121-22
    steeplechasing, 120-21
    trotting and harness racing, 125-27
Sredni Stog culture, 72-82
Standardbred (breed), 125-26
Star Pointer, 126
Steeplechasing, 120-21
Steppes, 68-76, 131, *132*, 134-35
Stirrups. *See* Tackle
Stud Book, 98
Suffolk (breed), 157
Sulkies, racing, 126
Sumerian use of horses, 61, 85
Sungir (Russia), 52, *53*
Swedish Warmblood (breed), 160
Swiss Warmblood (breed), 160
Systemodon, 20

T

Tackle
    Assyrian, 86
    bits, 8, 76-79, *80*, 110
    Egyptian, 86
    Kazak, 143
    saddles, 89, 90, 106, 111, 121, 143
    stirrups, 96
    words and phrases about, 8
Taillebourg (France), 50
Tang Dynasty, vi, 94, *95*
Tarpan, 64
Tarpan (breed, reconstructed), 170

Teeth, 4, 43, 47, 66, 73-74
  See also Bit wear; Dentition; Diet; Evolution; Grassland
    adaptations
Tennessee Walking Horse (breed), 167
Terra cotta army of Qin Shi Huang, 93-94
Territoriality of equids, 194
Tetraclaenodon, 16
Theriogenology, 186
Thoroughbred (breed), 98, 122-23, 124-25, 160, 165
Three-toed horses, 22-29
Thunder Gulch, iv, 124
Tito Bustillo (Spain), 48
Tomb burials, 91-94
Tournaments, jousting, 110-11
Training, 6, 106-08, 110, 111-14, 118
Trakehner (breed), 160
Trois Frères (France), 51
Trotting and harness racing, 125-27
Tutankhamen, 86, *87*

U

Ukraine, 72-75
Ungulates, 13
University of Pennsylvania, School of Veterinary Medicine,
    180-81, *182, 183*, 185-89
Utyëvka VI (Russia), *74*
Vehicles
    chariots, 62-63, 85-91, 105, 109
    Chinese bronze carriages, 93-94
    first appearance, 82
    Kazak, 143
    sulkies, racing, 126
Veterinary education, 178, 179, 180-81
    See also Medicine, equine
Vogelherd (Germany), 51, 53

W

War
    chariots in, 86-88, 90
    horses in, 3, 59, 80, 86-88, 96-100, 142; American
    Civil War, 178-79; American Revolutionary War, 178;
    Battle of Hastings, 96-97; Roman Empire, 90-91
Warmblood horses, 155, 159-61

  See also names of breeds
Washington, George, 123, 178, 204
Welfare of equines, 90, 91, 96, 177, 206-07
    humane treatment, 107-08, 110, 111-12, 118
Welsh Cob (breed), 172
Welsh Mountain Pony (breed), 172
Welsh Pony (breed), 172
Welsh Pony of Cob Type (breed), 172
Welsh Stud Book, 172

X, Y, AND Z

Xenophon, 5, 87-88, 101, 106-08

Yamna (Pit-Grave) culture, 75-76, 81-82
Yankee, 126
Yurt, 92, 138-41

Zebras, 194-97
    digestive system of, 193
    evolution of, 30, 32
    kinds: Burchell's, 196; Cape mountain, 197; Chapman's
        or Damara, 196; Grant's, 196; Grevy's, 194-95;
        Hartmann's, 197; Mountain, 194, 197; Plains,
        194, 195-96; Quagga, 196
Zooarchaeology, 63
Zoopraxiscope, 125